Women without Class

Women without Class

Girls, Race, and Identity

Julie Bettie

WITH A NEW INTRODUCTION

UNIVERSITY OF CALIFORNIA PRESS

University of California Press, one of the most distinguished university presses in the United States, enriches lives around the world by advancing scholarship in the humanities, social sciences, and natural sciences. Its activities are supported by the UC Press Foundation and by philanthropic contributions from individuals and institutions. For more information, visit www.ucpress.edu.

University of California Press
Oakland, California

Portions of this book have been adapted and reprinted from Julie Bettie, "Women without Class: Chicas, Cholas, Trash and the Presence/Absence of Class Identity," in *Signs: Journal of Women in Culture and Society,* vol. 26, no. 1, Autumn 2000, published by the University of Chicago Press. © 2000 by the University of Chicago. All rights reserved. Chapter 5 was adapted from Julie Bettie, "Exceptions to the Rule: Upwardly Mobile White and Mexican-American High School Girls," in *Gender & Society,* June 2002. © 2002 by Sage Publications. Reprinted by permission of Sage Publications. A brief portion of chapter 4 was adapted and reprinted from Julie Bettie, "Class Dismissed: *Roseanne* and the Changing Face of Working-Class Iconography," in *Social Text* 45, vol. 14, no. 4, Winter 1995. © 1995 by Duke University Press.

ISBN 978-0-520-28001-4 (paper)
ISBN 978-0-520-95724-4 (ebook)

The Library of Congress has cataloged an earlier edition of this book as follows:

Library of Congress Cataloging-in-Publication Data

Bettie, Julie, 1965–.
Women without class : girls, race, and identity / Julie Bettie.
p. cm.
Includes bibliographical references and index.
ISBN 978-0-520-23542-7 (pbk. : alk. paper)
1. White teenage girls—California—Race identity. 2. White teenage girls—California—Social conditions. 3. Mexican American teenage girls—California—Race identity. 4. Mexican American teenage girls—California—Social conditions. 5. High school students—California—Social conditions. 6. Mexican American students—California—Social conditions. 7. Social classes—California I. Title.

HQ798 .B425 2003
305.235—dc21 2001007757

Manufactured in the United States of America
23 22 21 20 19 18 17
10 9 8 7 6 5 4

In keeping with a commitment to support environmentally responsible and sustainable printing practices, UC Press has printed this book on Natures Natural, a fiber that contains 30% post-consumer waste and meets the minimum requirements of ANSI/NISO Z39.48-1992 (R 1997) (*Permanence of Paper*).

for Bettie Jean

Contents

Acknowledgments

I am deeply indebted to my mentors. Judith Stacey has been unwavering in her support, and I am profoundly grateful. Judith Newton, Vicki Smith, and, more recently, Herman Gray have been equally prized treasures. And it is thanks to Michael Blain that I began along this path.

I also wish to thank a number of friends and colleagues who gave me instructive feedback on this project, including Angela Valenzuela, Douglas Foley, Margaret Gibson, Dana Takagi, Caroline Persell, and Ricardo Stanton-Salazar. Carole Joffe provided invaluable contacts and favors, without which my work would have been ten times more difficult. My thanks also to the anonymous reviewers at University of California Press, University of Minnesota Press, *Signs: Journal of Women in Culture and Society,* and *Gender & Society,* all of whom offered important early critical feedback. And thank you to the fabulously smart members of my feminist theory seminars at the University of California, Santa Cruz, where I frequently found myself rejuvenated by conversation and debate. I am also grateful to my research assistants Kyre Atkinson, Esthela Bañuelos, Barbara Barnes, Clare Brown, Marycruz Diaz, and Jen Reck for their intellectual contributions, competency, and hours of (often tedious) work on this project. Thank you to Cheryl Van De Veer at UC Santa Cruz and Ellen F. Smith at UC Press, both of whom patiently assisted me with copyediting, and to Naomi Schneider, my editor at UC Press.

Friends (old and new), family, and fictive kin who have held my hand and supported me in various (and at times lifesaving) ways include Janet

Blaser, Diane Bridgeman, Lionel Cantú, Monica Casper, Christina Cicoletti, Betty Haase, Lyle Haase, David Hall, Matthew Henken, Michele Leedy, Barbara McKenna, Linda Meuret, Rosemary Powers, Craig Reinarman, Heidi Renteria (especially for her treasure-finding ability), Sadie Reynolds, Judith Stacey (again), Inger Stark, Michelle Witt (and Cece), Abigail Zoger, and the Sunday brunch crowd (for their nutritional fortitude). I am also grateful to Dominique for her insider perspective on girls' lives and her consumer expertise on popular culture. Thanks to Guenevere, who kept me company daily and nightly as I wrote, and who is gone now but had been my pal longest among all these fine friends. Finally, S's generosity, wisdom, and willingness to take comic risks made this an immensely more enjoyable journey; thanks, smart bear.

I owe much to the staff at "Waretown High School" for their good will. Considerations of confidentiality keep me from naming the school and the people, but I want to acknowledge the principal and the unit administrators, who gave me their trust, allowed me to conduct my research at their school, tolerated my presence, and made me feel welcome. Because I am narrating a story largely through the eyes of students and simply because I am performing a critical analysis, I "other" teachers at times, and I apologize for this necessary betrayal. These were warm people with the best intentions who, I recognize, were working very hard at their jobs. My analysis is not meant to be critical of individual people, but of the social systems, processes, and ideologies present in our culture that recruit individual actors and inform their actions. Thank you to all of the teachers and counselors for their time, their insights, and their willingness to have me just hanging around their classrooms and offices. P. D. was particularly generous and went beyond the call. And I am most indebted to A. M., who acted as my advocate and without whom this project would not have been possible.

Finally, my greatest debt is to the girls who trusted me with their stories and let me into their lives. They will likely never know how much they affected me or how much I learned from them. I apologize for the unintentional, yet inevitable, injuries that my intrusion into their lives might have caused. Many of them thanked me for taking an interest in their lives and for telling their stories. While I hope that I have not let them down, I am not that naive; I know that if they were to tell their own stories, their accounts would differ from mine. My hope, then, is that they might be one day be empowered to "talk back," to represent themselves without mediation. For those who might feel hurt by the content, I hope they can see that this story is not meant to be critical of individuals, all of whom I liked tremendously, but of social circumstances and forces that go far beyond individual lives. Likewise, what I have been able to give in return was less a benefit to the individual girls I came to know than to the larger project of understanding the many forces on young women's lives.

I also gratefully acknowledge the financial support for this project that came from the Woodrow Wilson National Fellowship Foundation, the National Women's Studies Association, research fellowships from the University of California at Davis, and grants from the Division of Social Sciences and the Academic Senate Committee on Research at the University of California at Santa Cruz. Finally, much of the writing was made possible by a grant from the Spencer Foundation. The views expressed are solely the responsibility of the author.

Introduction to the 2014 Edition

The past decade of stagnant wages for the 99 percent and million-dollar bonuses for the 1 percent has awakened the kids of the middle class to a national nightmare: the dream that coaxed their parents to meet the demands of work, school, mortgage payments, and tuition bills is shattered.
Down is the new up.

Richard Kim, "The Audacity of Occupy Wall Street"

In the ten years since since the publication of *Women without Class,* inequality has grown exponentially. In this introduction to the new edition, I briefly contextualize the book's empirical findings for a new historical context, considering economic crisis and class formation in the new economy, the emergence of postrace discourse, post–civil rights multiracialism, postfeminism, new femininities, and the queering of domestic life.

Since its publication, *Women without Class* has been employed in many literatures, including those of cultural studies and social theory, feminist studies, Latina/o studies, working-class studies, girls' studies, whiteness studies, and educational inequality. In this introduction I also reflect on the contributions that I think the book has made, suggesting why it has acquired a relatively broad and sustained audience for its content, and I note, with hindsight, some of its unexplored opportunities—namely, theorizing ethnicity more fully and employing queer theory more directly.

Finally, I comment on the continuing relevance of the book's cultural theory and a variety of its concepts, including the way it employs feminist poststructuralism and the concepts of performativity and intersectionality and works to resist theorizing its subjects as modern subjects. I also point to some new directions in cultural theory.

A NEW CONTEXT

For me, *Women without Class* is very much about cultural and political consciousness and interacting sociohistoric formations, about the cultural politics of how inequalities are reproduced and challenged and new subjectivities created. Though the book speaks to the role that educational processes play in the formation of inequality, I did not set out to do a study of educational inequality per se. Rather, my broad interest was in cultural politics and subject formation, asking specifically, what are the cultural gestures involved in the performance of class and how are they imbued with race, gender, and sexual meaning? For fortuitous reasons, the site I chose to explore this was a school. Consequently, *Women without Class* considers education less as an institution of reproduction than as one site of discursive formations and assemblages, where discourses of youth crisis, family values, compulsory heterosexuality, anti-immigration, individualism, self-esteem, promiscuity, teen pregnancy, postfeminism, and more recently neoliberalism, postrace, bullying, and sexualization circulate and participate in forming racialized, gendered, sexualized, and classed subjectivities specific to a historical moment. As *Women without Class* argues, these discourses have their source in a variety of historical changes under way, just as they also work as displacements from our focus on growing inequalities, deflecting attention from them.

In light of these original concerns, in what ways has history shifted, both inching along and quickly transforming, in the past ten years that would provide a new context for and reading of young people's lives, those of young women in particular? What kinds of citizen-subjects are now being created?

"Class" Formation in the New Economy

Unchecked capitalism had already produced the uneven processes of globalization, downsizing, privatization, underfunding education, mortgage fraud, and rising debt at the time I studied students' lives at Waretown High, but the inequalities that have resulted from these processes now rival those of the Great Depression. In tune with the long-standing critical tradition of studying the "reproduction of inequality," *Women without Class* argues that education is not, of course, the solution to inequality (as liberal discourse would have it) but rather that schools are routinely one of the institutional sites for that very reproduction (conceptualized now as imprecise and contingent). Consequently, *Women without Class,* along with other studies, suggests that the solution to our social ills most likely lies in the efforts of social justice movements and the complementary gestures of cultural politics to make both the nation-state and transnational corporate capital accountable to the citizenry and to inspire world citizens to behave ethically toward one another.

It was a bright moment for progressives to witness the political gestures of Occupy followed by the demonstrations for labor rights and democracy in Wisconsin in 2011. Given that mass demonstrations focusing attention on labor struggle per se had not been seen in a very long time in the United States, Wisconsin was surprising in that it turned out to be one of the largest pro-labor demonstrations in U.S. history (Nichols 2011, 14). The size and scope of current structural inequalities reached a tipping point, producing political consciousness as people came to see their personal trials as the result of large-scale social problems. What kinds of political consciousness and subjects created and have been created by this new moment in history? Was Occupy an episode of class struggle? What does "class struggle" look like now anyway?

According to one large survey of Occupy participants, it was people who believe that the legislative process is beyond repair, unable to solve the dilemmas that plague the nation, who flooded the streets, people who believed in the possibility of the change Barak Obama promised, that his very election had the potential to revolutionize America, but who were let down by politics as usual (Milkman, Luce, and Lewis 2013). A majority of those who organized were young adults, most of whom work in jobs that have never been unionized and come from families in which unions have never been central.

Women without Class heeded a call to forgo the predictions of totalizing social theories (one part of its address) and find class "where it lives" (Ortner 1993, 427), which, it turns out, is often found in gender, race, and sexual meaning, among other cultural discourses. During Occupy, it also appeared to live in the discourse on debt. A majority of Occupy participants were young people for whom a movement based on signifiers such as "class" or "labor" or "unionism" may feel much less relevant than one organized around indebtedness, a significant burden of the 99 percent. It appears, then, that it was not "class" identity or consciousness, understood as such, that mobilized people, but their shared "experience" of personal deficit.

Women without Class suggests that "class" as a signifier has problematically become a historically outdated code for white male industrial labor. Along with other works, *Women without Class* suggests that in a postindustrial economy, economic restructuring has made the working class invisible as working-class jobs have become less industrial, more service oriented, and more feminized, less dirty and more clean, ironically making it possible to maintain the myth of the great "middle." But in a post-postindustrial moment, among generations of young Americans, a majority (though not all) of whom are far removed from working-class industrial labor, the service economy now appears readily understood as downward mobility for the vast majority.

And while the largest survey shows that the majority of Occupiers (especially organizers) were white (Milkman, Luce, and Lewis 2013), here in Oakland and in other color-full cities across the United States, the face of Occupy was also visibly black, brown, and queer. Moreover, concerned that an awareness of neocolonialism and race making were absent from the movement, Native American activists pushed for renaming Occupy Oakland "Decolonize" to avoid a reinscription of settler colonialism, while Puerto Rico saw a push to rename the movement "(Un)Occupy" (Davis 2011). Perhaps white industrial blue-collar masculine labor is at last long gone as the "authentic" referent for the "working class."

Many demonstrators were underemployed young adults who not only had substantial debt but had also experienced recent job loss and were worried about access to education, money in politics, and corporate greed. Many felt inspired by the events that made up the Arab Spring and saw themselves as linked to a larger movement concerned with global capitalism (Milkman, Luce, and Lewis 2013). It appears, then, that Occupy's politics were based less on identity than on political desire, with "99%" a floating signifier that was effective in interpolating protest subjects. If social movements and intellectual shifts coincide, "no demands" might be imagined to represent a postparadigmatic epistemological zeitgeist, the desire for a different future without an articulation with arrogant certainty of a totalizing utopian vision of what it might look like. A monolithic, authentic, culturally distinct, noninclusive class politics depleted of ethnic, gender, sexual, and other meanings did not manifest Occupy, but neither did the "identity politics" that worried some among the old "new left" preclude it.

These young(ish) generations—some of their members Occupiers, others not—were sold the dream that an education bought on student loans promised a middle-class job and some security but are finding neither. *Women without Class* speaks to the disparity between those who have educational aspirations and those who can afford to have them. Now even those middle-class students with enough cultural and economic capital to get to college, once they are there, have to debate whether it makes sense to stay and acquire more debt or bail out. (Student loan debt averaged $18,650 in 2004 and rose to $26,600 in 2011 [Milkman, Luce, and Lewis 2013, 14].) Is it worth it to acquire tens of thousands of dollars in debt only to end up in a low-wage service job that offers no benefits or security and does not enable one to repay the very loans that got one there?

In sync with a larger neoliberal impulse, over the past decade, political conservatives have successfully argued for the state to divest from education, pushing for increased privatization. This has meant rising costs, increased class sizes, teacher and staff layoffs, elimination of programs, and high-stakes testing that punishes teachers and schools and, therefore, students. These conservative pressures on education are far from race neutral but rather reveal that education continues to be a key battleground for the racial restructuring of the United States (Omi and Winant 2012). Educational policy that includes relying on formulaic testing over teaching "adaptive and creative thought processes" abandons masses of low-income children, often black and brown, to permanent underemployment (Omi and Winant 2012, 322; see also Ravitch 2011; Zhao 2012; Ravitch 2013; Tienken and Orich 2013). *Women without Class* speaks to the fact that some working-class students and students of color hope to enter community colleges and then transfer to state or university schools to better their life chances. The rates of transfer have always been abysmally low. But today it is not even clear what the value of higher education is for those who do manage to transfer, even if there are slots to transfer into. In such a climate, the military remains, as it has always been, a seductive and risky alternative for the growing number who cannot afford college. (One girl whom I interviewed for *Women without Class* ten years ago, who was en route to the armed services, worried aloud to me, "I hope there's no war," unable to know that the United States would soon invade Iraq.) Moreover, the university is increasingly pressured to give "vocational" education, engaging its students in practical job training over critical learning. As *Women without Class* argues, education is not the cause or the cure for poverty. Schools and colleges can help produce skilled workers (whether vocational or professional), but when there are no living-wage jobs of either kind to fill, well . . .

College graduates, educated for careers that no longer exist, are now burdened with student loan debt that was supposed to lead to their mobility, are often on the brink of default, and face the likelihood that they will struggle to repay their debt well into their retirement (presuming they get one). We see home foreclosures not only among the working class but even in upper-middle-class neighborhoods, we witness rising credit card debt due to pay cuts and job loss, and we watch people file for bankruptcy because of their inability to afford their medical debts. In pursuit of the elusive American dream, Americans across all economic strata now borrow excessively to secure basic social goods, such as housing, education, and health care. These are the necessities that the middle class used to feel entitled to and that the left had long argued the state should make available to the disadvantaged among its citizens.

Achieving the American dream by working hard is now only a "remote possibility" for many, and for the now unprecedented numbers of transnational workers migrating to meet the huge demand for low-cost labor, citizenship is not necessarily a reward for their sacrifices (Vogel 2006, 39). Like Occupy, the Dreamers, youth activists who advocate the passage of the DREAM Act, also expose the hypocrisy of the American dream ideology. These are young people who, having migrated with their undocumented parents as children, received K–12 education in the United States and only later in adolescence came to understand their undocumented status and the shock of its meaning—their ineligibility to receive financial aid to attend college, in spite of their scholastic achievements and community contributions (Gonzalez 2011). Moreover, their ineligibility for legal work means that they can look forward only to sharing the same low-wage job opportunities as their parents. For migrant workers, poorly paid work in the informal economy is no longer, if it ever was, "an initiation into the mainstream U.S. working class" but is now only an invitation "to stay in the informal U.S. economy," and even then only for as long as they are needed, with deportation always a looming threat (Vogel 2006, 39).

"Middle class" is a social category that remains discursively present, as many claims to political legitimacy are based on it (Stout 2013), but it is increasingly ontologically absent, gone missing. Where *Women without Class* predicted harsh futures for working-class students, it suggested relatively middle-class futures for middle-class students. But what are the markers of "middle class" now? I recently asked a nineteen-year-old whose parents are college-educated working professionals if she was planning to go to college. She responded cynically, "Yeah, well, I work three jobs now, so I'm not sure where I'm supposed to fit that in." "Middle-class" Americans have neither the safety net nor the financial stability that the term previously suggested (Pruitt 2011), causing economic distinctions between the working and middle classes to fade while the gap between the superrich and the rest of us has grown more pronounced than ever. One consequence of the spectacle of Occupy was that economic class per se, which *Women without Class* demonstrates is typically discursively displaced, became centered in political debate, at least for a time. Mentions of "income inequality" began to rise in the media (Milkman, Luce, and Lewis 2013), perhaps momentarily contributing to a less class-blind social hierarchy.

But while the new economy has rendered terms such as *working class* and *middle class* even more anachronistic than they were just ten years ago, nonetheless distinct differences in income, wealth, and debt do, of course, remain, as some always weather the storm with less pain than others.

"Postrace" and New Ethnicities

How do "race" and ethnicity "intersect" with class formation in relation to these processes? What kinds of racial projects are under way, and what kinds of new racial/ethnic subjects are being created by current social and cultural forces?

Over the past decade the term *postrace* emerged in many arenas, being employed with multiple and contradictory meanings. One line of thinking considers *postrace* synonymous with *color-blind discourse*. Here, the election of an African American to the presidency helped produced a discourse of "postracial optimism" that bolstered the already present color-blind discourse, which posits that the solution to racism is to ignore race (Omi and Winant 2012, 309). Like color-blind discourse, postrace ideology is a sleight of hand, a discursive trick whereby the route to making race a less salient force is to renounce racial categorizations, all the while ignoring the ongoing structural effects that categories of race have manifested and continue to manifest. Postrace, then, is characterized by both the repudiation of race and its constant recognition. It has become a strategy of racial formation, a new way of manifesting racial projects and inequalities, ironically by not making explicit references to race, because in commonsense thinking, the very fact of a black president means we are now "beyond that."

Women without Class makes good use of this notion of color-blind discourse in its analysis of racial formation, particularly in its focus on Proposition 209's attention to economic differences over racial categories as an ill-informed means of remedying inequality. The long-term effects of Proposition 209 can be examined now that its passage (in 1996) was almost two decades ago. The news is that, according to a study of those attending the University of California, the proportion of Latina/o and African American students has in fact declined, revealing that the proposition's color-blind intent was far from race neutral in its effects. The admissions process was, of course, only "partially mediated" by affirmative action prior to 209 to begin with (Santos, Cabrera, and Fosnacht 2010, 617). "Even when race *was* a consideration in the admissions process," it was never able to fully eliminate unequal access but only to "ameliorate the disparate impact [of race-based unequal access] that occurs in the admission process" (624).

These findings suggest that the lack of affirmative action since the passage of Proposition 209 has had a cooling effect on underrepresented students of color, dissuading Latina/o and African American students from applying for admission to begin with as campuses may now appear less than welcoming to them. And while progressive admission policies that seek out students of color post-209 have partially mitigated the proposition's impact, they have been "insufficient [as] substitutes for race-conscious admissions" (Santos, Cabrera, and Fosnacht 2010, 625).

One finding that *Women without Class* offers is that while students of color are relatively equipped with a discourse on race to describe the institutionalized barriers that impact their lives due to racism, working-class whites can only engage in self-blame for their "failure," because a discourse on class, which would help them explain their struggle, is so absent and displaced in our culture. But in a postrace discursive environment, which suggests the end of racism, the ability of young people of color to appeal to either interpersonal experiences of racism or institutionalized racial barriers as affecting their life choices may fast be becoming "illegitimate." Meanwhile, women and men of color, including those who are immigrants, are still overrepresented among the poor, separated from the "middle" by both income and wealth. Both postrace and a strengthening neoliberal discourse of choice that blames individuals rather than social forces and promotes an ideology of self-sufficiency and individual responsibility have strengthened right when the ground has shifted under these young people's feet.

Postrace as color-blind ideology aside, there is yet another, less prevalent potential meaning of *postrace*, better named post–civil rights, which *Women without Class* began to point to in its analysis of racial performativity. In other arenas, people have focused on the positive potential that an alternative idea of postrace might offer to undermine the essentialism of racial categories. For example, the term *post-Blackness* came out of the Harlem art world in the late 1990s, where it signified a generational shift. It described those artists who wanted neither to be labeled "black artists" nor to be restricted by this categorization even though their work was rooted in notions of blackness, which it was deeply about redefining (Touré 2011). The term was often widely misunderstood as a repudiation of blackness, but post-Blackness was meant to recognize a shift away from an older generation's attachment to identity politics and the notion of a unified authentic black culture and a younger generation's emotional distance from past struggles. This shift enabled young artists to foreground irreverence (toward both a white gaze and a black civil rights gaze) as a strategy of engaging in cultural politics.

Employing the term *post–civil rights* in order to speak to new ethnicities (not only blackness), not as a postrace ideology but as a periodizing concept, works to signify the distance that younger generations may have from conceptualizations of race and ethnicity rooted in a particular era of identity politics and particular historical experiences of racial trauma. Without an intent to deflect attention from the negative power of its more common, color-blind meaning, this alternative understanding of *postrace* as "post–civil rights" does point to a new generation's growing, and soon to be widespread, experience of being multiracial/ethnic or "mixed race." This experience often ignites youth's acute awareness of the malleability of race. While we are all "interracial" in the long arm of history, never having belonged to discrete racial categories, in the short arm of history, since the end of miscegenation laws and the rise of post–civil rights voluntary sexual unions, multiracial membership has been on the rise. (The "multiracial" population grew by 30 percent from 2000 to 2010, with 18 percent of the United States now considering itself so. In places like California it is quickly becoming a norm. By 2025, California will be barely half "white" [Almaguer 2012].) These new categorizations and the ways of experiencing one's racial/ethnic self that accompany them enable us to question what it means to be white, black,

Asian, Latina/o, Native, and so on in startlingly new ways and with answers that differ from those of previous generations. Post–civil rights class mobility, increased global migration, and the greater visibility of LGBTQ communities of color manifest a range of new identifications. Thus, these answers often bring forth "a more expansive notion" of Chicana/o-ness, whiteness, and the like than before (Touré 2011, 204). In this line of thinking, postrace as post–civil rights would mean signifying not the (false) end of blackness, Latina/o-ness, and so on but the "end of the reign of a narrow, single notion of" such categorizations (Dyson 2011, xv), offering connotations far different from *postrace*'s association with color-blind discourse.

Post–civil rights as a signifier of a historical moment, one characterized by deessentialized racial/ethnic gestures that recognize race as a historical construct yet with temporal attachments, fits with the way race and ethnicity are thought through in *Women without Class* and is consistent with Hall's description of new ethnicities (2000). *Women without Class* explores its recognition of race and ethnicity as fictional and temporal yet persistent and obdurate in part through the notion of racial performativity. My point here is that increasingly, any analysis of the way we experience our racial/ethnic selves will have to contend with this growing postmodern experience of "mixedness," new ethnicities and new forms of racialized embodiment (to which I will return as relates to performance theory). While in many ways obvious, in studies of educational inequality, the invisibility of multiracial students persists, especially at the policy level (Caballero, Haynes, and Tikly 2007), and *Women without Class* only anecdotally begins to make it visible.

The existence of such a large population who identify as "multi" impacts not only those who identify with it or are identified as it but the entire culture's thinking about the fiction of race, and challenges us in our thinking about ethnicity as cultural difference as well. The point of research to make this invisibility visible would be to understand race as both historically and interactionally constructed, to explore racialized performances as context specific within both the long arm of history and the course of daily life, and to analyze performance as becoming. In everyday interaction, race and ethnicity are situational and protean (Rockquemore and Brunsma 2007), with large impact as global schemas of race and ethnicity are "challenged and recreated in . . . transnational space," where transnational migration affects changes in personal and collective views of racial classification in both the home and host societies (Roth 2012, 10). The widespread existence and experience of post–civil rights multiracial/multiethnic subjectivities has the potential to challenge notions of racial authenticity, but only when an understanding of it sidesteps the naïve assertion that "mixed race" will conveniently and automatically create a harmonious, color-blind society (Gilbert 2005, 58).

Considering post–civil rights and postrace discourses in tandem, Obama's election might be said to have both diminished and intensified notions of race. His visibility, his "mixed" race status, and his racial performance raise an awareness of the malleability of race while revealing its polarizing impact as racism has been brought to the fore in the backlash against him. An increase of interracialness can at once produce a softening of categories of race and point to tensions around racial categories and potentially embattled identities.

"Postfeminism" and New Femininities

Women without Class puts racial formation theory into conversation with feminist theories of intersectionality, working to incorporate a missing analysis of gender and sexuality (see Kandaswamy 2012 for a celebratory yet critical overview of Omi and Winant's [1986] foundational text along these lines). *Women without Class* asks how gender and sexual formations "intersect" with race and class ones. What kinds of new gender and sexual subjects are being created by current social and cultural forces?

Not wholly unlike the emergent discourse of postrace, *postfeminist* is a signifier that has appeared on both the popular and the scholarly stage over the past decades. It was meant and taken by some as a label for a conservative, antifeminist impulse that suggests feminist politics is no longer necessary now that gender equality has supposedly been achieved, and thus it inspired the (troubled) retort "I'll be a postfeminist in postpatriarchy," which rejects any utility the concept of postfeminsm might have. An alternative, and far more useful, meaning of the term signifies a historical moment (akin to *postmodern*) that marks not the death of feminism but "the simultaneous incorporation, revision, and depoliticization of many of the central goals of second-wave feminism" (Stacey 1990, 8), indicating both its success and its demise. Here *postfeminism*, as a periodizing concept, perhaps more carefully named *post–second wave*, refers to "the consciousness and strategies that increasing numbers of women [and men] have developed in response to the new difficulties and opportunities of postindustrial society" (Stacey 1990, 8).

In short, a range of economic and cultural transformations have created new categories of womanhood and made an array of new gender and sexual subjectivities possible for younger generations. This recognition of how historical forces produce important generational differences in women's lives has led over the past decade to an avalanche of scholarship on "third-wave feminisms," "new femininities," and "girls' studies."

The content of these works varies, with those coming out of popular psychology and therapeutic practice (often written for trade audiences) reading far differently than those informed by cultural studies scholarship. The latter, including *Women without Class*, work to explore how girls adeptly negotiate popular culture, and they provide a complex reading of young womens' and girls' lives. My point here is to express concern over the increasing popularity of the former, which participate in media constructions of girls, and especially girls' sexuality, as a social problem. Such accounts patronizingly describe girls largely as victims of "the media" and "popular culture," both of which are given far too much explanatory weight, and neglect the influence of other social forces on their lives. In fact, *Women without Class* opens with a critical reading of the popular trade text *Reviving Ophelia* (Pipher 1994), as a foil pointing, as many others also now have, to the problematic construction and generalization of girlhood as white middle-class heterosexual victimhood. Over the past decade we have witnessed a proliferation of texts and popular discourses in this genre of "Ophelia narratives," which routinely articulate a "cohesive picture of adolescent girlhood as traumatic" and presents "adolescent femininity as a state of injury" (Marshall 2007, 717, 707). Girls' "empowerment" (as liberal subjects) arrives through the help of adults who are their "self-appointed moral guardians" (McRobbie 1991, x).

This discourse on female adolescence generally continues to neglect any recognition of female desire, too often promotes an asexual ideal for girls, and routinely scapegoats and pathologizes femininity. Moreover, it ignores many other dimensions of girls' lives. Too often the texts that generate this public discourse, when describing new generational subjects, continue to tend toward gender reductionism, suggesting that the experience of a generation, a collective of people, is all the same. While it is the case that a generation or cohort (across age, class, race/ethnicity, nationality, sexuality, geographic location, and so on) does share a historical moment, it is crucial to recognize the uneven experiences of it, as *Women without Class* and many others have worked to show (see Lopez 2002; Denner and Dunbar 2004; Carter 2005; Miller 2008; Jones 2009; Pasco 2011; Garcia 2012). Where heterosexual middle-class white girls star in this discourse, as about-to-be fallen women in need of rescue, working-class girls and girls of color cameo less often (and lesbian, bi, trans, or questioning girls almost never), as in need of help, always already oversexualized, part of the problem, or not conceptualized as worthy "victims."

The current oversimplified "sexualization" thesis in popular discourse (which circulates widely in these trade texts, in the media, at schools, and among parents), and is present in some scholarly discourse as well, too often buys rather wholesale into the puritan ideals of a sex-negative culture, tending to promote a problematic "politics of respectability" (Higgenbotham 1993) as a solution to the supposed "problem" of girls' sexuality. These texts work as cautionary tales, telling girls (and their parents and teachers) that female sexual desire and pleasure are fundamentally dangerous. We hear primarily the voices of those public commentators who can see only in dubious negative terms the "pornification" of culture and the "sexualization" of young women. Girls as sexually desiring subjects are invisible, their sexuality primarily visible only when they are imagined as victims, sensationalizing their "tragic" behavior. Perhaps the real tragedy is that these discourses provide such a narrow rage of sexual subjectivities for young women to identify with.

Absent, for example, is any consideration that some of the cultural shifts we are witnessing might also be read as signs of the queering of domestic life or of a potentially more sex-positive, sexually open, and queer culture (to which I will return). In contrast, sexualities scholars point more neutrally to larger historical shifts under way, such as the postmodernization of sexuality. This is marked by a shift away from relational sexuality, based on a dating, romance, and a marriage script, toward a "recreational sexual ethic," which is based on pleasure and manifests "new erotic dispositions" (Bernstein 2007, 4–6). While we have in fact witnessed an increase in representations of sexuality, including its increased commodification, this does not automatically translate into "promiscuity, pathology, and deficiency" (Egan 2013, 5). The extent to which these cultural shifts re-create or challenge inequalities is a question whose answer should be explored, not presumed. Where, for example, are the stories of overt sexuality as confrontational by design? Where are the stories of girls whose failure to meet conservative norms is experienced not as failing at "femininity" or as evidence of low "self-esteem" but as purposeful violations of the regulation of their sexuality, as refusals of middle-class notions of "adolescence" and morality, or as mere expressions of ethnic, class, and sexual variations?

In this cultural context, sexuality—female sexuality in particular, especially that of young women and girls—continues to be a site of strong cultural contestation, reproducing a society that has long been two-faced about sexuality, which is at once highly visible and repressed. Because these cultural shifts have the potential to uproot the ongoing regulation of female sexuality, we daily witness "sex panics" (Lancaster 2011) over young female sexuality. The ongoing invisibility of girls' (and women's) desire reveals a long-standing cultural refusal to accept girls as sexual citizens (Willis 2008). These sex panics cannot be understood apart from other social formations. The regulation of female sexuality is always inflected with discourses of class, race, and heteronormativity, reproducing middle-class white heterosexual norms of femininity (Marshall 2007). The regulation of sexuality has always also been a strategy of regulating people of color, the working class, and queer communities (Puri 1999; Ferguson 2004; Cantú 2009; Moore 2011). Even the focus on keeping sexuality "age appropriate" is coded by race, class, and nation, imposing normative ideals of twentieth-century white Western childhood, failing to recognize that childhood itself is historically and socially constructed.

In short, over the past decade, the "girl" has become "an assemblage of social and cultural issues and questions rather than a field of physical facts" (Driscoll 2002, 14). Or as R. Danielle Egan describes it, the sexualized girl now figures as a "monster," a "metaphor for our cultural condition," representing the erosion of the traditional family, challenges to heteronormativity, middle-class decline and fear of class contagion through the perceived "eroticism of the working class," fear over the "racialization of sexual innocence," fear of "unbounded female heterosexuality," challenges to the historic valorization of whiteness, challenges to Western notions of childhood, and cultural anxiety over children's eroticism (2013, 17, 135). The girl as monster has its source in a variety of historical changes under way, just as it works as a displacement, deflecting attention from them.

Setting this popular discourse on "sexualization" aside and coming from a different site—cultural studies scholarship—others have offered up a different concern, that neoliberal forces now coincide with gender formation to help construct a new key subjectivity for young women as consumer-citizens (McRobbie 2008; Banet-Weiser 2012). To the extent that young women, some far more than others, have benefited from second-wave feminism and genuinely do experience a degree of greater cultural and economic power, capital has envisioned them as empowered agents who are free to make choices in work, family, and sexuality that are at once entrepreneurial and consumer choices. The caution here is to look for how liberal feminist ideas of "empowerment, independence, and choice" may at times be appropriated and co-opted in the service of individualizing neoliberal narratives of mobility and how they may become "a key 'technology' through which the self is lived" (Ringrose 2013, 68, 9).

I have asked what new kinds of citizen-subjects are being created and have only gestured here toward some answers, as relates to the themes that are prevalent in *Women without Class*, along with naming some of the discursive formations and materialities that have made them possible. History is always working to make new subject positions available for temporal attachment. I turn now to a more direct consideration of the critique of the modernist understanding of the social subject that is present (perhaps more often implicitly than explicitly) in *Women without Class,* via its use of cultural theory.

CULTURAL THEORY

Poststructuralisms and Performativity

Women without Class was written in a time and place where the interdisciplinary training in feminist studies, feminisms of color, and cultural studies that I and others received produced a preoccupation among many scholars with both intersectionality and poststructuralist theory. Where much of feminist and cultural studies had both created and embraced insights of poststructuralism, it was not yet an accepted kind of analysis within most of sociology (and perhaps still is not). While not explicitly stated, one goal of mine was to share what I found to be the usefulness of poststructuralist theory with a sociological audience, as well as with those who were focused on intersectionality but without the insights that would lead to a noncategorical, more processual way of imagining it.

Concerned with the politics of theory, *Women without Class* works purposefully to try to recognize and give credit to feminisms, especially feminisms of color, for the labor of theory production, for generating many insights that at the time were (and likely still are) too often attributed only to "postmodern theorists," and to show that these categories are not neatly distinct, that the critique of the modern subject was in fact produced by the critique of the center that came from the recognition and representation of those who had been marginalized in multiple ways.

This recognition of postmodern subjectivity is not unrelated to methodology, and *Women without Class* is also preoccupied, as many were at the time, with the crisis of ethnographic representation. How to represent ethnography in light of postmodern epistemological shifts produced a wide range of "experimental" ethnographic textual representations and has since given over to concerns that center on not only how to represent the "other" but also how to represent the "self," resulting in autoethnography, polyphonic texts, ethnographic fiction, performance ethnography, a reskilling of intellectual culture, and new academic subjectivities (Bettie 2014).

For me the use that *Women without Class* makes of a variety of kinds of cultural theory; the way it pushes concepts (such as performativity, class consciousness, discourse, resistance, materiality, and cultural capital) up against the "empirical" world to see if they work, so to speak, and attempts to alter them when they don't; and its insistence that theory, as Clifford Geertz (1973, 55–56) suggested, "stay rather close to the ground" or "hover" low over the ethnographic site, are some of its strengths. Also, the book's attempt to collapse "micro" and "macro," by making an ethnographic account of everyday practices and the creation of subjectivity coterminous with an explication of cultural, discursive, and material forces—its on-the-ground examination of "structurally embedded agency" and "intention-filled structures" (Ortner 1996, 12)—seems key to its value.

Women without Class shows that the social formations that produce inequality persist less as static structures than as fluid processes in formation while not ignoring the ways in which they become obdurate, stubborn, and material, yet always potentially impermanent. Poststructuralist theory enabled a move away from a previously too-rigid notion of structures and institutions to an analysis of structures as discourses and, increasingly many would add, "assemblages" (Deleuze and Guatarri 1983). Moreover, the focus on structure as discourse, and as abiding only in an interim—not an essential or ahistorical—way invites a (Foucaultian) conceptualization of power as fields that can be tapped into as subjects consciously and unconsciously enact socially produced "selves." These theoretical tools allowed *Women without Class* to work to conceptualize young people's "agency" less through the liberal lens of "empowered" subjects, of autonomous selves, than to imagine agency as the possibility of a particular historical contingency, a social creation of the particular articulation of elements that come together at a given historical conjuncture in a way that makes change always one possible outcome.

It is now especially crucial to consider a reconceptualization of agency, given the strengthening of a neoliberal discourse of choice (Ringrose 2013). To do so suggests an account of agency that does not search "for sustained, rational accounts from unitary coherent actors" but rather locates "critical moments of subjective flux" (112) as historical shifts make new "kinds" of people and new cultural gestures possible. Newer vocabularies of theory are being put to use that move us even further outside the dialectic of structure and agency as cultural analysts search less for "resistance," a concept that has long been overladen, than for "lines of flight" (Deleuze and Guatarri 2004 [1984]) and moments of rupture based on fantasy and desire (Ringrose 2013). *Women without Class* works to attend ethnographically to how discourse enters people's lives, both invading them and being challenged by them.

Related is the conceptual distinction that *Women without Class* offers between performativity (structure) as unconscious iteration and performance (agency) as conscious, knowing display. One way of putting theory to work that *Women without Class* meant to do was to deessentialize race via an analysis of it using performance theory. While Judith Butler's theory of gender performativity was, of course, used by many at the time of my original writing, I found little work that extended this concept to race beyond textual analyses. I was unaware at the time of John L. Jackson Jr.'s *Harlemworld* (2001), which does this ethnographic work. There are other writings that explore race as performance that appeared around the time *Women without Class* was published and many that have emerged since (Mirón and Inda 2000; Mahtani 2002; Carbado and Gulati 2003; Ehlers 2003; Johnson 2003a; Johnson 2003b; Butler 2004; Rich 2004; Ehlers 2006; Nayak 2006; Youdell 2006; Veninga 2009; Butler 2010; Fleetwood 2011; Ehlers 2012; Chadderton 2013).

Where *Women without Class* just barely began thinking through an analysis of race/ethnicity as performance in school settings, others have pushed further. Catherine Veninga, for example, critiquing the "ontological commitments of critical race theory," asks how students "mobilize their bodies to negotiate belongings ostensibly foreclosed by the primacy of phenotype" (2009, 107). Like *Women without Class*, this scholarship works to bridge the performativity and materiality of bodies, revealing how people who have an ambiguous phenotype "strategically deploy racialized performances to mobilize readings of their mixed-race bodies that disrupt" social expectations of racial categories (Veninga

2009, 118; see also Mahtani 2002). For example, a white body's performance of (perceived) "blackness" "constitutes an ontological crisis" (Veninga 2009, 121; see also Ehlers 2006; Ehlers 2012). In such instances, people perform social identities against prescribed social rules that assign racial identity based on phenotype, and access identities from which they would otherwise be prohibited if they had announced their racial "truth" (Ehlers 2006). Given that the cultural imperative is to embody one's supposed racial "truth," such an "embodied performance is *always* a space of crisis" (156).

Thinking through race as performative reveals that the body is a "malleable site that actually provides rather than precludes access to alternative racial scripts" (Veninga 2009, 124). A self-understanding of race as performed offers new interpretations of cultural gestures against oversimplified interpretations of such practices as merely a matter of assimilation or appropriation. It provides a narration of the self that resists a modernist impulse on "identity" and allows "a change of self-recognition . . . the emergence into visibility of a new subject," a recognition that race/ethnicity is always in a state of becoming (Hall 2000, 204), in both history and the space of everyday practices. *Women without Class* began to "map the specificity of becomings" (Ringrose 2013, 83) in these performances of self, to reveal context-specific shifting processes of identification. In its focus on racial performativity, *Women without Class* both employed racial formation theory at the level of political and state discourse and located it in the intimate microcosm of everyday life and individual cultural gestures.

Feminist uses of poststructuralism at the time when I was writing *Women without Class* were in part a response to the problematic ontological underpinnings of standpoint theory. Feminist materialists, or "new materialists," have often articulated poststructuralism's limitations regarding the role of materiality, the body, and ontology over the past decade (Coole and Frost 2010; Puar 2012). While this might be seen as the pendulum swinging back again, it could rather qualify as a move in a post-poststructuralist direction. The authors that I cite here work to demonstrate, like *Women without Class,* how to conceptualize performativity without ignoring materiality (such as phenotype, the sexed body, or economic capital), bridging the discursive and the material, all the while recognizing that embodiment is always or almost always apprehended through culture (Butler 1993).

At the time when I was writing *Women without Class*, I could find no work that extended the concept of performativity to class, save for the concept of "doing difference" in a different theoretical tradition within sociology (West and Fenstermaker 1995), and so doing this truly felt like exploration. *Women without Class* has since been cited among a handful of works written during a boomlet of new scholarship on class, much of which provides a reading of class that incorporates poststructuralism (Skeggs 1997; Cobble 2005), queers grand narratives of capitalism (Gibson-Graham 1996), and speaks to class performativity (Rottenburg 2004; Cobble 2005; Pruitt 2011). (Though it might be said that Paul Willis, among others in his cohort, offered a much earlier, embryonic version of thinking through class as performance.)

I was also very much interested in exploring class less as a political consciousness than as a lived cultural "identity" experienced as much through leisure, consumption, and social relations as it is through work, and there was a tradition within (mostly British) cultural studies that assisted me in doing so. *Women without Class* employs Raymond Williams's (1970) "structure of feeling" concept to think through class as an unarticulated injury rather than only a political consciousness or identity, to consider how inequality is felt but not politically articulated. Since the "affective turn" (Massumi 2002; Ahmed 2004; Clough and Halley 2007), many have elaborated on affective states that are not readily named in language and that, again, in a critique of some versions of poststructuralism, challenge its nonontological impulse through a focus on that which might be prediscursive, along with collective trauma, public feeling, and political emotion (Berlant 1997; Cvetkovich 2003; Berlant 2008; Gould 2009; Berlant 2011; Cvetkovich 2012). (It should be noted that along with R. Williams 1970, Sennett and Cobb's [1972] notion of "hidden injuries" and the work of a long list of feminist scholars, most notably Arlie Hochschild [1983], have been inchoate precursors to this new study of affect.) As Sara Ahmed (2004) aptly describes, affective states help create the subject positions that people identify with and feel a sense of belonging to.

Ethnographic work on this front and related to class per se includes that which asks: how do class positioning and mobility feel (Walley 2013)? Noelle Stout (2013) explores how affective states are not mere superstructure but rather work to structure neoliberalism and vice versa. She describes, for example, how under the conditions of a wide-scale mortgage crisis, shame has characterized homeowner subjectivity for many homeowners, as the inability to pay one's debt has been publically constructed as an individual moral failing. Shame has long been a felt experience of class, a displacement of sorts, a "hidden injury" (Sennett and Cobb 1972). Stout asks, when might this negative affect be productive? When does despair form communities of resistance? Through Occupy, this private shame showed the potential to be turned into collective public outrage and the displacement was revealed.

Class shame, of course, cannot be uncoupled from other articulations, as color continues to signify exclusion from the "respectable" classes and the genders and sexualities that compose them. The inability to perform "respectable femininity" or "masculinity" (read: white heterosexual middle class) is a "burden" for many. Sexuality and gender, then, have long been used to pathologize "minority" cultures, as nonheteronormative family structures and sexual behavior are both taken to be causes of economic failure (Ferguson 2004).

Lisa R. Pruitt (2011) too speaks to these felt injuries manifested as public feelings in her description of the class culture gap that fuels the culture wars. Resonant with *Women without Class*'s depiction of rural/small-town, working-class culture, she names the rural/urban class coding and displacement found in the discourse of middle-class liberals and "coastal elites" who have carelessly spewed decades of casual insults to rural working people (seen, for example, in media pundits' condescending image of Sara Palin as a big-game hunter). Likewise, *Women without Class* argues that an analysis of class not as political consciousness but as culture, as a sense of group belonging, and a race/ethnic–specific one at that, may be necessary to the creation of any sense of political community. This culture of casual insults is fuel for class resentment (J. Williams 2010), and these felt injuries to one's cultural dignity work hard to preclude the political unity that progressives desire.

Troubling the Metaphor

Although the term *intersectionality* now circulates widely, the concept often carries some worrisome baggage. While these problems are not necessarily inherent to Kimberlé Crenshaw's formulation of intersectionality as "method and disposition, a heuristic and analytic tool" (Carbado et al. 2013, 312; see also Crenshaw 1989; Crenshaw 1991; Bilge 2013), when we examine its travelogue we find that with some regularity, intersectionality has been employed in ways that are limiting and lack complexity and/or are depoliticized. Too much work that uses this terminology conceptualizes social formations and identities as ahistoric and static rather than processual, relational, and temporal (see overviews in McCall 2005; Choo and Ferree 2010; Grzanka 2014). Unfortunately, the list of subject positions (race, gender, class, sexuality, etc.) that often accompany the analytical tool of intersectionality are too often invoked to imply static social locations or identity categories rather than being understood as dynamic historical forces and processes. Alternatively, the languages of racialization, colonialism, capitalism, neoliberalism, and so on are more likely to suggest impermanent and moving social forces.

In other instances, organizations have appropriated and mainstreamed the meaning of *intersectionality,* co-opting its more radical meaning for neoliberal "diversity" politics. Here, instrumental approaches to considering multiple forms of diversity enable corporations and social justice organizations to "accrue 'liberal capital'" (Ward 2008, 6; see also Duggan 2002). Again, these troublesome uses do not necessarily originate with the concept itself, and intersectionality continues to be put to use, its limitations discovered and its utility maximized. Crenshaw herself suggested that it is best understood not as a theory of identity but as a heuristic device with which to *do* things (Carbado et al. 2013). Thus it is not useful to conflate intersectionality, as some have, with standpoint theory, identity politics, or a modernist epistemology.

Recently, others working to articulate a poststructuralist theory of intersectionality have reread intersectionality as coproduced "assemblages" (a la Deleuze), messy multidirectional networks and collections of multiplicities, organic and nonorganic forces that cannot be analytically disassembled, alongside a recognition that to do so "betrays the founding impulse of intersectionality, that identities cannot be so easily cleaved" (Puar 2007, 212; see also Puar 2012).

Moreover, identity as a modernist understanding of the self suggests starting with static positions and then considering movement. Instead we might begin with the primacy of process, to conceptualize the self not as being but as endless becomings. This direction of thinking then produces "wonder that there can be stasis" at all (Massumi 2002, 6); thus the subject is conceived as an ongoing event, an effect, "a capture" (Puar 2007, 215). Bringing ontology back in, sociality would also be conceived as "encounters between bodies, rather than simply entities and attributes of subjects" (Puar 2012, 58).

In short, intersectionality as an analytical tool has never precluded a critique of the modern subject and does not force an analysis of the intersections of static identities but has always already allowed the recognition of moving social formations that produce protean and historically temporal subjects. It is ironic that a tool meant to decenter the normative (modern) subject of feminism has been employed at times in a way that does not critique that very subject. Many of the "cherished categories of the intersectional mantra . . . are the products of modernist colonial agendas and . . . a Western/Euro-American epistemological formation through which the notion of discrete identity has emerged" (Puar 2012, 54). Thus, lengthening the laundry list of subjectivities can replicate the very problem at hand. The challenge for social theory, of course, is how to critique the modernist understanding of the social subject and liberal notions of social change while insisting on politics, albeit politics reimagined.

Some of the richest work that has been done under the sign of intersectionality recognizes that social forces are not precise, analogous formations that develop in isolation and then intersect but rather are imbricated, such that the meaning of each is realized through the others; as well as demonstrates that these various forces are both material and discursive. Even when all this is understood to be true in principle, representing this complexity, whether it is articulated as intersections or conjunctures or assemblages, can be a daunting task.

Women without Class tries to show this coproduction at the level of social formations and this discursive imbrication, suggesting that race and gender and sexuality are some of the languages through which we talk about class, class and gender and sexuality are some of the languages through which we talk about race, and so on. Because they are coconstituted, each social force cannot be effectively thought through apart from the others. Each is routinely articulated through and inflected by the others, gaining its meaning and the material that goes with it through reference to them (Kandaswamy 2012).

Queering the Tripartite

Keeping in mind the "poststructuralist fatigue around the notion of the subject itself" and the fact that the focus on "difference" merely produces "new subjects of inquiry that infinitely multiply exclusion in order to promote inclusion" (Puar 2012, 62, 54), it is nonetheless the case that the "race, gender, and class" tripartite was momentarily effective in challenging the blind spots of ethnic studies, feminist studies, and Marxisms by asking them to be in conversation with one another. But inevitably this tripartite produced key absences. Generational differences often are not accounted for. Often neither race nor ethnicity captures the forces of geography, nation, religion, or sovereignty. Gender too often continues to mean cisgender (nontransgender) female- or male-bodied people and at times even remains a proxy for heterosexual female-bodied people in particular. Routinely, work under the sign of gender fails to think through the ways in which gender is sexualized and sexuality is gendered, due to a failure to incorporate the insights of queer theory, which is too often thought irrelevant to heterogender performances.

Some of the richest work has gone far beyond the limitations of race, gender, and class to a nuanced unpacking of densely imbricated social forces, often through a queer critique, revealing, for example, a queer political economy of migration that demonstrates how heteronormative immigration laws and border enforcement regulate sexuality (Cantú 2009). Or showing how the regulation of sexuality unfortunately has been used to establish heteropatriarchal legitimacy in communities of color: for example, through the marginalization of gay men and lesbians (Kandaswamy 2012) or by placing erotic restrictions on women (Puri 1999; Espiritu 2001).

This work has also unpacked the process by which acceptance, equality, and citizenship have been contingent on heterosexuality and gender and sexual conformity. As the nation demanded white heteropatriarchal kinship structures yet made them impossible for many, the intersection of capitalism and heteronormativity worked to make the working class, communities of color, and immigrant communities always already queer, forced to operate outside heteropatriarchy (Ferguson 2004). *Women without Class* argues, along with others, that capital creates not merely "empty places" to be filled but also gendered and racialized subjects to fill them. Complicating this further, Ferguson 2004 shows how the gender and sexual transgressions of nonwhite people have been constitutive of nonwhite labor, since migration, globalization, and heteronormativity shape the very configuration of class.

Moreover, those who operate outside heteropatriarchy—not just LGBTQ communities but other sexual "deviants," including sex workers and consumers among other nonnormative sexual practitioners—are routinely criminalized as noncitizens as national policies on sex tourism, HIV/AIDS, and cultural definitions of respectable sexualities vastly shape economic inequality in ways that cannot be ignored. In short, heteronormativity and the politics of respectability are part of the narrative of national belonging, as one's domestic character and sexual practices are always in question as part of citizenship (Moore 2011). Sexuality has historically been a part of the creation of "classes," as subjects are created for class slots, revealing the imbrication of class with constructions of sexual "deviance." These works reveal how sexuality structures capital and vice versa, recognizing that capital has a sexual politics. They show that macroeconomic shifts manifest in the most intimate realms of daily life and that intimacy, gender, domesticity, sexuality, and race are at the heart of empire. These works go far in complicating models of intersectionality by disarticulating race, gender, class, nationalisms, sovereignty, tradition, modernity, sexualities, ethnicity, colonialisms, neoliberalisms, and so on in deep, careful, nuanced ways.

Women without Class does better in its analysis of some of these social forces than of others. I want to point directly to two unexplored opportunities I see in *Women without Class*. The racial formation theory that it employs dovetails with its poststructuralist impulse, exploring racial categories and institutions as historicized, temporal, and in process. It focuses on how the very construction of categories of racial difference, and their articulation through institutional practices, produces material inequality. One absence is that *Women without Class* does not sufficiently think through ethnicity as cultural difference per se. While nation, tradition, and colonialism are not absent from the text, it does not explore ethnicity in depth. This is because the analysis of race/ethnicity in the study primarily employs racial formation theory, which focuses on color and phenotype, discouraging an analysis of ethnicity through its rightful dismissal of sociology's earlier, embarrassingly colonialist, ethnicity paradigm (a la Robert Park).

But this runs the risk of throwing the baby out with the bathwater. Although Michael Omi and Howard Winant's (1986) account of the role of color and phenotype in the ongoing construction of racial difference in the United States remains compelling (see HoSang, LaBennett, and Pulido 2012), this does not mean that there are no (crafted, impermanent) cultural differences among different racial/ethnic groups that are relevant to the analysis of our lives. Must we set aside the study of cultural difference altogether, from fear of essentialism in our analysis or fear of being associated with politically ill-intended "culture of poverty" arguments? This may be an especially relevant question for Latina/os, who, relative to other racial/ethnic groups of color, do often have an evident shared ethnic background, anchored in a shared religion and language (Almaguer 2012, 146). In short, Latina/os have always occupied a unique place between "race" and ethnicity.

Second, the focus of *Women without Class* is primarily self-defined cisgender heterosexual girls, and while their heterosexuality is not invisible in the analysis (as *Women without Class* emphasizes the heterosexual imperative of the discourse on family values that shaped their lives), it was perhaps conceived of as somewhat more categorical than race, gender, or class at the level of identity. Where school officials misread the students' gender and sexual performances as mere evidence of their heterosexual concerns, I did not, pointing instead to the race and class meanings of their feminine sexual gestures as well. While this was useful, I might also have explored those gender and sexual performances as possibly mere "fledging heterosexual" identities (Valocchi 2005, 763) rather than already fixed heterosexual identities, in spite of the students' self-definitions.

At the level of social formation, while *Women without Class* demonstrates the way in which the heterosexual nuclear family is the idealized family unit for the nation, the push for compulsory heterosexuality, and the raced and classed meanings of "family values," it doesn't explicitly name its undoing as "queer" where it could have. While the identity discourse of the girls (save for one or two) was clearly heterosexual, their practices were queer, in the sense of resisting heteronormative family structures in imagining their futures without men and in the homosocial cultural rituals in which they engaged with one another. That is, they realized they "can get affection, intimacy, and family without marriage or without a relationship where they will be dependent," thus revealing that they already have an "ambivalent relationship to normative heterosexuality" (Valocchi 2005, 763). This can be an effect of both their class and their race position, since it is working-class families, families of color, and migrant families that are often at the forefront of new family formations (Stacey 1990). The middle class often follows their lead, because shifts in the economy impact working-class whites and people of color first. As racialized and working-class subjects, las chicas at Waretown High were unknowingly participating in the queering of domestic life. Kinship is queered whether girls choose or are economically forced to forgo economic dependence on men. This queering is part of a larger disruption of the heteropatriarchal system that the U.S. class structure has been built on.

Women without Class does show that lesbian and gay performances of gender and sexuality are linked to class, as students' violations of heterosexuality at times resulted in their peer group membership among the lowest rank of students at the school. The "poor white trash" clique of students for a variety of reasons (whether it be that they were poor, queer, or racially "mixed") did not perform either their whiteness or their gender "appropriately," and their gender and sexual "deviancy" could readily lead them to subordinate class futures. Race, class, and sexuality are expressed through a rejection of normative conventions of gender that routinely mark femininity as "deviant" or unrespectable when it is brown, working class, and/or queer.

POSTEMPIRE "AMERICAN" DREAMS

The discourse of heteronormative family values and the class, sexual, and racial meanings that accompany it were strong presences in Waretown and across the country at the beginning of the previous decade, in spite of large-scale empirical shifts in kinship structures, or the queering of domestic life, that was well under way. Kinship can be said to be queered as we witness these social shifts: The erosion of the "traditional" family, which includes a "delay" in the ages of marriage and childbearing, with younger generations increasingly choosing to do neither. Hetero marriage rates are on the decline, even though gay and interracial marriage rates are on the rise, and same-sex couples are more likely than heterosexual ones to be interracial. We see the market availability of what used to be the reproductive labor of the "private" sphere, including domestic labor, fertility options, and sexual commerce (which is on the rise), consumer options that are routinely dependent on the labor of (global) women of color. Increasingly visible and acceptable is sexuality that operates outside marriage and monogamy sanctioned by the church and/or state, and not just in LGBTQ communities. Heterosexual sexual relations are increasingly (if unevenly) less stigmatized for failing to revolve around the monogamous married unit either, producing greater sexual permissiveness, more pluralistic sexual practices, and new kinds of heterosexualities. Queer cultural changes do not just affect sexual "minorities" but open up a rethinking of the right to kinship diversity, sexual diversity, sexual pleasure, and sexual citizenship for everyone. Due to both women's increased paid labor and earning power and men's declining wages, there has been a shift among heterosexuals in the patriarchal bargain that historically made women economically dependent on men, upsetting what had become normalized "gender roles" in hetero relations. This, of course, is precisely what fuels certain reactionary social policies and movements among conservatives who take these progressive changes as evidence of the "decline" in civilization.

In marked contrast, Judith Halberstam has provocatively suggested a queering of time and place in which uses of both time and space develop "in opposition to the institutions of family, heteronormativity, and reproduction" (2005, 1). In the West, the idea of a "normal" life course is imbued with heteronormative, among other, assumptions: it presumes that people have access to college and jobs and want marriage and children, and all in a particular order. For most, this imagined life cycle is nonsensical. Brown, black, impoverished, migrant, and queer life trajectories look quite otherwise, whether due to structural constraints or a purposeful attempt to challenge undesirable cultural norms. As the coproduced shifting class formation and queering of domestic life have unfolded over the past decades, such a normative life cycle has become increasingly untenable for even white middle-classes youth.

In public discourse there is a tendency to measure the current state of affairs by asking if the kids are all right, often taking adolescents and young adults as a barometer of the state of the economy, the culture, and the nation by considering when they are able to arrive at various "appropriate" markers of adulthood. But those markers have always been imbricated with other, often discursively invisible social forces. For example, *Women without Class* shows that middle-class youth experience an extended adolescence via college, while working-class youth begin their adult lives (going to work, experiencing racism in the job market, being laid off, having children, struggling with child care, managing work/family tensions, and so on) much earlier. Too often the fact that adulthood and life-span are already affected by class, race, ethnicity, gender, sexuality, culture, migration, geography, and so on remains invisible while cultural commentators worry about whether U.S. youth are living up to a historically specific, middle-class norm modeled on the heteronormative place and time of the now defunct "modern family" and twentieth-century Western notions of childhood.

Women without Class suggests that the focus on youth, "youth crisis," and "family values" and all that accompanies it often works as a displacement, taking the focus away from social formations that continue to deepen economic and cultural inequality. This erases other life trajectories and narrowly blames social problems on individuals, racial/ethnic groups, migrant workers, sexual "deviants," and failed family types. Where some continue to scapegoat, others point to the obvious fact that these social forces have now impacted the middle too, as there are too few middle-income occupations (with or without a college degree) to inhabit, leaving even middle-class youth unable to secure jobs, own cars, or afford marriages, kids, and homes. Only when "class" inequality becomes extreme enough to impact the middle class does the cultural consciousness shift and some blame is placed on social forces rather than failing individuals. Over the past decade this individualizing tendency was mediated by the vast, impossible to ignore, large-scale economic shifts and inequality that made it a bit easier to locate young people's lives in historical relation to those of their parents and grandparents. Arguably, this produced a temporary cultural consciousness around economic inequality that impacted the middle classes. For Others, this "economic" inequality had always already manifested over and over, through colonialism, racialization, gender and sexual formation, and so on.

Occupy, along with the Dreamers, posed a serious challenge to the rhetoric of the American dream, deconstructing it in multiple ways. But on rejecting these historically specific, Western white middle-class nonqueer markers of adulthood and success, the question becomes: what are appropriate, globally fair, postempire "American" dreams for new generations?

Might the failure to reach certain "accomplishments" in a timely fashion simply look, from a future perspective, like a new version of adulthood? *Women without Class* points to the changing labor market and declining wages that await generations of youth, and while as workers they without a doubt continue to need health care and living wages, they have other needs that, if met, may change the face of twenty-first-century Western "adulthood," change the way we view ourselves, and create new kinds of adult global citizens.

Working-class communities, communities of color, immigrant communities, and LGBTQ communities continue to invent and reinvent "family" and kinship in light of the denial of citizenship rights they face and economic decline that impacts them long before it affects the white middle class (Stacey 2012; Heath 2012). As the middle class goes missing economically, it continues to catch up in nonnormative kinship formation (Stacey 1990). Perhaps the patriarchal, heteronormative family as the necessary backbone of the nation, having been slowly eroded, is finally being seriously challenged in culture, law, and policy. For many of us, this is a large part of a new American dream, to be sure.

Moreover, new American dreams perhaps may no longer include ecologically unfriendly car ownership and commutes to the suburbs, may mean forgoing the geographic and financial commitment of homeownership and either delaying or forgoing marriage and children for more flexible kinship structures. In the aftermath of the "great social debacle" that the West called economic prosperity (Halberstam 2013), and the exclusions and wounds it produced, new dreams may include the desire, for the sake of greater global fairness, to live simply, to own less, to live green, and to forgo modernist and oppressive notions of "family" that make economic dependency unproblematic and let the nation-state and global capital off the hook for their failure to provide for the world's citizen-workers.

J. Bettie
Oakland, California
May 2014

I thank Victoria Smith, Stephen Valocchi, Christina Anderson-Zavala, and two anonymous reviewers at University of California Press for their comments on this writing.

CHAPTER 1

Portraying Waretown High

As a new school year was about to begin, I spent many hours on the phone, chatting with high school teachers in California's Central Valley about my research interest. I was trying to find an advocate who would help me gain entrance into a school to conduct a comparative study of girls from different class and racial/ethnic locations.[1] When I explained my interests, many of the teachers (all women) suggested I read Mary Pipher's 1994 bestseller *Reviving Ophelia: Saving the Selves of Adolescent Girls,* popular among school teachers and parents. One even exclaimed, "Oh, you absolutely *have* to read this book if you are going to study girls." But I was too consumed with arranging access to a site and, once I made my way into a school, with getting to know several groups of girls to spend much time reading.

It was not until several months later that I picked up Pipher's book. By this time, I had come to know approximately sixty senior girls in multiple class- and race-organized cliques at the school I call Waretown High. Reading *Reviving Ophelia,* I found that some of the stories Pipher tells in her examination of that crucial transition between girlhood and adolescence resonated with Waretown girls' accounts of the trials they had suffered in junior high and early high school.[2] Yet I felt uncomfortable with her summation of the influences on girls' lives.

THE LIMITATIONS OF GENDER

Pipher's title refers to the story of Ophelia, in Shakespeare's *Hamlet,* which "shows the destructive forces that affect young women. As a girl, Ophelia is happy and free, but with adolescence she loses herself. When she falls in love with Hamlet, she lives only for his approval. She has no inner direction. . . . When Hamlet spurns her, . . . she goes mad with grief. Dressed in elegant clothes that weigh her down, she drowns in a stream filled with flowers" (20). Pipher laments over girls who only a year before ran and played sports, unconcerned about their appearance; girls who on reaching puberty became obsessed with body image and whose self-esteem plummeted as they were indoctrinated in the "junk values of mass culture." She tells stories of low self-esteem, eating disorders, difficulties with friendship, use and abuse of drugs and alcohol, sexual assault, suicide attempts, and at times, confusion over racial/ethnic belonging. Pipher asks why drugs and alcohol are so common among seventh-graders, why girls hate their parents, and what the meaning of body piercing may be. Other problems she lists as "less dangerous" but "more puzzling" are "school refusal" and "underachievement." Although I could not disagree with her finding that we live in "a girl-poisoning culture," I was disturbed by the way she framed the stories of girls she had counseled.

The week before, I had talked with a white girl named Tara, whom I found in the lunchroom, skipping class. A far cry from the blue-eyed, innocently vulnerable-looking adolescent girl on the cover of *Reviving Ophelia,* Tara had her purple-dyed hair tucked up messily in a rubber band, her short fingernails were painted black, and she wore two charcoal smudges of eye shadow, in a rather outdated-punk statement of nihilism. As she explained, "I wear black, 'cause it describes my mood." On top of her head sat her trademark sunglasses, which she usually hid behind in school but had lifted for our conversation. She wore torn-up cut-off jeans, combat boots (pseudo-brand Doc Martens), and an oversized tan polyester leisure-suit jacket she'd "scored" at the thrift store. Tara was regularly "tweaked" on crank; she was currently grounded for getting "an F+ and improving" on her report card (as she said with a proud chuckle); and she had told me that as a sophomore she "was throwing up all the time" (bulimic behavior). Now she was explaining that her last boyfriend, John, "taught me how to drink high class . . . you know, drinking wine with food or something." This comment came on the heels of telling me about a fight she had had with a onetime friend named Jill: "I was pounding her head against the cement when the crowd broke it up." Jill's mother had recently married, and the stepfather's income had made a vacation to Hawaii possible. Tara was invited along, but her parents could not afford to pay for her trip, so Jill had taken another friend. After the trip, Tara reported, Jill "had all these new clothes. And she, I don't know, just changed. She stopped smokin' and started callin' us losers and lowlifes all the time." Tara, who expected she might have to return for a fifth year of high school in order to graduate, had made no plans beyond high school.

I had also spoken that week with Lorena, a Mexican-American girl I'd known for several months. As we sat at the concrete lunch tables in the courtyard, she played with her hair, running her fingers through it, tucking it up into a white scrunchy, only to pull it out again a minute later, tossing her head to direct the hair back over her shoulders out of the way. Her eyelashes were thick with mascara, her long nails were a deep burgundy color, and her lips were painted to match and carefully outlined with a darker shade. She wore white platform shoes, hip-hugger bell bottom jeans, and a tight cropped knit top, all in tune with the recent Seventies retro fashion trend. We had just come from a sewing class composed of white and Mexican-American girls, discussing, as one white girl put it, how "ridiculously dressed up some girls get just to go to the mall." She had carried on about how she preferred to dress very casually for shopping, in her most comfortable old jeans and a sweatshirt. Many in the group concurred, but I noted Lorena's silence. When I asked her about it, her answer pointed to the salience of being brown and the meanings associated with it: "I always dress up for the mall. Otherwise they think I'm shoplifting." A group of white girls walked past us, and Lorena began explaining to me why she "can't stand those rich girls." Using her best "valley girl" accent, she mimicked them saying, "Ohmigod, like I can't believe I left my cell phone in my car." Lorena had missed school three days that week because her father had hurt his back lifting a heavy carton on the loading dock at work. Her mother could not afford to miss work; neither could her older brother, who still lived at home and contributed to the family income with money he made working at the car wash. Consequently, Lorena was the only one able to stay home and care for her dad while he was down.

As she told me this, we walked past a wall display of poetry by students in an English literature class, one of which read: "College should reflect the dedication of the few, / for they all started in the same classroom, / and were given the same work to do." In casual conversation with her peers Lorena spoke of plans to attend the university and an interest in law. In reality, she had not taken the required courses for university admission; she hoped to go to a nearby community college after graduation but wasn't sure her parents could afford it.[3]

Tara and Lorena were each members of friendship groups I came to know well, and these two groups of girls, along with many other groups, were on my mind as I read Pipher's description of girls' lives. During the months I had spent at Waretown High I had not come to see Tara and Lorena as mere victims of a mass culture that promotes their subordination based on gender. To do so would have been to define them solely by their gender and even within that to see them solely as victims. One thing Tara and Lorena had in common, in spite of their many differences, was that by their own naming they were not "preps," the predominantly white middle-class college-preparatory girls they so despised. As I read *Reviving Ophelia,* it struck me that Pipher's account of the "well-adjusted" girl, who exists before the alleged moment of poisoning or gender-subordinate indoctrination by mass culture, sounded suspiciously like a "prep," one of those girls at the high school who tended to be heavily involved in athletics or some other school-sanctioned extracurricular activity, who were high academic achievers, who usually wore looser, more unisex clothing and little or no makeup, and who were favored by teachers. In short, they were girls who performed a school-sanctioned version of femininity. Applauding girls with these characteristics, Pipher tells us that "androgynous adults are the most well adjusted . . . since they are free to act without worrying if their behavior is feminine or masculine" (18).

But the girls I came to know, both white and Mexican-American, were not only worried about whether their actions were masculine or feminine; they were equally concerned with the race and, in a more convoluted way, the class meanings of their practices, or "performances," which, if they mimicked preps, would set them up in a competition where they could only fail. Less (or not only) victims of mass culture than creative users of it, girls who did not meet prep norms created alternative symbolic economies in which they earned and wore different "badges of dignity" (Sennett and Cobb 1972; MacLeod 1987). Their alternative versions of gender performance were shaped by a nascent knowledge of racial/ethnic and class hierarchies.

I confess—somewhat apologetically—that I am presenting Pipher as a straw person of sorts. (Admittedly, my knee jerked each time her tone suggested a girl in lipstick was in need of counseling.) But the fact that her book spent 154 weeks on the *New York Times* bestseller list, ending in August 1998, justifies a close consideration of it. What I recognized as I read the book and thought about girls like Tara and Lorena was that Pipher's account of girls is too often void of the broader social context in which they live. Yet it is not surprising that such a book would find much appeal in our culture, where popular understandings of social phenomena are dominated by individualistic, psychological explanations and routinely lack any consideration of the effect of social structural forces on individual lives.

Although Pipher admits she is generationally far removed from girls today and so is uncertain of the meaning of their practices, a bigger limitation is perhaps less about generation than her unwillingness to more fully analyze the multiple social forces that shape girls' lives. Reminiscent of Carol Gilligan's (1982) early work, gender appears here as the most significant dimension of girls' selves, leaving race/ethnicity, class, and sexuality analytically subordinate. In centering gender, Pipher does not adequately explore the ways that girls' practices, especially the ones that disturb her (such as makeup, tattoos, piercing, drugs, school refusal), often mark hierarchical class and racial/ethnic relations among girls themselves and are not solely the consequence of gender inequality. The girls I had come to admire most, girls who faced the biggest odds in our multi-stratified society and whose strength and creative resistances inspired me, were not simply poisoned by a mass culture that teaches them gender inferiority. Girls do not define themselves only in relationship to boys in a heterosexual matrix; "one can 'become a woman' in opposition to other women" (Alarcón 1990, 360).

This is, of course, not to deny that discourses on gender are at work in shaping the identities and structuring the futures of the girls I came to know. But studies of girls often focus on early adolescence, describing young girls first encountering societal strictures on their gendered performances, whereas I spoke with young women who had come out on the other side with multiple ways of negotiating gender, along with other creative negotiations required by their living in a society stratified by race/ethnicity, class, and sexuality as much as gender. Girls performed different versions of femininity that were integrally linked to and inseparable from their class and racial/ethnic performances. Multiple social hierarchies were at work in the "styles" that girls like Tara, Lorena, and others employed.

The same week I read *Reviving Ophelia,* the author was featured on the front page of a *USA Weekend* insert in my local paper as a promoter of "family values." Contributing to the current moral panic about youth and fanning the flame of family values politics, Pipher, along with other moral entrepreneurs, decries elements of mass culture such as rap music, television, and pop psychology books as evidence that "our culture is at war with families" (quoted in Turner 1996, 4). The article notes that the family values "chorus" is "coming from all corners" and that Pipher's (1996) version has a liberal face. Indeed, although naming "family breakdown" as the cause for virtually all social ills is based on dubious social science, it has become a rallying cry across the political spectrum. As Judith Stacey explains, the "revisionist campaign for family values" of the political left (read centrist), like the political right, promotes the claim that two-parent heterosexual married couples and their biological children are superior families. But where the right tends to be explicitly antifeminist and homophobic, centrists opt for a "post-feminist family ethic" (1996, 52), which accommodates feminist ideals of gender equality by taking for granted that women have a right to education, equal wages, and a career, but then goes on to argue that women should *choose* to place familial needs above career (presuming that families have the luxury to make such a choice, which working-class families do not). This, they argue, is what is good for kids, good for families, good for America.[4] The nostalgia present in family values discourse holds, among other things, a desire for youth to adhere to a middle-class ideal of appropriately timed life stages that includes an extended adolescence. Such a norm can be achieved when entry into the full-time job market can be delayed by extending school years to include college. But, of course, this is a route that working-class kids have historically rarely followed, entering adult roles sooner than their middle-class peers.

Coupled with the discourse on "family values" is the so-called "youth crisis," often coded black (and at times brown), which presumably includes too much sex (think teen pregnancy) and violence (think gangs). In political debate this "youth crisis" is rarely linked to the fact of downward mobility among middle-income working-class people, which has produced more low-income youth with uncertain futures and, in particular, an overrepresentation of youth of color among them. "Family values" discourse displaces a discussion of the increasingly gender- and race-shaped class hierarchy, shifting the focus from economic well-being to family structure. In addition to scapegoating family types, it makes youth itself a threatening enemy to be feared. Indeed, the shift of focus toward youth also works to displace finer analyses of growing inequality.[5] All this became evident to me as I discovered that the lives of the girl-women I was studying were not so different from adult women's lives, as they too had encountered race discrimination in the job market, low wages in sex-segregated jobs, life choices shaped by avoiding abusive partners, partners who refused to accept parenting responsibilities, a search for low-cost child care, and a struggle to combine parenthood with work and school.

This book, then, presents an ethnographic portrait of working-class white and Mexican-American girls in their senior year of high school in a town in California's Central Valley. The context of these young women's lives includes a deindustrializing economy; the growth of service-sector occupations held largely by men and women of color and by white women; the related family revolutions of the twentieth century; the elimination of affirmative action; a rise in anti-immigrant sentiment; and changing cultural representations and iconographies of class, race, and gender meanings. These are social forces that render the very term "working class" anachronistic. My goal was to learn how these young women experience and understand class differences in their peer culture and how their and their parents' class location and racial/ethnic identity shaped the girls' perceptions of social differences at school and the possibilities for their futures.

I examined girls' experience of class difference and identity by documenting and analyzing the "common-sense" categories they used and created to describe and explain class-based differences among themselves.[6] I documented the unspoken boundary work that was a part of everyday interaction among students; the kinds of interaction that reveal symbolic class distinctions and differences in "cultural capital" between working-class and middle-class girls.[7] Most importantly, I have investigated the ways in which these common-sense class categories are infused with and intersect with gender and racial/ethnic meanings. While the most recent turns in feminist theorizing on identity and experience argue for a stronger understanding of how women's gender identity differs within the category "woman" across racial/ethnic and class lines, at the time of my writing, the race-class-gender trinity remains more often asserted and thought through theoretically, textually, and historically than it is *ethnographically* explored. It is my hope to advance this body of theory by bringing ethnographic data to it, as I describe the lived experience of these intersections in the lives of the young women I studied and the discourses that construct those experiences.

THE SOCIAL GEOGRAPHY OF WARETOWN

I began my project at a community college in Sacramento, because my main interest was in women from working-class families across racial/ethnic identities and I knew it was there that I would find those students who, for economic and/or academic reasons, had been unable to attend a four-year institution right out of high school. Instructors allowed me into their classrooms to describe my research and to ask for volunteers to be interviewed. I explained that I was interested in the educational experiences of women who were the first generation of their families to go to college. Heads nodded as I spoke, and my list of interviewees grew long. These women (and sometimes men too, who asked to be involved) expressed pleasure that someone cared to talk to them about this experience. I spoke as well with students from my university who had come from working-class families, some of whom had transferred in from community colleges and who told stories of both the stigma associated with this and the interactional work they performed to conceal it when they could. All these college women spoke at length about differences among girls that manifested in clique membership, style, curriculum choice, and participation in school rituals, topics that would later inform the questions I used at Waretown High.

But it wasn't long into the process of interviewing community college women that I became frustrated by the fact that their descriptions of themselves and their high school peers were devoid of context for me. I had to rely on what each of them could *tell* me of their respective high school experiences. What their stories held in common was the description of a youth culture specific to California in the 1990s and no doubt specific to some degree to the largely small-town/rural Central Valley geography. Through their narratives they constructed race and class identities for themselves which were relational, clearly defined by the context of the communities from which they came. But I could not *see* for myself what they meant and where they fit in to the high school and community hierarchy they described. Furthermore, missing from this sample were the experiences of high school students who didn't even make it to the community college.

And so I began making the necessary calls to find a high school in which to conduct my research. I had the good fortune to find a teacher who became an invaluable advocate, helping me gain entrance into Waretown High. Although it wasn't originally part of my criteria, I came to believe it was fortunate that Waretown had a rural setting, rather than suburban or urban, since this reflected my own schooling experience. I felt at home in Waretown in many ways. It had the look and feel of my own Midwestern farming town: lots of four-by-four trucks with mud and manure on the tires and plenty of American-made cars. I shared this "habitus" (Bourdieu 1984):[8] the intangible dimension of culture such as smells, sounds, and the rhythm of the voices of rural white people. The difference I felt from Mexican American girls challenged me in many ways, while the commonalities I shared with all Waretown girls informed my analysis in "insider" ways that might have been missing if I were located in another (more urban) context. I was well aware of and could easily relate to the stigma students felt as a consequence of being from a small rural town, from nowhere that matters. Further, I was glad to be able to uncouple the study of working-class and poor youth from an urban setting, since in media accounts they are so often portrayed as one and the same.

Waretown has a population of approximately forty thousand people. The high school reflects the town demographically, being about 60 percent white and 40 percent Mexican American, with other people of color composing less than 2 percent of the population. Approximately 16 percent of the Mexican-American students are Mexican-born, while the remainder are second- and third-generation residents. Located in California's Central Valley, the town was built on agriculture and the industries that support it. The parents of most of the second-generation Mexican-American girls had immigrated as teens or young adults under the Bracero Program for recruiting farmworkers (in effect from 1942 to 1964).[9] They joined a stable working- and lower-middle-class Mexican-American community in Waretown, which had been established during an earlier wave of immigration (1920–30) and whose members had become small business owners, labor contractors, and field supervisors. The fathers of white working-class girls I knew often worked in blue-collar industries that support farming such as irrigation, farm machinery, and trucking. Among Mexican-American working-class girls, fathers' work included occupations similar to working-class whites but also sometimes field labor, and mothers too at times worked in the fields or in canneries. On my back road commute to Waretown each morning, I watched dozens of groups of farmworkers beginning their day's work in the surrounding fields. In the early fall and late spring months, the relentless Central Valley sun was already warm enough by eight in the morning that I would have rolled down the window of my car.

During the 1980s several large distribution centers settled in the area to warehouse and distribute products to nearby discount department stores such as Target, Kmart, and PayLess. These centers and stores are now the largest employers in the town, especially for a younger generation of workers. The distribution centers employ primarily men doing warehouse work and trucking while women work in lower-paid retail jobs at the department stores or perform clerical work in the stores and in small businesses around town. The school system, a local hospital, a convalescent home, large grocery stores, smaller department stores, and a variety of small businesses in the shopping mall and around town employ people at various levels of training and consequent income. The children of middle-class professionals were a visible minority at the school. Most were white, but a few were Mexican-American. Their parents worked as teachers, doctors, lawyers, professors, counselors, administrators, or business owners.

About 30 percent of high school students are on the free or reduced-price lunch program. School administrators agreed, however, that this number could be doubled if all eligible students were to apply. One obvious reason that many do not is the stigma associated with standing in a separate lunch line. Almost all students who are in this line daily are Mexican-American, usually sophomores and juniors. Most seniors, white and Mexican-American, leave the school grounds during lunch time (the ability to do so being a status marker) and choose to spend their own money on fast food.

This expenditure was somewhat surprising, as was the fact that many of the students drove their own cars. But almost all of the students with whom I spoke—nearly all of them seniors—had jobs, and I learned that it was economically prudent for even relatively low-income parents to help their teen purchase an inexpensive car. Along with the independence that came with owning one's own car came an expectation from parents that their teens would provide for themselves. While some students from middle-income families were expected to earn their own money for luxury items like designer-brand clothes, most students I spoke with worked and earned money to pay for their car, insurance, gas, food (at least lunch), clothes, shoes, and school expenses (such as a yearbook, senior pictures, and the prom), and also tried to save money for junior college. For some students, parents made it explicit that this contribution was expected, while others explained that although their parents "never said it," they observed the financial strain their parents were under, and they "just knew" they had to take care of themselves. Several of these students worked nearly thirty hours per week. In short, they made a not insignificant contribution to their family economy by being somewhat self-supporting before they were even adults. It goes without saying that such a work schedule affected students' academic performance and often made it impossible for them to participate in extracurricular school activities.

About 53 percent of Waretown high school graduates go to community colleges, either with plans to complete a one-to-two-year vocational certificate program or with the hope of transferring to a four-year institution. Despite these hopes, the rate of transfer from community colleges to four-year schools nationally is only 20 percent (Grubb 1991), and Waretown students' transfer rate appears to be even lower. Another 28 percent of Waretown graduates go directly to four-year schools; 3 percent attend trade schools; and the remaining 16 percent are without plans for post-secondary education. The status associated with having money for nicer cars and clothes, along with the status differences associated with aspirations for four-year college vs. community college and, related to that, with participation in a vocational vs. college-preparatory curriculum, was a clear source of class and race resentment and helped shape membership in friendship groups.

Waretown consists of many neighborhoods of lower-middle-class and stable working-class homes (both owned and rented). There is some residential segregation by race and class. One neighborhood near the railroad tracks houses mostly impoverished second- and third-generation Mexican Americans, and a sprawling one-story low-income housing project behind the cannery, known as "the projects," is primarily an immigrant community. A white neighborhood near the hospital was usually described as "nice" or "rich," and within it is a private elementary school. A single high school of fifteen hundred students serves the town, but there are several elementary schools, and at times students linked one another's social status with the geographic location of the elementary school they had attended. The one private elementary school is the only private schooling option in Waretown. Thus, both middle-class and working-class students are educated together in middle and high school years.

Over my nine months of participant observation and interviewing, I came to know the clique structure or informal peer hierarchy among students at the school; this was the primary way students understood class and racial/ethnic differences among themselves. Labels and descriptions of each group varied, of course, depending on the social location of the student providing the description. Nonetheless, there was a general mapping, which almost all students agreed on and provided readily and easily when asked. Although there were exceptions, the groups were largely segregated by race/ethnicity and class. Among whites there were "preps," "hicks," and "smokers/rockers/trash"; among Mexican-American students, "Mexican preps" and "cholas/cholos" or "hardcores." There was also a considerable number of students, both white and Mexican-American, who didn't fit well into any of these categories and were often simply labeled as "others." At times the white "others" were labeled "skaters/alternatives," and the self-referent for the group of female Mexican-American "others" I came to know was "las chicas" (the girls).

I found students quite happy and willing to talk about this aspect of their social world. In fact, students were appreciative that I found their peer structure important, for this is an aspect of their lives and of their school experience that many adults (school personnel and parents) either don't take seriously, dismiss as stereotyping, or avoid talking about in an effort to enact a color-blind and, less consciously, a class-blind social environment. Schools, of course, reflect larger society, and school personnel, in tune with the color-blind political impulse of the times, often took a category-blind approach toward managing social hierarchy among students. Sometimes students too bought into this blindness: they knew the categories were there, but they also knew it was supposedly wrong to acknowledge them. Both students and teachers held many contradictions and expressed much confusion in how they perceived students as individuals versus as members of social groups. This difficulty resulted not only from feeling compelled to think in a category-blind way, but also from the fact that exceptions to the rule came easily to mind. The high visibility of these exceptions to larger patterns challenged the ability of school personnel and students to see the basic class and race patterns of group membership at all. For example, the presence of one Mexican-American student in a clique with nine whites would result in that group's being most readily identified as "racially mixed."

When I met students who were exceptions, who didn't seem to fit into the group they were in, I pushed for explanations and found important insights into how racial/ethnic, gender, and sexual subjectivity intersect with class. I will return to these exceptions in later chapters, but here I want to provide a cursory sketch of students at Waretown High through brief descriptions of the race and class composition of the social groups and also point to patterns of membership. Although I am primarily interested in employing a *relational* conceptualization of class, where class is understood as a historical process of class conflict and action, always in formation (class as a relationship, not a thing [E. P. Thompson 1963]), it is useful here to employ a *categorical* notion of class (where class is "socioeconomic status," an aggregate of categories based on occupation, income, and educational attainment, a structure represented a priori). Although I hope to make such a fixed class taxonomy problematic, I do name girls as working-class or middle-class in origin throughout the book, and the sketches below will help readers understand what variables I used to place girls in such categories.

In presenting these groups, I draw on Joseph Howell's useful distinction between two types of working-class lives in his ethnography of white working-class families (1973). "Settled-living" families are supported by jobs that have relative security, higher pay, and, at times, health benefits. Settled-living lifestyles are orderly and predictable and sometimes include the ownership of a modest home. "Hard-living" families are supported by low-paying, less stable occupations that lack health care benefits and make home ownership impossible—self-employed work, non-union labor, service work—and have lifestyles that are chaotic and unpredictable. Instability in one area of life often contributes to instability in another: a rough marriage might lead to drinking or drug use, which in turn leads to missing work and job loss. Or losing a job might lead to drinking or drug use, an eviction and marital crisis. Hard-living is not desired or intentional, but is a consequence of the difficulties of trying to establish a settled life. For those with minimal education and subsequent low income, there was often too little to be gained from following socially conservative norms. The minimal payoff is often not perceived to be worth the sacrifices involved. Hard-living arose out of this constraining set of life circumstances.

Smokers

The group of mostly white students at the school who were usually referred to as "the smokers" (because they smoked cigarettes), but sometimes "the rockers" (due to their taste for heavy metal music), and occasionally "white trash," were most often from hard-living families. These were Tara's friends. They had parents who did not finish or barely finished high school. Typical jobs for mothers included nurse's aide, grocery store stocker, secretary, and beautician. Fathers' occupations included a self-employed truck driver, a self-employed vendor, a retired wood-mill worker, a Vietnam veteran on disability, a non-union janitor, and a port-a-potty installer. Sometimes hard-living students hinted at illegal income–generating strategies as well. It was difficult to find seniors among this group, as many had dropped out or had been kicked out of school. These students generally did not have plans beyond high school, as they were just hoping to graduate.

Cholas and Cholos

The cholas and cholos (or chola/os) also often called "hard-cores," were primarily Mexican-American students from hard-living families. Both terms were often used to indicate that a student was in or wanted to be in a "gang," and therefore dressed the part. In actuality, chola/o refers to a Mexican-American street style that sometimes marks identification with gangs but can merely mark racial/ethnic belonging; the actual degree of commitment to a gang exists on a continuum. Nonetheless, cholas/os, like pachucas and pachucos a generation before them, are—often wrongly—assumed to be engaged in criminal behavior.[10] Fathers commonly worked in the fields or as dishwashers or doing food delivery; mothers, in the cannery, in the fields, as caretakers, and as domestics. There were two groupings of cholas/os, which represented two gang affiliations: *sureño* (south) and *norteño* (north). The sureños tended to be immigrant students who primarily spoke Spanish, while the norteños tended to be second-generation Mexican Americans whose primary language at school was English. Consequently, there was a pattern of class difference between these two groups, although there were exceptions to every pattern.

Because I was interested in young women's transition to adult lives and class futures, I limited my sample to studying girls in their senior year. Significantly, although there were senior boys in this category, there were no senior girls. Girls who performed chola identity in junior high and into early high school years had left the high school to attend either a continuation high school in Waretown or an adult education program, both of which offered diplomas more quickly for fewer credit hours. Those with babies had chosen this option because the shorter classroom hours made it easier to combine school with parenting. Some, like their male counterparts, were forced to try to complete high school in an alternative fashion after being kicked out of Waretown High for a variety of school "violations."

Las Chicas

Other Mexican-American girls, like Lorena, who had performed chola identity in their earlier years, simply "matured out" (Vigil 1988) and remained in high school.[11] They were part of the "others" that had no obvious distinction, but they labeled themselves "las chicas." Many of las chicas were identified by other students as gang-affiliated. In truth, las chicas disapproved of gang violence but were sympathetic to the plight of boys who were involved because these were their brothers and friends, boys they had grown up with. Thus, their style was explicitly linked to a racial/ethnic politic, identification with a gang, without commitment to gang violence. These girls tended to be from settled-living families. Their parents had sometimes finished high school and managed to secure one stable job between them. They sometimes owned modest homes, and often at least one parent's job provided the family with health care benefits. Mothers worked in occupations such as seasonal cannery or field work, other factory work, as a dental assistant, a mail sorter, or a nurse's aide in a retirement home. Occupations of fathers included a garbage man, a fieldwork foreman, a janitor, a painter, a tractor equipment company foreman, a car salesman, a utility company serviceman, and a truck driver. These girls hoped to go to vocational business schools to complete one-to-two-year programs or to community colleges to complete certificate programs; a few hoped to transfer to four-year schools.

Skaters

The largest mass of white students were those who didn't fit easily into any well-defined clique, but who self-identified as "alternative" or "skaters." Like las chicas, they were from settled-living families that had modest homes and health care benefits. Their parents had usually finished high school. Some had gone, later in life, to a community college for a one-to-two-year training program—usually the mothers, entering programs in secretarial science, word processing, dental assistance, or accounting. Mothers' work included clerical and accounting jobs at local businesses, a dental hygienist, and an administrative assistant. Examples of fathers' work were a mechanic, a disabled Vietnam veteran, a groundskeeper, a maintenance man, a warehouse foreman, a telephone truck serviceman, and a beer factory worker. These girls planned to go to community colleges with the explicit goal of transferring to four-year schools, and a few planned to go directly to four-year state schools.

Hicks

The "hicks" were mostly white students distinguished by an interest in agriculture. Some came from farming families, while others lived in town, their interest in agriculture and animals not linked to family work. These students ranged from hard-living to settled-living, depending on parents' jobs and incomes. Mothers' jobs included manager of a beauty salon, school-lunchroom worker, and administrative assistant. Examples of fathers' work included an electrician, a self-employed painter, a police officer, and a post office clerk. Most of these students planned to go to community college; some of the boys planned to apprentice in blue-collar industries right out of high school.

Preps

The "preps" were primarily white students who were the most middle-class of all students at the school. Their parents were often college educated, although some families had gained income and community prestige by having done quite well over the generations in some blue-collar industry. Mothers worked, for example, as a general contractor, a teacher, a nurse, a small-business manager, a special education teacher, and a junior college teacher. Fathers' work included a professor, a contractor, a business owner, a banker, a teacher, a lawyer, and an accountant. These students had aspirations to attend private colleges or public universities.

ON METHOD AND ETHNOGRAPHIC REFLEXIVITY

My research included "hanging out" with girls in classrooms and hallways, during lunch hours, at school dances, sports events, Future Homemakers of America (FHA) meetings, a Future Farmers of America (FFA) hay-bucking contest and similar events, meetings of MEChA (Movimiento Estudiantil Chicano de Aztlán, the Chicano student movement organization), in coffee shops, restaurants, and the shopping mall, in the school parking lot, near the bleachers behind the school, at birthday parties, and sometimes sitting cross-legged on the floor of girls' bedrooms "just talkin'." During the school year, I spent almost every day at the school, often returning in the evening to attend an extracurricular event and sometimes on weekends to meet and "kick it" with girls. I came to know more than sixty girls well, about half of which were Mexican-American and half of which were white, and many more as acquaintances. I talked with them about such details of their lives as dating, friendships, partying, clothes, makeup, popular culture, school, family, work, and their hopes and expectations for the future. I asked them numerous questions about their families, such as their parents' and grandparents' educational and occupational history and income. I asked them how much time their parents spent working and what they did for leisure, what various family members watched on television and did or did not read, where they shopped, what they believed their parents' political views were, how parents seemed similar to or different from their teachers. And I asked questions about what cars the family owned, the meals they ate, the vacations they did or did not take, the neighborhoods they lived in, and whether or not they had health insurance. As indicators of educational achievement, I documented which track each girl was on and how she came to be placed there, which girls made it to graduation and which did not, and each girl's post–high school plans for work, vocational schooling, or college. At the end of the school year, I compared girls' plans to the reality of what colleges they were accepted at and/or what jobs they secured. In short, I spent much time just wandering about the school, not really an insider but not a complete outsider either, making mental notes of who was where and doing what, and looking for students who had free time to talk. I'd routinely slip into the bathroom where I hid behind a stall door and recorded observations in my notebook.

Because it was my goal to compare girls across race and class locations, the most difficult task was attempting to enter the life-world of so many different social actors. The fact that I was crossing cliques was an enormous added worry for me, concerned as I was that this transgression would inhibit the various groups of girls from opening up and thus jeopardize my ability to establish trust. Being identified as a "researcher" seemed at times to engender trust, however. When I asked Lisa, a white girl, if she felt uncomfortable talking to me about her perception of the Mexican-American girls we were discussing, she responded, "No. It is okay because you are the objective researcher." I decided that this was not the time to explain to her the crisis of ethnographic authority and the challenges it poses to the ideal of an impartial science. In her mind, her description of me as "objective" made her feel it was safe to talk, as it meant that I was not going to tell the Mexican-American girls what she said about them, that I was not engaged in the network of gossip that students generally were. I listened, and I asked questions, but I did not talk about other students.

My awkward status as someone without any clear institutionalized role at the school was a source of discomfort at first; this lessened with time but never fully went away. I feel indebted to Penelope Eckert (1989), to whose book I retreated each time I worried that this kind of study was an impossibility. It eased my mind to read her description of her role at the school where she studied "jocks and burnouts," with its many parallels to my daily experience. I couldn't help but think that the process would have been much easier if I had been there to talk to teachers, since our shared "adult" status removed us from the social world of students for whom daily school life and its microscopically observed interactions were emotionally consequential in large ways. And, as noted, it would have been easier had I been there to befriend only one particular group of girls, rather than trying to negotiate relationships with several groups of girls who did not view each other in friendly ways. Instead, I had no social home and was a transgressor of a kind, crossing all social categories, and always potentially perceived as a betrayer of confidence (both across groups of girls and across the student/teacher divide). This was difficult terrain to negotiate and an uncomfortable space to inhabit on a daily basis; I would come home exhausted. But I was probably more concerned about my role at the school than anyone there was. The last week of school, when I thanked one of the administrators for her help and for tolerating my presence, she commented, "You really became a piece of the landscape here." It was reassuring to hear that I had not been as conspicuous as I felt.

I managed the student/teacher divide by avoiding teachers as much as possible. Gaining student confidence required that I distance myself from adult school personnel. So I waited to interview teachers, counselors, and administrators formally until the last month of school. When I did interview them, I did so in private places like faculty lounges where we would not be seen by students.

Managing the clique divide proved more difficult. At times, it felt remarkably easy because of the degree to which students in cliques physically segregated themselves at the school, parceling the school into geographic territories. I could easily spend time with preps in the student government class, with hicks in the "ag" department or the far end of the parking lot, with las chicas in the business building, and with smokers behind the school. But sites that were ambiguous territory caused problems. One day as I walked between class periods, across the center of the school toward las chicas who watched me approaching, I was intercepted by Jennifer, a prep girl, who made kind of public claim to me, greeting me with a hug, and saying loudly, "Hi, Julie! Do you want to talk again today? Talking to me was particularly helpful, wasn't it?" On another day I saw the shock on the face of Amber, a prep girl, when she spotted me walking to the parking lot with Lorena, whom preps perceived as a "hard-core." And Shelly, a self-defined "hick," stopped talking to me after she saw me talking and laughing, having a good time, with a group of Mexican-American girls in the lunchroom one day. The lunchroom and "hallways" (the outdoor spaces between buildings full of classrooms) were difficult spaces to negotiate, and while I spent much time at the beginning of the year making observations there, as I began to get close to each group of girls, I found myself avoiding such mixed areas until after the bell rang and everyone was in their place for the hour. Everyone knew, of course, that I was crossing groups, and as the year went on, an unspoken understanding was enacted, where each group of girls and I exchanged only pleasant "hello's" in mixed settings and reserved further interaction for when I came to visit them in their "home" at the school.

I met the preps through a teacher who taught a college-prep class and in whose class I made a formal presentation on who I was and what my project was about and asked for volunteers. This worked well with this group, who were the kind of students likely to volunteer, but was not the most feasible approach for working-class students, who were likely to count themselves out of such an activity. These students were much harder to get to know, and therefore I had to use a variety of strategies for meeting them. I sometimes met them through a trusted teacher or the school nurse, but usually, and most effectively, through other students, as I interviewed girls in a network of friendship circles. It only took getting to know one girl in a clique to open up the whole group to me. In fact, I came to know a majority of the girls through other girls, and this helped distance me from the adult authority status of school personnel. For the most part I introduced myself as "a student from the university" doing "a study of high school girls." After explaining to students in a variety of contexts who I was and why I was there, I gave them a consent form to sign, which stated my guarantee of anonymity and confidentiality; I also gave them a consent form for their parents to sign.

In order to disguise the identities of these girls, I have, of course, changed their names and altered information about each girl, for example, switching occupations of one girl's parents with those of another in parallel social locations. This means that although a given characteristic of or a specific incident involving a particular girl might seem to members of the Waretown community to make that girl identifiable, in fact the various events, beliefs, and statements associated with a name in this book cannot be assumed to belong to any one girl. Finally, I have also used pseudonyms for and altered facts about teachers and other school personnel when it was necessary to do so for the sake of anonymity.

I was thirty-one the year of my fieldwork, but probably looked younger. I never lied about my age, extent of education, or other facts of my life, but didn't disclose much unless asked. I was often mistaken by teachers and administrators for a student, mostly because I dressed like one. My appearance worked as both an advantage and a disadvantage. On the one hand, looking youthful helped distance me from teachers and parents and adults in general and therefore probably did help students feel comfortable with me. Further, we shared the status of "student" (albeit from different institutions), and this category seemed to be key, suggesting that one has not yet begun adult life and is subordinate to someone older and with more authority. The distinction between graduate and undergraduate status was lost on many of the girls. On the other hand, I had to be careful not to look too close in age or dress, which could have backfired by making me come across as disingenuous, trying too hard to pass myself off as something I wasn't. I didn't try to adjust to each group I spent time with, but rather wore a generic "costume" that was virtually the same everyday. I wore Levi's (not too baggy, not too tight) and the cheap version ($9.99 at Payless Shoes) of basic brown leather clunky-heeled shoes that were in fashion at the moment. I wore variously colored scoop-necked T-shirts and in the winter an open flannel shirt over them. In an effort to acknowledge my difference and not look like I was trying too hard to fit in, I chose to carry my canvas shoulder bag rather than the backpack that most prep students favored.

In short, I looked like an "other" of sorts, but not terribly "hip," which I believed was the safest category to occupy. Students' perceptions of me varied depending on who they were. Preps seemed to believe I was one of them. After all, I was working on a degree at a university, something they planned to do, and they seemed to be quite comfortable with me. This was ironic given that they were one of the groups of girls I felt most uncomfortable with. I was not college-prep when I was in high school, and I found myself in awe (at times even intimidated) at the amount of knowledge they had at such an early age. I admit I also experienced occasional pangs of resentment toward them because of the cultural capital they took for granted.

Working-class students, I believe, saw me as a college student who was learning how to be a counselor or psychologist, one of these occupations that work with "troubled" teens. This was evident one day when Tara attempted to get out of class by telling a teacher she wanted to go talk to "the counselor lady." Her strategy of deception with the teacher was to give me more status than she knew I had by deeming me a counselor already, as opposed to a student, and by making me older than she thought I was by defining me as a lady.

I felt far closer to white working-class students in experience, but this was not necessarily reciprocated. Given my mobility upward from my own settled-living location, I knew these students perceived me as other. Explaining where I originally came from was not necessarily the best strategy for establishing trust, since it could serve to increase their feelings of failure. This is where I feel the most ambivalence about class mobility. There is no way around the fact that I unintentionally inflicted class injury, as people who are exceptions often do. Nonetheless, these girls also often appreciated and benefited from my attention. Working-class girls, across race, were happy that I was not studying only the preps, that they too counted as worthy of being talked to. And my attention sometimes gave them status among other students; they mattered in this thing I was doing as much as preps did.

For my part, the most complicated relationship was the one I had with Mexican-American girls. I had a certain amount of automatic legitimacy based on the fact that the teacher who was my advocate at the school was a white woman whose racial politics they trusted (so much so that students considered asking her to teach a Chicano studies class). White liberals were hardly thick on the ground in this community, and the mere fact that I was willing to speak openly on and ask frank questions about race seemed to automatically engender a certain level of trust among these girls. I asked them directly how they felt about me as a "white girl" from the university writing a story about them, attempting to represent them. Though they occasionally wondered if the multiple factors influencing their lives might be hard for me as a cultural outsider to understand, they also were concerned that I might choose not to include their stories. Ana explained, "You can't just write about the white girls. It would only be half a story, half a book." And Marisol added, "Besides, you are studying girls. And so we have that in common." For the most part, these girls generally expressed to me that I should not worry about my outsider status. And that is what made me worry most of all.

I came of age intellectually during the crisis of ethnographic authority and fully felt the associated angst and paralysis, wondering if I could or should study anyone socially located in places which are other to myself. The critique of authority and the exploration of experimental ways of writing ethnography reflexively have come from interdisciplinary feminist and ethnic studies and from postmodern theory.[12] This relatively recent transformation in social theory has been, in part, a consequence of the civil rights and women's liberation movements, in which disenfranchised people began to gain some access to higher education and to challenge conservative scholarship that had, either explicitly or implicitly, validated the status quo of inequality. The intervention that feminist and ethnic studies scholars made was to identify the androcentrism and ethnocentrism of much of what passed as value-free science and to argue instead that all knowledge is perspectival.

In terms of qualitative research, this led to a questioning of the ethnographer's ability to offer an objective account. In other words, this turn toward antifoundationalism meant recognizing that language does not *reflect* reality but is *constitutive* of it. That is, the ethnographic text is not a transparent account of reality but a product of the interaction and negotiation between researcher and researched. As Daphne Patai describes it, the interview is "a point of intersection between two subjectivities—theirs and mine, their cultural assumptions and mine, their memories and my questions, their sense of self and my own, their hesitations and my encouraging words or gestures (or sometimes vice versa), and much much more" (1988, 146). To acknowledge the possibility of profound cultural differences between researcher and researched means recognizing that the "intersubjective ground for objective forms of knowledge is precisely what is [or may be] missing" in the ethnographic encounter (Clifford 1988, 35). Consequently, the written product might then be better understood as a "partial truth" (Clifford 1998), since an author cannot just pretend to be letting her subjects tell their story or supposedly give them voice without her analytical mediation. Reflexive ethnography demands that as ethnographers we point to our own subjectivity, acknowledge that it undoubtedly shapes the story we tell, and—most importantly—recognize the fact of the power we wield, the power of interpretation. The text is not simply the result of an even negotiation between ethnographer and subject, because in the end authority literally remains with the ethnographer, as *author* of that text.

In other words, to perform reflexive ethnography means to recognize that the ethnographer does not offer a "view from nowhere" (Bordo 1990) or what Donna Haraway (1988) calls the "god trick," the ideal of an objective, value-free, aperspectival knowledge. What is required instead is a radical reflexivity that acknowledges that there is always a *place* from which we speak. Unfortunately, this refutation of impartial knowledge has been widely misunderstood as a celebration of relativism, that all perspectives are equal. Indeed, they are not. Rather, what postmodern theory poses is a challenge to *contextualize* (P. Williams 1991). It is not that all perspectives are equal, but that they are all situated, contextual, from a place invested with more or less power. From this perspective, reflexive ethnographic practice might lead, as Haraway explains, toward the "joining of partial views," "ongoing critical interpretation among 'fields' of interpreters" (communities, not individuals), with the recognition that some views are institutionally and culturally more empowered than others (1988, 590).

The concern over the lack of intersubjectivity, the division of intellectual labor, and an imbalance of power between a researcher and her subjects has, in contemporary work, been most often discussed in relationship to racial/ethnic difference and the difference of first-world/third-world global inequality (although early on feminists were quick to point out the problematic lack of intersubjectivity between researcher and subject based on gender). Within feminist studies, a series of concerns has been expressed about white Western women studying women in the third world and white women studying women of color in the United States, which I want to point to here. The key problem was/is a kind of essentialism whereby white Western feminists assumed similarities with third-world women on the basis of gender, ignoring important differences among women across culture, history, and geography.[13]

Attempts to correct for this manifested yet another problem, which Marnia Lazreg has appropriately labeled "essentializing otherness." This occurs when the recognition of difference is paramount but includes a tendency to define "others" as all the same: "on the other side of difference, they must be, they are, all alike" (1988, 93). The concern here is that third-world women were/are represented by cultural outsiders in ways that portrayed them as eternal victims. This denied them selfhood and presented them as persons without agency, often as women overdetermined by religion, tradition, and patriarchy, where those three phenomena are given privileged explanatory power and are conceptualized as static and unchanging: on the other side of difference, history, it seems, stands still (Mohanty 1991). Here "others" are "made into the bearers of unexplained categories," having no existence or individuality outside of those categories (Lazreg 1988, 94).

In short, there was/is among white Western feminists a failure to see that "others" are for themselves and not for "us"; they are not here to prove universalist theories of patriarchy, which was the project of an early second-wave feminism that desired global sisterhood. Pointing out to white women the arrogance and power that inheres in their claims of sameness with women of color, Elizabeth Spelman has explained that "women of color have been distrustful of white women who point to similarities between them when it seems politically expedient to do so and to dissimilarities when it does not" (1988, 139). Consequently, the critics of feminist essentialism have asserted the need for vigilant attentiveness to the *specificity* of the kinds of struggles and the kinds of resistances women engage and for a focus on differences among women and the salience of social forces of domination, beyond gender, to women's lives. In my account of Mexican-American and white girls, I make claims of *both* similarity and difference between them, attending as best I can to the implications of such claims. My hope is that this work makes a contribution to the joining of partial views.

The critiques of essentialized subjects also lead to a scholarship that prioritizes deconstructing monolithic notions of racial subjects and the notion of an authentic Chicano (for example) cultural identity.[14] Rosa Linda Fregoso and Angie Chabram, while attending to the political utility of naming a shared culture, shared conditions of oppression, and a shared history of conquest, point simultaneously to differences within the category Chicana/o. Attention to differences *within* is requisite in order to recognize the historically constructed nature of racial/ethnic subjectivity. Difference between Chicanos and Chicanas based on gender is a key issue raised by Chicana feminists, but beyond this they point to the many other variables that must be considered, such as "the heterogeneous experiences of migration, conquest, and regional variation" (1990, 206) as well as sexuality, generation, Spanish fluency, and skin color. In short, Chicana/o identity is an ongoing production, historically changing, and not an accomplished and static fact. Echoing Lazreg, Fregoso and Chabram explain that it is crucial not to make the mistake of taking all people of color as "different" from the "humanist" subject and assume that they are transparent among themselves.

The ethnographic dilemma I faced was that my cultural identity as a white woman might result in an analysis that was not sensitive to Mexican-American culture and racial/ethnic identity, either, on the one hand, by failing to *recognize* cultural specificity or, on the other hand, by *reducing* girls to their ethnicity, whereby everything they do can be attributed to and is overdetermined by "their" culture, ignoring intracultural variation. I felt more certain about my ability to avoid the latter pitfall. As I listened to Mexican-American girls narrate their life stories, differences proliferated among them, and their lives defied common ideas about Mexican-American culture. (There were divorced parents, working mothers, small families, an occasional abortion, parents with as high expectations for their daughter as their son, and in one case a family of practicing Jehovah's Witnesses.) Regarding the former pitfall, I did feel uncertain about my representation of Mexican-American girls' lives, and I contemplated daily the possible ways in which my own white, settled-living cultural identity shaped both my interaction with the girls and my textual representation of them. But as Fred Pfeil helps me explain, I believe we can attempt to understand the exploitative relations that people who are other to us are embedded in "well enough to serve them in a struggle against those relations" (1994, 226).

In the end, the uncertainty I felt about representing Mexican-American girls' lives led me to believe that I had a false sense of certainty about my ability to represent white voices. It is very easy to be deceived by what *appears* as cultural sameness. But when we begin to unpack racial/ethnic categories, including whiteness, it becomes clear that racial/ethnic sameness is not enough to lay claims to intersubjectivity. Class differences in particular, as manifested within a U.S. population (as opposed to a first-world/third-world global class divide), have not often been considered in the literature on reflexive ethnography, since class, as a basis for identity politics, has not commonly been made salient in the politics of theory. Racial difference was far and away not the only axis of my identity that mattered, not the only difference on the basis of which I felt challenged about my position to say anything about a particular girl's life. I often felt like an outsider around experiences of sexuality, family abuse, and class. At other times, I felt like an insider on the basis of those same topics. The logic of an identity politics in which identity is conceptualized as static and clearly bounded doesn't easily acknowledge the *continuum* of experience, *relative* sameness and difference, and *degrees* of intersubjectivity that allow for emotional empathy and political alliance. Discussions of the uneven power relations embedded in ethnography usually focus on the ethnographer's unavoidable exploitation of her "subjects." Ironically, I feel I betrayed the more privileged preps the most because I knew my emotional allegiance was to working-class girls, and I knew I would often portray preps through the eyes of working-class students, for whom they are villains of a sort.

Chabram and Fregoso go on to draw our attention yet closer to the power differentials embedded in theory when they note the irony of the fact that the racialized other in much postmodern theorizing of the subject is discussed as an abstraction, while in reality this other is actually very concrete and in physical proximity to those who theorize about her/him. The traditional site for ethnographic work, the "third world," is now less isolated from the "first world," causing some anthropologists to begin doing ethnography "at home." Consequently, what was always true for the sociologist is increasingly true for the anthropologist: the subject is no longer out there, far removed in time and space from the ethnographer and her textual production, but is here at home and likely to be cleaning her office or busing her table. Moreover, with the gains (limited and reversible though they may be) of the civil rights era, the other is increasingly present in the academic institution in the person of students and/or colleagues, ready to talk back, to make interventions into theories and assumptions that fail to recognize the partiality of perspective. It was/is easier to support the fallacy of an objective researcher when subjects were not empowered to talk back, because of either a lack of geographic proximity or a lack of cultural and economic power (Chabram 1990). This was never more clear to me than when just one year after completing my ethnographic work, one of the (white middle-class) girls from my study showed up as a student in my university classroom, able to raise her hand and deny my authority as I spoke about my research, a situation I both feared and welcomed. Ethnographers cannot take for granted a radical separation between the world of academe and the ethnographic site. We cannot "presuppose a geographical, geopolitical, and intellectual distance between the worlds of the researcher and the subject[s]" of our research (Chabram 1990, 238).

With this one exception, the young women in my classroom are not the actual girls I studied, though occasionally there are girls who represent the girls I studied, who could easily have been them—a middle-class Chicana or the rare and exceptional Chicana or white girl from a working-class family. But by and large this does not happen because, with few exceptions, working-class girls do not make it to the university. The colonizing aspect of ethnography where the ethnographer writes about subjects who are not empowered to talk back is present in my text. Even as people of color had become increasingly represented in academe (though that now appears to be reversing), working-class people, of any color, are rarely present here.

The stories I've written are inevitably informed by my cultural identity. My text is "situated knowledge" (Haraway 1988) because it cannot be otherwise. But while all knowledge is perspectival, it is based not only on one's cultural identity but also on one's political identity. An early form of identity politics seemed to suggest that an author might provide to readers a list of her identity categories with an assumption that this made visible to the reader how she perceived the world and, most importantly, what her blind spots were. But such an idea is based on the notion that identity is fixed and static rather than fluid and historicized, and presumes that one's knowledge of the world is based on some kind of raw experience unmediated by cultural and political discourse. As debates in identity politics wore on and the need for alliances became more urgent, the limitation of this kind of conceptualization of identity politics where one's political position is assumed to flow rather automatically from one's cultural identity began to appear. Some argued for a move beyond this most constraining, and perhaps naive, version of identity politics, suggesting instead that one can—indeed one *must,* to achieve social transformation—learn to read the world critically, as persons who are other to you might do.[15]

Valerie Walkerdine usefully explains why a confession of one's identity categories is an inadequate tool to provide to a reader when she says, "I had to take seriously the position from which I thought, felt, observed, wrote. But that position was not a fixed place, which told me that because I was born white, female, and working class, that I should see the world in a particular way, but that the ways I had been brought up to see the world, my very subjectivity, was created, produced, regulated in the social realm itself. There was not even some certain 'I' to do the observing, even if I took the step to present myself" (1997, 59). Where Walkerdine then inserts herself prolifically into her text, exploring the possible effects of her fluid class identity (from working to middle) and her self as the product of postwar class formation, I choose to insert myself only occasionally. Although my identity shapes my text, this happens in ways that are not necessarily transparent to me, and making them so would require layers of analysis of the ways in which I have been historically produced as a racialized, classed, sexual, gendered, and political subject. Though I see the value in the most reflexive ethnographies, which some dismiss as egocentric, I prefer in this book to state my recognition that my text is inevitably shaped by my cultural and political identity and then get on with the business of producing a book about the girls I came to know at Waretown.

A NOTE ON GENDER AND METHOD

Having read ethnographic accounts of youth subcultures in which researchers described and privileged "hanging out" in public spaces as the method for acquiring data and gaining insider status, I went into this project expecting to do the same. Certainly girls do hang out, as boys do, and I gleaned much information from being with them in public places. But the ways girls hang out or, as it is more contemporarily expressed, "kick it" and spend time with one another were such that sitting in the corner of the library with Blanca talking intimacies, or having an hour-long phone conversation with Maggie or a two-and-a-half hour conversation in a coffee shop with Amber and Jennifer, or talking at the kitchen table with girls at Lorena's house did not feel like artificial environments for "interviews." Since girls do "girl talk," often in sets of twos or threes, this was equally participant observation, as I was "doing" high school girl identity. A male colleague challenged me when he scoffed, "Talking on the phone is hardly ethnography." But how could it not be when a large part of what girls do is to talk one-on-one, and at great length?

Girls' pleasure in "just talking" and the blurring of this boundary between participant observation and formal interviewing became apparent one day when Lorena and I spent a two-hour block of time talking on the lawn in front of the school. When the period ended, she said, "Let's go meet the girls, they are coming out of class." When we met them, Lorena bragged, "We talked for so long, the tape stopped twice!" And Blanca competed, "When we talked yesterday, it was so long the batteries died and we kept havin' ta change them." On another occasion, as I wandered the halls with two girls who were skipping class, we were confronted by a teacher, who asked, "Why aren't you girls in class?" Wendy attempted an excuse, which the teacher interrupted, saying, "Oh sure. So you weren't just out here talking huh?" In other words, he knew that what we were doing that kept us from our class, our violation, was "talking."

This is, no doubt, a significant part of the reason why the issue of betrayal among girls is so pronounced. Girl talk, the disclosure of emotional injuries and insecurities, is often the basis for friendship and is what bonds girls. Therefore, to be seen doing the same, to be talking with another girl who is not a friend, is a potential act of betrayal. Donna Gaines explains this well in her ethnography of suburban teens. "Rule is, the street belongs to the boys. They are more public in orientation—they'll talk to anybody about anything. . . . But the girls are a little different. They're insular; they mostly hang out in pairs, rarely more than trios. They won't let you penetrate unless they see you every day, and then it's just friendly and polite. You have to be a best friend to get really close. Their conversations tend to be more local, personal, private. The girls are a subculture within a subculture" (1990, 63).

My entrée into dialogues with girls was a very gendered experience. Where Douglas Foley (1990), for example, notes that he spent much time hanging out in the gym playing hoops with the boys, my connection with girls was not mediated by a physical activity that would enable us to interact casually without much personal dialogue. I got to know girls while hanging out, talking more than doing, where we connected in conversations about things we saw in women's magazines, about boyfriends, whether or not we plan to have kids, and fashion. What we were wearing was often a topic of conversation. The silver rings I wore turned out to be a common opener for benign conversation. But clothing was a tricky subject to navigate; inevitably it revolved around an unarticulated awareness of body image, since girls this age (or perhaps women of almost all ages) are interminably and unfortunately aware of their body size and shape in relationship to unreasonable beauty norms and to each other. I found myself each morning trying to dress in ways that were appealing, yet not competitive or threatening.

At first I had questioned whether I was hanging out effectively, whether I had found the "action," but as the school year went by, I began to rethink what I first imagined as my own social ineptness or lack of ability as a researcher as more likely a consequence of a masculine bias in the literature on methodology. An integral part of this bias is the sensationalism of male youth violence, or at least of danger, and the ethnographer's desire to be where the action is, what Judith Stacey has dubbed "action-hero ethnography."[16] But the danger and violence experienced by women often occurs in private spaces and is often experienced as a solitary event. For example, in contrast to the many films primarily about male youth, *Girlstown* (1995) provides an alternative representation: we come to know a girl who was raped in the back seat of a car and another who is battered by her child's father. In the film the girls learn of each other's experiences through girl talk and then are empowered to collectively confront those who violated them. Similarly, Lisa Lewis (1990) offers an analysis of music videos in which she finds images that suggest to girls two kinds of intervention: "access signs," in which girls, aware of the attendant dangers, collectively take over male public space; but also "discovery signs," in which girls are found taking pleasure in each other's company in private spaces. The invisibility or lack of legitimacy given by school ethnographers to girl talk or "bedroom culture" reveals the privileging of public over private spheres of life as that which is important ethno to graph.

ABOUT THIS BOOK

Chapter 2 provides an overview of the academic theory debates that I both employ and critique in my analysis. Readers less interested in those debates might choose to skip this chapter. Chapters 3–5 present the ethnographic descriptions of the groups of girls I came to know. Chapter 3 focuses on working-class Mexican-American girls, and chapter 4 on working-class white girls. Chapter 5 looks at both white and Mexican-American working-class girls who are exceptional in that they are taking college-prep classes and plan to attend four-year institutions. In chapter 6 I explore relationships between various groups of girls across class and race. In the concluding chapter, I speak to the larger social and historical forces that shape the lives of this particular generation of young women and draw conclusions about the utility of the concepts of performance and performativity.

This organization deliberately decenters white middle-class girls, although they remain present in the analysis. It is no surprise, however, that preps were centered at the school—quite literally, as their hanging-out territory was at the middle of the campus in front of the library and near the buildings that house most of the college-prep courses. They were centered by school personnel as well, by the mere fact that, of all the students at Waretown High, they best met the normative ideal held out for student success, which is college attendance. On my first day at the school an administrator took me to an honors classroom saying,

"These are our best and our brightest." There I met Rhonda, who invited me to tag along as she went about the school putting up posters of student government candidates. As we walked around the grounds, she pointed out and named each building as she told me about her family's summer vacation, which included trips to various universities she was considering. When we passed by a building she had failed to identify and I asked what it was, she commented, "Oh, those are home economics courses. I don't know *what* those people do in there." When I asked about a group of white girls standing inside the door, she looked at me quizzically, then smiled at my naïveté, and explained, "Oh, they're smokers. They won't talk to you." And later, when I asked about another group of girls standing near the business building, she was again perplexed by my interest and responded, "Oh, well, those are *Mexican* girls," as if to say, they don't count; if you are here to study girls (read white, middle-class, normal), you are here to study us. At the end of our tour, she politely offered her assistance: "Let me know which of my friends you want to talk to."

CHAPTER 2

Women without Class

Recent scholarship reveals a renewed interest in class, and this growing literature involves various investments in class as a conceptual tool.[1] My intent is not to reassert the primacy of class, but to reconfigure it as an analytic category in light of the foregrounding of gender and race in feminist and ethnic studies and a related antifoundationalist turn in social theory. I enter this discussion wary of the investments of nostalgic leftists who offer a return to class analysis as a solution to the supposed problems of identity politics, and I hope to demonstrate a move away from reductionist ways of theorizing class. In this chapter I discuss literatures that frame my own work and that both assist and hinder understanding class as a cultural identity and the class subjectivity of women in particular. I explore the relationship between the symbolic economy of class—that is, the various class meanings that circulate in the supposedly separate domains of political, popular, and social science discourse—and the formation of subjective class identity among groups of high school girls. My goal in exploring the relationship between class symbolism and identity formation is to understand "the complex and contradictory ways" in which class subjectivity is constructed in relationship to gender and racial/ethnic identity under late capitalism (Long 1989, 428).

The book and chapter title "Women without Class" has multiple meanings. First, and most simply, it reflects my interest in young women from families of modest means and low educational attainment, who therefore have little cultural capital to enable class mobility. Other meanings speak to the theory debates I engage. A second meaning refers, in particular, to the fact that class analysis and social theory remained, until recently perhaps, insufficiently transformed by feminist theory, unable to conceptualize women as class subjects. Ignoring women's experience of class results in a profound androcentric bias, such that women are routinely invisible as class subjects. In much leftist analysis women are assumed to be without class, as these theorists often remain unable to see the category "working class" unless it is marked white and male. Such biases promote the invisibility of both white women and women of color as class subjects.[2]

This has happened in different ways. The failure to perceive women as class subjects, or as racial/ethnic subjects, has been part of the "youth and social class couplet" (McRobbie 1994, 181) of subculture studies and the school ethnographies of cultural marxists.[3] While there is a long tradition of school ethnographies in the overlapping fields of sociology, anthropology, education, and cultural studies, these studies have focused almost exclusively on the experiences and identities of boys, describing (and at times romanticizing) rituals of resistance to class reproduction at school, at work, and on the street. I work to redress the androcentric and ethnocentric biases found in the conceptual apparatuses of much of this scholarship. As has been pointed out by feminist critics of this body of work, such a public bias renders girls marginal as class subjects and neglects "contexts in which girls might be participating in 'equivalent rituals, response, and negotiations' " (Long 1989, 427).

Among studies of the class structure, women may have been included in class taxonomies, but without any theorization of gender, as in the early work of E. O. Wright (1985).[4] Or, more simply, the category "working class" was invisible unless it was marked white, male, and/or blue-collar industrial, indicated by the fact that studies of "the working class" often focused on men's lives (and at times women in blue-collar labor).[5] In other words, marxists were slow at times to recognize sex-segregated pink-collar occupations as working-class and to use gender to theorize class by exploring the ways in which gender shapes class formation.

In the symbolic economy of class the (now outdated) popular-culture icon Archie Bunker typified the working-class folk hero. Archie "just happened" to be white and male because the working class "was conceived in masculine terms," since "work, and especially manual labor, was still considered a masculine activity" (Ehrenreich 1989, 109). But this folk hero also turned up in academic work at the time, where white working-class men became the newest exotic anthropological subjects, even though the working class was increasingly composed of women and people of color. The pervasiveness of this identification of the working class as white and male might reflect the fact that for white liberal middle-class men, the primary producers of such images, "the blue-collar stereotype could never be such a distant 'other' as the poor, especially the black poor" (121) and could never be such a "distant 'other'" as women, and especially working-class women.

For example, the cover of Richard Sennett and Jonathan Cobb's *The Hidden Injuries of Class* (1972) featured the torso of a muscular white man in a denim shirt operating a jackhammer, participating in the historic and continuing cultural reification of the working class as white and male. I'd like to say this was a sign of the times, but a visual survey of book jackets in my university bookstore reveals this class iconography has not changed in response to the changing demographics of labor. The cover of an anthology on "work in America" featured male construction workers, and a 1995 anthology of "working people in California" featured a welder. The gender of this second worker is less discernible as his/her face is hidden behind a protective mask (though a head scarf suggests the worker may be female). In either case, "work" itself remains symbolically linked to blue-collar industrial labor.

When *is* class a visible characteristic of women? Two more book jackets, both introductory overviews of classic and contemporary theorizing on class, show a woman (one middle-aged and one elderly) in the coach car of a train; a sign above each of them reads "First," clearly marking their class locations. It is curious to most feminists, I'm sure, that the most despised creature in the leftist imagination appears not to be, say, a greedy white male CEO, but a middle-class or upper-class *unproductive* white woman. Perhaps it is no surprise that she is chosen, then, as the working class's most distant other. Where the male worker is romantically invoked as the revolutionary subject, she can only be treated with disdain. Such women can be represented as the bourgeoisie so long as class remains primary and gender invisible, and so long as working-class work is imagined only as the domain of men. Women make the stage as class subjects, it seems, when they represent consumption and leisure, not work.

The failure of social theory to theorize women as class subjects is repeated in and perhaps assisted by political discourse, where women's class location and identity is often obscured in contemporary discourse on "the family." Here, impoverished women are seen not as *poor* women, but as women *in between* men, encouraging the perception of women's class location in terms of family disruption. By shifting the focus away from women's economic well-being to the morality or immorality of family structure, this public discourse aids in underwriting a gender-blind imaginary of class, precluding us from viewing women in class terms apart from attachments with men.

Ironically, some versions of feminism have been complicit in constructing women as without class or racial/ethnic subjectivity. On a third level, then, my title considers debates within feminist theory and refers to feminist accounts that, while working as a corrective to androcentric biases and class reduction, tend toward gender reductionism, focusing primarily on the differences between boys and girls or women and men, failing to account for gender differences within sex categories across race, class, and sexuality. Historically, such studies have focused on white middle-class girls or women, but failed to define them as such. Thus, they too were perceived and presented not as class or racial/ethnic subjects, but only gendered.

Race/ethnicity and class do appear in newer books on girls, but while these concepts are named, often only gender is theorized.[6] These new books, some written as crossover books that hope to appeal to both an academic and a popular audience, as Mary Pipher's (1994) did, often have as their goal to disrupt gender reductionist thinking by pointing to race, class, and at times sexual difference. But race/ethnicity and class are too often presented as "categorical" variables (Connell 1987), essentially *there* rather than *created.* Minimal attention is given to the ways in which race and class are politically, historically, and situationally constructed (and performed) in relationship to gender.

For example, building on the American Association of University Women (AAUW) self-esteem study of girls (1992), Peggy Orenstein's (1994) study of schoolgirls points to the importance of class and includes girls from diverse class locations, but after her introductory discussion of its importance, class receives minimal analytical attention. Moreover, her choice of one school that is populated by primarily suburban white middle-class students and another that is populated by primarily urban working-class students of color reifies the false dichotomy that all white students are middle-class and all students of color are urban working-class. To her credit Orenstein does discuss the importance of racial differences between the two groups of girls at their respective schools, and she eschews a gender-reductionist analysis by suggesting that at times issues of racism and poverty can overshadow gender differences. But the dichotomy remains as she fails to discuss differences that may exist *among* African-American girls or *among* Latinas, based on class or generational status (i.e., how many generations removed from immigration), for example.

Refreshingly, Joan Jacobs Brumberg's (1997) historical study of girls' "body projects" refuses to conflate race with class, noting that some of the differences about body image between white girls and girls of color may be in part related to class. While she studies primarily white middle-class girls, Brumberg understands and articulates the way in which class meaning (and at times race) is relational, with each group defined in opposition to one another. She highlights the centrality of class in historical constructions of "beauty": Victorian middle-class girls defined themselves through a series of contrasts to the labor and dirt associated with working-class girls.

Some of these books also make an attempt to see contemporary girls in historical context, recognizing generational (i.e., age cohort) differences in the experience of girlhood, and thus they at times make an evaluation as to whether things are "better" or "worse" for girls today. Unfortunately, Brumberg reveals an admiration for "the world we have lost," presenting contemporary girls not as negotiators of culture, but as primarily victims (of manipulative business, biology, sexual liberalism and feminism, and shifts in parenting and mentoring). She fails to discuss girls' contextualization in peer groups, which results in her misreading, in my opinion, of some subcultural youth practices, such as piercing. Like Pipher, she seems unable to see the possibility that these practices might be forms of resistance to the authority and approval of adults and race and class hierarchies. To her credit, Orenstein's study does a better job of acknowledging girls' agency, suggesting that what many take as evidence of girls' victimhood (eating disorders, self-cutting, and disengagement from school) can also be fruitfully seen as displays of anger and protests against unachievable standards.

Naomi Wolf's (1997) book on girls' sexuality makes a deliberate attempt to bridge a possible generation gap among feminists; her goal is to offer an account of girlhood during rather than before the 1960s sexual revolution. However, she makes gross generalizations from her own white upper-middle-class experience and appears to believe that hers is "ordinary" and representative of the norm. Pointing to the liberating effects of claiming a "bad girl" identity, she fails to see the historic and contemporary race and class meanings associated with active sexuality among girls and women and how the label "bad girl" is applied differentially across race and class lines and with varying effects. Moreover, she argues that women are "naturally" more sexual than men, ignoring in large part the historical, cultural, and political construction of sexuality.

More recently, Lyn Mikel Brown's (1998) study of "the politics of girls' anger" makes an explicit attempt to dismantle the assumption that all working-class girls are of color and that all white girls are middle-class. She studies only white working-class girls and keenly demonstrates the ways in which class inflects femininity and girls' anger and resistance. She provides an important corrective to theories of a self-esteem crisis among girls by arguing against presenting girls as passive victims and demonstrating ways in which anger is a political emotion, but she does not idealize girls' resistance. However, while gender is explored as an unstable construct, class and race both remain static, undefined, and analytically subordinate to gender. As with so many books on girls, to the extent that race (whiteness in this case) and class appear, they do so as demographic variables, not social and political constructs.

The critique of gender reductionism is, of course, old news in feminist theory; "third-world" (Mohanty 1991)[7] and "critical race" feminism[8] have long since posed serious challenges to the gendered subject of "white middle-class" feminism.[9] Feminist work that is informed by the incisive race critique asserted (most often) by women of color has led to a clearer understanding of how multiple social formations and identities intersect.

While third-world feminism has refused gender reductionism, exploring the variety of possible differences and similarities, divisions and alliances within the category Woman, across race, ethnicity, nation, and sexuality, little attention appears to have been paid to cross-racial analysis of class. Quantitative studies often compare race and class as "variables," but comparative ethnographic work is rarer, with a few notable exceptions (Higgenbothem and Weber 1992; Luttrell 1993, 1997). Within contemporary feminist theory and empirical work, it seems there has been a trend toward dichotomizing white middle-class women and working-class women of color.[10] Few have offered a "working-class feminism" (and I suggest this along with, not instead of, third-world feminism) that would speak to the similarity of working-class experiences women might have across race and thereby teach us something about how class operates, and that would show the limits of those similarities and thereby lend more clarity to how race operates independent of class and why it cannot be reduced to it. Like popular discourse, feminist theory and U.S. cultural studies, at times, suffer from a conflation and confusion of race/ethnicity and class, where they are reduced to each other, such that we fail to see how both social forces operate independently yet intersect. I suggest these comparisons should be made, but also point to the need for vigilant attentiveness to the risks involved in making claims of similarity and difference and to the politics of theory and the dangers of appropriation.[11]

This conflation may be due in part to the fact that within U.S. feminist theory and cultural studies, *class* as a topic seems tainted, perhaps perceived as outdated and unfashionable, relegated to either prefeminist marxism or to socialist feminism. Socialist feminism never failed to examine class, of course, but it was lacking at times in analyses of race. Race was too often understood only as the difference of class in the leftist tradition of reducing race to class. Further, class was often explored by socialist feminists more at the level of abstract systems (capitalism, patriarchy) than as a cultural identity and subjective experience.[12]

In spite of their own limitations, feminists and scholars of race and ethnicity have worked to correct the biases in class analysis that fail to theorize women as class subjects and that are a consequence of two separate but related problems: first, the focus on male (white and/or nonwhite) subjects; and second, the employment of conceptual schemes that not only fail to adequately explain the production of women's experience of class but also make gender and race epiphenomenal to class formation. With regard to subculture studies, these biases can be seen not only in the focus on primarily male youth in public places, but also in the use of normative conceptions of "class consciousness" as defined by relations of production, by the focus on youth's transition to work identity, and by the failure to consider gender, family futures and pasts, and racial/ethnic identity as shapers of class subjectivity.

Paul Willis's classic work *Learning to Labour: How Working Class Kids Get Working Class Jobs* (1977), was a welcome improvement over structural determinist arguments,[13] arguing for the "relative autonomy of culture" and recognizing that structural forces are always mediated by a cultural milieu. Willis even recognized that gender meanings were part of that cultural milieu, as he explained how the link between masculinity and manual labor inhibited male youth from taking an interest in other kinds of labor that they imagined as feminized and inferior.

Further, Willis offered up racial meanings as part of the recipe, suggesting "the lads'" sense of white superiority "softened the blow" of their obtaining only working-class jobs. In so doing, he showed how cultural resources are used to make sense of inherited structural and material conditions.

But in the end Willis's account failed feminism. He presents his male subjects "as though they were *the* working class" (Holland and Eisenhart 1990, 34), describing working-class culture as valuing manual labor and physical prowess, the sexual domination of women, and oppression of people of color. In so doing Willis played down internal class divisions along gender and racial/ethnic lines, remaining blind to gender- and racial/ethnic-specific culture and domains. Although he discusses the relevance of their meanings to the development of the lads' class identity, his awareness of these organizing variables of inequality has no consequence for his overall theory (Holland and Eisenhart 1990). While he conceptualized class in the historic terms of class formation, he conceptualized race and gender as categorical or static, essentially there rather than historically composed, and so failed to explore their co-creation with class. When analyzing class, he understood culture holistically as expressive practices, but when speaking to gender and race/ethnicity, culture appears as mere ideology masking the workings of class reproduction. In short, gender and race projects are not seen to be as central as class struggle.[14]

Early feminist critiques of marxism sought to add considerations of "patriarchy" to analyses of capitalism, asserting that these dual systems were separate but interacting (layered or additive). This too often led to a description of patriarchy as transhistorical and transcultural, while capitalism remained understood as historical, dynamic, and unfortunately gender neutral. But by 1975, Gayle Rubin had suggested that "sex/gender systems" were historically specific ways of organizing sexuality and reproduction, and by 1984 she had made sex and gender analytically separate, pointing to sexuality, a hierarchy of desire, as a distinct social formation. Heidi Hartmann (1979) provided a lucid critique of marxism's theory of the development of "empty places," exemplifying the partnership of patriarchy and capitalism through a case study of labor unions that revealed how gender ideology was used to support the demand for better wages, a "family wage," for working-class men at women's expense through the collusion of white male capitalists and white male workers. In short, marxist categories of analysis do not explain why particular kinds of people (gendered, racialized) fill particular occupational places. Hartmann demonstrated that class is not the only agent of history and pointed toward the need for parallel analyses of the ways in which gender and racial logic inform capitalism (though she did not explore the latter). Many have since worked to demonstrate the ways in which gender helps to constitute class relations and vice versa, where gender is not assumed as an essential category that exists prior to its historically specific and politically influenced emergence.[15]

Likewise, Joan Acker (1988) clearly pointed to the limitations of a marxist class analysis that suggests people participate in capitalism as either an owner or a non-owner of the means of production. This fails to acknowledge, she argues, that historically women were not allowed to be full citizens because they were denied the right to vote or own property. Thus, the question becomes who is free to even participate in capitalism. This denial of citizenship based on the logic of gender—and, we must of course add, the logic of race—is outside of and preexists capitalist class inequality.

Simultaneously, scholars of race and ethnicity have offered parallel challenges to analyses of class formation. Most usefully, Michael Omi and Howard Winant (1994) have created and employed the concept of "racial formation," describing racial/ethnic categories not as preexisting but as emerging from "racial projects" in which the content and salience of racial categories are politically constructed and work to secure white privilege. Many have pointed to the historic racialized struggles that white men have engaged in (and white women benefited from) with populations of color to secure their privileged status, demonstrating a collusion among whites across class divisions.[16] As Tomás Almaguer explains, there was an " 'elective affinity' between the material interests of whites at different class levels and the racial ideologies that simultaneously structured" an Anglo-dominated society (1994, 3). And Lisa Lowe challenges marxism's theory of empty places by demonstrating that U.S. "capital has historically accumulated and profited through the *differentiation* of labor rather than through its homogenization" (1996, 159). When we explore the connection between "*how* . . . jobs are defined and *who* is sought after for the jobs" (Mohanty 1997, 11), it becomes apparent that occupational categories are not randomly filled by a homogenized working class. Rather, we witness the impact of immigration and globalization on the very configuration of class, as racialized and gendered subjects are created to fill class slots.

White privileges have historically been established and maintained under the sign of citizenship. Immigration and naturalization laws, and social and welfare policies, are informed by ideologies of race as racial categorizations shift over time in part as a function of the U.S. need to exploit labor (Mohanty 1991). Historically U.S. capital has demanded cheap labor, and the state's denial of citizenship and the elimination of welfare benefits has worked to keep people illegal and dependent, unable to refuse low-wage work. The state allows capital to extract cheap labor from workers, yet evades responsibility for the welfare of exploited workers and their children; workers are dehumanized by the effective denial that they have families and family needs such as education and health services (Chang 1994). Both citizenship status and racial identification have been used to legitimate paying people of color substandard wages, and both voluntary and involuntary immigrant populations of color have been denied citizenship rights despite sweat and blood contributions to the U.S. economy and national defense efforts.

Because of this history, color itself can come to signify questionable citizenship status, with "American" national identity popularly imagined as white. This ill-gotten conflation of whiteness and citizenship is a disturbingly pervasive ideology. As Clara, a second-generation Mexican-American girl, said to me one day, "We don't have as equal a life as an American person, I mean, a white person."

In short, both gender and race inform class formation; women are still too often conceptualized in the nation's mind not as workers, but as wives and mothers, and people of color are not imagined as full citizens or *true* Americans and are therefore believed to deserve only the lowest rung of occupations. This, of course, places women of color in the worst of situations, as global capital takes advantage of preexisting formations of race and gender.

CLASS AS CULTURE

My interest in exploring the intersections of race, class, gender, and sexuality spans both the macro level of social formation, where these processes are mutually constitutive, and the micro level of identity formation, where the circulation of cultural meanings produces the material that makes various subjectivities possible. Mindful of the theory debates and empirical gaps reviewed above, I set off to explore if and how young women experience and understand class differences among themselves, and specifically how girls' experience of gender and race was shaped by class difference and class meaning. I foreground, but do not privilege, class as I examine how gender, sexual identity, color, and ethnicity intersect with and shape class as a lived culture and subjective identity. Rather than presuming that "class consciousness" unfolds automatically from the relations of production, I choose to explore it as a learned position (Steedman 1986), arguing that class identity comes to be known equally by markers that exist outside of discovering one's position in paid labor, as an identity lived out in private life and personal relations—in short, class culture. One's experience of class may be expressed not only in terms of work identity and income but also in terms of familial relations, social relations unrelated to those of employment (such as school and peer relations), and in leisure and consumption practices, including the "identity formation material" (McRobbie 1994) offered up by popular culture. Cultural marxism has done this, but not by beginning with women's lives. The production of women's experience in these "non-work" sites and women's relationship to production and consumption have historically differed from men's and thus must be examined in order to give an account of the gender-specific experience of class identity and expression of class culture, and to assist an exploration of how gender meanings shape class formation itself. We must also examine the symbolic boundaries that mark the difference between racial/ethnic-specific working- and middle-class performances of gender, to understand how racial/ethnic meanings shape class formation.

In thinking through class as a cultural identity, I want to foreground consumption as a defining class activity and, in particular, style and women's traditional concern with shopping and buying. While studies have focused on men's consumption and leisure as a way of understanding class as a cultural identity, these inquiries are not parallel. It is ironic that most of the studies of subcultural style have been about boys, when style and fashion are, or are at least perceived to be, so central to girls' identity. Lisa Lewis notes that, historically, an underlying assumption within the subculture literature viewed "the marketplace as the antithesis of authentic cultural expression (as essentially a mechanism of capitalist reproduction)." Given that the "domestic division of labour has long positioned women as the primary consumption workers . . . [and] consumption work has been largely framed by Marxists as non-productive labour," such an assumption makes it difficult to consider "consumer girl culture" as a site of resistance at all; participation in it can only be understood as a kind of false consciousness (1990, 98–99). In class reductionist thinking, when consumption is aligned with femininity and consumption is inherently the antithesis of resistance, then girls, it seems, cannot "resist."

If women express the symbolic boundaries of class culture through consumption practices and commodities targeted at women, then the gender-specific "hidden injuries of class" experienced by women often have to do with these markers. "Hidden injuries" refers to the social-psychological burdens of class status anxiety, "the feeling of vulnerability in contrasting oneself to others at a higher social level, the buried sense of inadequacy" that affects "those who lose the most by being classified" (Sennett and Cobb 1972).[17] Carolyn Steedman explores the gender specificity of such injuries, using her mother's desire for "a New Look skirt" as a metaphor to think through the "politics of envy" and the "culture of longing" her mother experienced. The masculinization in class analysis has almost wholly ignored the transitional objects of women's experience of class identity and mobility, "the material stepping stones of our escape: clothes, shoes, makeup" (1986, 15). Moving beyond personal style, women's consumption practices have not been peripheral to their class identities (as defined by production); rather they have historically been a part of their productive (or what socialist feminists called reproductive) labor within families.

Focusing on class as identity distinguishes my project from other inquiries into the formation of class consciousness, which employ normative marxist notions of what constitutes class consciousness, that is, that class belonging hinges on an understanding of one's relationship to production and the development of a political consciousness. Conceiving class as an identity rather than a consciousness reveals two important points: first, that such an identity may not necessarily be a politicized one, and second, that class is only one among many identities that might mobilize people.

Even cultural marxists, though they employed a more holistic definition of culture as everyday ways of life rather than as ideology, still too often tended to define working-class community and culture "in the restricted sense of a political community" (Foley 1990, 165). In contrast, I mean a class identity that is not to be understood as a politicized identity (class-for-itself) but as a sense of one's place(s) in a cultural economy of meaning—that is, a sense of place or difference that may or may not contain a feeling of opposition or antagonism and that may or may not (more often the latter) be commonly named and known as "class." I'm interested in people's implicit recognition of cultural difference, in the everyday symbolic boundaries that people employ to understand their own and others sense of place(s), and the way in which understandings of place are intertwined with gender and racial/ethnic meanings. Such expressive cultural practices and class identities cannot be understood as unmediated by racial/ethnic, gender, and sexual cultures (among other salient identities) and by history, but rather might be better explored as "ethnic-gender-class" cultures and identities (Clarke 1991).

The persistent question raised and debated by this distinction between class identity / class culture and class consciousness is "Does a working class culture have to have class consciousness to be a class culture or not?" (Foley 1990, 167). I suggest, as others have, that expressive cultural styles and, of particular interest to me here, their manifestation in the performances of youth subcultures, have their source in and are reflections of class (though not only class) realities, regardless of whether they are articulated as such. The expression of self through one's relationship to and creative use of commodities (both artifacts and the discourses of popular culture) is a central practice in capitalist society. These modes of expression can represent antibourgeois, antipatriarchal, or antiracist meanings even when social actors don't articulate them as such. As we will see, students were very able to communicate a sense of unfairness, a "structure of feeling" (R. Williams, 1965),[18] where inequalities were felt but not politically articulated. Rejecting a limited definition of culture as ideology, we can see it as less the conscious ideas people are taught than the "unreflective way we treat each other" (Foley 1990, 168). In short, the political economy behind our everyday relationships is routinely hidden from us, mediated by commodities so that the struggle is often waged less over explicit political ideologies than over modes of identity expression, which "does not necessarily culminate in a progressive class acting 'for' itself politically" (186).

There is a degree of overlap between the idea of class culture found in cultural marxism and the idea of class as a status group found in Weberian sociology. However, as Douglas Foley (1990) explains, an unfortunate false dichotomy has been constructed between the idea of status groups of different lifestyles and status displays on the one hand, and economic classes on the other. While Bourdieu (1984) works through this by linking status groups with class, describing "social classes as cultural status display groups" (Foley 1990, 170), the relationship is overdetermined in his account (where cultural capital too readily determines class location).[19] I use *class* instead of *status group* because I want to point to the fact that membership in groups was largely shaped by class, and even when it was not, group membership had significant consequences for students' class futures; *status* is too benign a term to express this.[20] Directing our attention to class culture and identity "is a way of focusing class analysis on the *cultural politics* of how economic classes are culturally reproduced and resisted" (Foley 1990, 170; emphasis mine) and on how those cultural politics are mutually inflected by race and gender. As Foley suggests (1990, 191), paying attention to differences in consumption and expression does not have to mean (although it unfortunately does in some scholarship) forgoing classes as competing economic groups. Further, linking class culture with gender and racial/ethnic culture assists us in explaining how class inequality is organized by race and gender projects.

SUBCULTURAL STYLE: CLASS-BARELY-AWARE-OF-ITSELF

Studies of subcultural meaning and style done by cultural marxists have come primarily from Great Britain,[21] since in the United States such creative youth were treated instead under the rubric of deviance and delinquency.[22] A subculture is understood as a shared aesthetic or preferred style, including dress, accessories, speech, and demeanor. Subcultures grow out of multiple structures of inequality, though class has usually been analytically privileged, and are generally understood as simultaneously resistances to and reproductions of those inequities. As creative responses to the injuries of inequality and attempts to maintain dignity, they are often "intentionally confrontational and disturbing styles," which pose a "perceived threat to civil order and morality" until they are co-opted and commodified by the culture industry, which then markets the styles for mass consumption (Ferrell and Sanders 1995, 8, 16), thus diffusing any subversive potential they may have had.[23] But if such expressions of cultural resistance quickly become co-opted and commercialized, new generations just as quickly create and recreate new expressions. As one white girl described her cohort, "This crowd used to be the rockers, then they were punks, now I don't know what we're called." And a Mexican-American girl explained, "The granddaddies were the zoot suiters, and then there were the pachucos, they were our parents. Now, well, I guess it's gangs."

The criminalization of and "moral panics" (Cohen 1972) over these styles, as happened with the mods and rockers, for example, in Great Britain, with zoot suiters and bikers, among others, in the United States, and, most contemporarily, with hip-hop style and music, "deflect attention from larger and more complex political problems like economic and ethnic inequality" and uncertain futures (Ferrell and Sanders 1995,10). But, further, any potential awareness of gender inequality is deflected both by the media's focus on and sensationalizing of male youth violence and by the masculinism of social science analysis. Angela McRobbie notes the "urban romanticism" and "masculinist overtones" of subculture studies (1991, 20), where the supposedly gender-neutral term "youth" actually stands for male.

Girls' only sensationalized parallel to the media's focus on youthful male violence is the media-fabricated "epidemic" of teen pregnancy, from which boys are curiously absent. As Kristin Luker (1996) explains, in actuality most teens having babies are legal adults of eighteen and nineteen, and currently teens make up a declining portion of unwed mothers. The media and the conservative right make gender (and biological gender in particular) more salient than other aspects of girls' identities when they perennially fail to consider class as a causal variable in explaining teen pregnancy. Teen pregnancy does not cause poverty but vice versa: girls who become pregnant early (and especially those who go ahead and give birth) are more often than not poor to begin with. Race *is* made salient in depictions of teen pregnancy, though not, as I would hope, because of the recognition that teen pregnancy is linked to poverty and poverty is linked to institutionalized racism. The cause of teen pregnancy is imagined not as a consequence of being poor but as a perceived consequence of poor family values among people of color. Teen pregnancy, among Latinas and African-American women in particular, invokes white fears of "overbreeding" among women of color, as white women are imagined as the only legitimate reproducers of the nation and women of color are imagined as a welfare burden.

But by and large, in order to envision themselves as class or race subjects, girls must routinely read themselves as boys in media accounts of "youth." The subtitle of a cover story in the *San Francisco Examiner Magazine* on the topic of "wiggas" (which the article explains is shorthand for "white niggers"; Wagner 1996) reads "suburban kidz hip-hop across the color line." The story is about white youth who appropriate hip-hop culture and perform "black" identity. The cover picture is a collage of magazine cutouts of white kids with blue eyes and blond hair (functioning as a code for racial purity) wearing hip-hop fashion and standing in front of a white picket fence behind which sits a charming two-story house and an apple tree. Although there is a girl *pictured* on the front, girls are absent from the story itself.

Similarly, in a 1993 episode of the television talk show *Oprah* on the same topic, several groups of boys, white and black, sat on the stage. The audience was confounded by the young black man who, as one guest explained, "looks like he walked out of Eddie Bauer" and by the young white boys in hip-hop style who "grew up in the 'hood,' " as the participants debated what it meant to dress black or dress white. During the course of the hour-long program all parties failed to note that, race and ethnicity aside, these were different versions of masculinity and girls were once again missing from a story about "youth."

Until recently, the role of girls in subcultures had been left largely unaddressed.[24] McRobbie (1991) is an exception in her early posing of the questions: What is girls' role in subcultures? Are they actually missing or marginal, or does the masculinist bias of past analyses simply fail to explore their role? Do their resistances mimic those of boys, or do girls employ strategies unique to their gender culture?[25] McRobbie's answers (42–48) suggest that a "girl culture" among working-class girls—focused on fashion, beauty, and heterosexual romance—and patterns of "quiet non-cooperation," "gentle undermining," "subtle redefinition," "immersion in private concerns," "tactics of silence," and expression of "unambiguous boredom" in the classroom all work as forms of resistance (or "accommodation," according to Joan Anyon [1984]) that girls employ to reject official school activities and, by association, middle-class cultural norms. That is, girls may resist school without violently confronting it, and their strategies, often less sensational than those of boys, are easily overlooked. Still others (such as Dorothy Holland and Margaret Eisenhart [1990]) reject this idea, arguing that the girl culture McRobbie describes, far from constituting "resistance," is the very problem to be reckoned with, as girls are "educated in romance" and competitive heterosexuality, which puts women on a sexual auction block and recreates the sexual division of labor. I will suggest that it is, of course, both.

But beyond the invisibility of gender in media accounts, there is also a failure to "think class" with much clarity. On the *Oprah* show, as on the magazine cover, the same set of binaries surface repeatedly: white is middle-class is suburban; black is lower-class is urban. But a slippage occurs in which class references are dropped out, and white stands in for middle where black stands in for lower, or suburban stands in for white and urban for black. Class and racial/ethnic signifiers are melded together in such a way that "authentic" black, and sometimes brown, identity is imagined as lower-class, urban, and often violent—and male as well. These are the overly simplified identity categories offered, but they do not reflect the complexity of life. Middle-class youth of color (however statistically small in number) are missing, for example, as are multiracial/multiethnic identity and small-town or rural poverty. The racial/ethnic and class subject positions offered by the "identity formation material" (McRobbie 1994, 192) of popular culture often do not allow for more nuanced social locations.

Since much subcultural theory and ethnographic work has its origins in Great Britain, it is important when making its translation to the United States to note that our class-blind discourse means there is even less chance here that working-class youth would be able to articulate class identity, although students of color might do so more readily than white students. The logic of leftist social theory routinely reduces race and gender to class (which is presumed more fundamental), failing to see either race or gender as autonomous fields of social conflict or fundamental axes of social organization. However, in popular discourse we regularly see just the opposite, where class is not a present category of thought at all or is present but understood only as a difference of money and as temporary, given the U.S. ideology of upward mobility. Sherry Ortner (1991, 1993, 1998) helps us considerably in understanding the common-sense ways of describing class differences in everyday talk. What primarily characterizes popular understandings of class is that class itself is "not a central category of cultural discourse" in the United States. "It does appear in native discourse . . . just not in terms we recognize as 'about class.' " That is to say, class is often expressed through categories of difference which are "*taken to be* 'locked into' individuals—gender, race, ethnic origin, and so forth" (1991, 169–71; emphasis mine). Thus, discourses on gender and race, which traditionally position these categories as fixed and natural, have offered sites on which class issues are articulated in other terms and have helped sustain the long-standing ideological representation of the United States as a classless society.

Ortner suggests that most people cannot or will not think with the category *class*. That is, people appear "discursively disabled" from talking about class, and "class has a fleeting quality" as it is "barely textualized" in their talk. Consequently, she suggests that we must learn to find class discourse "where it lives," in the discourse of success, money, values, intelligence, gender, race, ethnicity (1993, 423, 427) and, I would add, among youth in subcultural styles. Because of the various and many displacements of class in everyday talk, it would be wrong to conclude that class meanings are absent for people if the common-sense categories of cultural difference they use are not named as *class*. But the lack of an available public discourse on class makes it difficult to "think class," to put a label on this difference.

Clearly, Ortner's and my use of the term *displacement* is not to be confused with a move to privilege class and put gender and race back in their place, so to speak. Setting aside any conventional leftist fear that class as a category of analysis is being replaced by race and gender analysis, we do need to consider the ways in which popular understandings of class, from which social science discourse may not be so far removed, contain race and gender codes that shape and are shaped by our understandings of class difference. They are always already mutually implicated in one another.

CLASS AS PERFORMANCE AND PERFORMATIVE

I entered the field with a good deal of cynicism about subcultural styles in the United States, in particular among white youth, assuming they would not be linked in any way to class politics. I was prepared to find that youth of color would be more able to articulate race awareness, and a related nascent class awareness, through a politics of style. For the most part, I expected to find that subcultural genres were politically vacuous styles performed by middle-class youth who were victims of the mass culture industry. In short, I did not go looking to romanticize subculture style as resistance, and especially not among girls.

But a primary way students understand class and racial/ethnic differences among themselves is through their informal peer hierarchy, with cliques and their corresponding styles largely organized by racial/ethnic and class identities. The social roles linked to group membership include curriculum choices (whether a student is on the college-prep or vocational track) and extracurricular activities (whether a student was involved in what are considered either college-prep or non-prep activities). These courses and activities combine to shape class futures, leading some girls to four-year colleges, others to vocational programs at community colleges, and still others directly to low-wage jobs directly out of high school.

While there is a strong correlation between a girl's class of "origin" (by which I mean her parents socioeconomic status), and her class performance at school (which includes academic achievement, prep or non-prep activities, and membership in friendship groups and their corresponding style), it is an imperfect one, and there are exceptions where middle-class girls perform working-class identity and vice versa. In other words, in a kind of class "passing," some students choose to perform class identities which are sometimes not their "own."

Although clique membership is not entirely determined by class, there was certainly "a polarization of attitudes toward class characteristics," and group categories (such as preps, smokers, and chola/os) were "embodiment[s] of the middle and working class[es]" (Eckert 1989, 4–5) and led to differential class futures. On the one hand, embracing and publicly performing a particular class culture mattered significantly more than origins in terms of a student's aspirations, her treatment by teachers and other students, and potentially her class future. On the other hand, class origins did matter, of course, as girls drew upon different resources from home, both economic and cultural, which shaped their life chances. Families are a crucial site where cultural capital is acquired and where class identity is formed, which individuals then bring to mixed-class settings. Class-differentiated experiences within the family provide us with different sets of symbolic and material resources (Roman 1988) and shape our experience of mixed-class public settings like schools, peer culture, and sites of leisure and consumption, where we then routinely experience and inflict class injuries upon each other. It is important to explore the way in which the construction of self is shaped by family and community life, and the way in which the family contributes to the "ideological construction of 'other' " (Weis 1990).

Because of the imperfect correlation, I came to define students not only as working- or middle-class in origin (problematic in itself), but also as working- or middle-class *performers* (and synonymously as non-prep or prep students). Girls who were passing, or metaphorically cross-dressing, had to negotiate their "inherited" identity from home with their "chosen" public identity at school.[26] There was a disparity for them between what people looked like and talked like at home, and their own class performance at school and what their friends' parents were like. As I came to understand these negotiations of class as cultural (not political) identities, it became useful to conceptualize class not only as a material location, but also as a performance. Although my reference to middle-class and working-class performers is cumbersome, I choose it nonetheless as a constant reminder to the reader of my point that class can be conceptualized, in part, as a performance and that there are exceptions to the class-origin-equals-class-performance rule. Many educational ethnographies make claims and generalizations about working-class students and middle-class students. If I employ the same terminology, my work may be indistinguishable from those, and my key point about class as performance and about exceptions may be lost by the end of the reading.

Exceptions to the rule aside, social actors largely display the cultural capital that is a consequence of the material and cultural resources to which they have had access. Cultural performances most often reflect one's *habitus*—that is, our unconsciously enacted, socially learned dispositions, which are not natural or inherent or prior to the social organization of class inequality, but are in fact produced by it. Here it is useful to think of class as *performative,* in the sense that class as cultural identity is an *effect* of social structure.

Little attention has been paid to thinking about *class* as a performance or as performative. To conceptualize class in this way is not to ignore its materiality. There is always the materiality of the body in thinking about race and gender (the continua of phenotype and of sex), whose meaning is negotiated and made more or less salient by culture (or, more strongly, whose materiality is created by culture). And with class there is the materiality of economic and cultural resources about which we make meaning. Cultural and political discourses that naturalize and sanction kinds of class relations and normalize institutionalized class inequality produce kinds of class subjects (poor, working, middle, rich, etc.) and material inequalities. In turn, those class subjects and material inequalities produce discourses that naturalize and normalize class inequality.

The normalization of class inequality and its institutionalization regulates class performances. For example, class-specific styles of speech, such as the use of standard or nonstandard grammar, accents, mannerisms, and dress (all of which are also racially/ethnically and regionally specific), are learned sets of expressive cultural practices that express class membership. Group categories at school require different class performances, and students engage in practices of exclusion based on authentic class performances (Foley 1990).[27] Cultural differences in class (linked to both education and income) are key to the middle-class practices of exclusion that make school "success" difficult for working-class students across color and ethnicity. Class can be conceptualized as performative in that there is no interior difference (innate and inferior "intelligence" or "taste," for example) that is being expressed, but rather institutionalized class inequality *creates* class subjects who display differences in cultural capital. Bourdieu suggests that while children from the working class can through mobility "acquire the social, linguistic, and cultural competencies which characterize the upper-middle and middle class, they can never achieve the 'natural' familiarity of those born to these classes and are academically penalized on this basis" (Lamont and Lareau 1988, 156). This explains the discomfort and anxiety associated with passing often described by those who have been upwardly mobile.

In short, what is necessary to understand about my use of and distinction between the terms *performance* and *performative* is that the former refers to agency and a conscious attempt at passing. Applied to class this might mean consciously imitating middle-class expressions of cultural capital in an attempt at mobility. *Performativity,* on the other hand, refers to the fact that class subjects are the effects of the social structure of class inequality, caught in unconscious displays of cultural capital that are a consequence of class origin or habitus. Here there is no "doer behind the deed" (Hood-Williams and Harrison 1998). The dual concepts of performance and performativity thus allow me analytical room to explain the extent to which class identity is both fluid and fixed.

Within a poststructuralist, radically constructionist formulation of identity there is no real, eternal, essential, fixed subject, but only one that is given meaning in context (both in the long arm of history and in the short arm of interaction). On the one hand, we are all always performing our cultural identities, and the performance *is* the self. Performance is all there is, because no identities are natural; they are all constructed. But, on the other hand, those constructed subjectivities are institutionalized, made into structures that have an autonomy apart from the interactional performance. So there is a fixity to those identities, which is what makes it possible for people to have a provisional, temporal "real" self that, in turn, is what makes it possible for them to *feel* like they are passing, in drag, momentarily acting like someone other than who they "really" are. In short, there are times when one's performance does not align with one's notion of an "authentic" true self; one's performance can be incongruent with who one thinks one really is.

In fact, although postmodern theory tells us there is no real self, people often tend to feel they have one. That is, social actors routinely understand and explain themselves (though not exclusively) in essentialist ways. I do not mean to reassert a modern subject, but rather, in the context of recognizing that identity and experience are always constructed discursively, I wish to emphasize here an "understanding of identity as self-presence" (Fuss 1989, 103) to point to the less theorized, spontaneous understanding of identity and experience of everyday actors. In short, identities are "points of temporary attachment to the subject positions which discursive practices construct for us" (S. Hall 1996, 6). In a poststructuralist formulation, passing, it seems, would not be possible, because the concept assumes there is an objective referent that is being evaded. But by passing I do not mean to infer an essential subject that is being covered up, but rather this institutionalized temporal "real" self that is indeed constructed, but not routinely taken to be so by the social actor. It is cultural and material structures that make these subjectivities possible, and while those structures are historical and contingent, not inevitable, but constantly being reproduced in practice, it may not always feel like it. The fiction of an essential or real self aids in the reproduction of inequality because it masks the fact that all subjectivities are constructed and that they are institutionalized and regulated (Butler 1990). In other words, race, class, sexuality, and gender are not properties of individuals, but axes of social organization that are shifting and fluid. But there is a *temporal* fixity, bound by the context of history and culture, and these identities are routinely embraced as real by social actors (i.e., I am Mexican-American, I am white, I am a girl) and are real in their consequences.

The work on performativity that comes out of cultural studies and poststructuralist feminism (Butler 1990, 1993, in particular), both of which offer a radical constructionist analysis of gender, race, and sexuality, holds something in common with the constructionism of symbolic interactionist sociology and ethnomethodology (Goffman 1959, 1967, 1974; and West and Fenstermaker 1995, in particular). There are important differences between the two, however, which are reflected in the long-standing structure/agency debate. Symbolic interactionist sociology and ethnomethodology have been long critiqued for tending toward a subject too readily construed as an active agent outside of the autonomy of social structures that preexist and produce various performances.[28] A widespread misreading of Judith Butler's notion of performance also conceptualizes actors as agents who are free to choose identity performances. In actuality, in her poststructuralist framework there is no actor/agent who preexists the performance; rather the subject is constructed by the performance. Within the latter understanding, poststructuralism has been criticized for tending toward an overdetermined subject, one who is always already interpellated by discourse. I attempt to address both this fixity and fluidity, structure and agency, as I query how girls are constructed by and construct themselves in and with cultural discourses.

By discourse I do not simply mean language in practice. Rather, discourses are "competing ways of giving meaning to the world, which imply differences in the organization of social power" and have implications for the social practices in which we engage (Weedon 1987). I employ the concept of discourse because it is a way of deconstructing a binary division between the material and the ideal and reflects a shift from a foundationalist to an antifoundationalist epistemology. That is, the concept of discourse suggests that "ideology has a material existence as it is always materialized in practices . . . it organizes action" (Mouffe 1979). By discourse, then, I mean constellations of "knowledge," together with institutionalized social practices, which are politicized and result in an array of possible subjectivities.

Discourses, or public meaning systems (political, social science, popular culture, etc.), are the material for identity formation. We deploy these discourses to construct our identities but from a limited range of options. Consequently, some identities are readily made possible while others are not, and in this way we are somewhat overdetermined by the meaning systems that preexist us as individuals.

I know from the misreadings of Butler that class as performance/performative will sound too flimsy or voluntaristic to some, that at times my analysis might be taken to mean that girls are wholly choosing their race-class-gender performance. Let me hasten to point out to readers that I focus on the production of identity via discursive frameworks and institutional forces and constraints.[29] The decision on whether to highlight structure over agency or agency over structure is, in part, dependent on one's conceptualization of audience. When I write for an academic audience of social scientists who have little problem envisioning social actors as shaped by social structures, and in fact are perhaps likely to see them in an overdetermined fashion, highlighting agency and resistance seem useful. But when I imagine a popular audience for my work, who would be likely to read through the lens of a pervasive ideology of individualism and personal responsibility, highlighting the restrictions on girls' choices proves the important agenda. I can have it both ways because, indeed, it is both ways. I find a poststructuralist focus on repeating structures but with historical contingency a useful tool here and an improvement on reproduction theory. Categories of identity and structures of inequality are not automatic but must be constantly reproduced in practice, and so there is a moment of possibility for social change. The reproduction of structure is not automatic, but contingent on its repetition or iteration.

Ortner usefully suggests the need for a new language to dissolve some of these unproductive binaries, offering "structurally embedded agency" and "intention-filled structures" (1996, 12). Importantly, she suggests that some theorists (i.e., Giddens and Bourdieu) tend to offer a vision of structure and agency as a "loop" or reflexive relationship: structures producing subjects who in turn produce structures. But she suggests the political desires of feminist, subaltern, minority, and postcolonial theory result in our "choos[ing] to avoid the loop, to look for the slippages in reproduction, the erosions of long-standing patterns, the moments of disorder and of outright 'resistance' " (17) "with everything slightly—but not completely—tilted toward incompleteness, instability, and change" (18). In this vein, what I try to do here is to go beyond a common poststructuralist deconstruction of public discourses "to attend *ethnographically* to the ways in which discourses enter into people's lives, both invading them in a Bourdieuian, even Foucauldian, sense and being implicitly or explicitly challenged by them in the course of practices that always go beyond discursive constraints" (Ortner 1998, 14; emphasis mine).[30]

I proceed by asking: What are the cultural gestures involved in the performance of class? How is class "authenticity" accomplished? And how is it imbued with racial/ethnic, sexual, and gender meaning?[31] I hope to provide a "thick description" (Geertz 1973) of these performative intersections. Little attention has been paid to the ways in which class subjectivity, as a cultural identity, is experienced in relationship to the cultural meanings of race/ethnicity, gender, and sexuality.[32] These various gestures of class performance never exist outside of and are always imbued with race and gender meanings. For example, as we will see among Mexican-American students, class performance was made complex by the ongoing negotiation between themselves, peers, and parents around the meanings of and links between class mobility, assimilation, and a race-based politic and identity. Because middle- or working-class performances were experienced differently across race/ethnicity, and further, because those performances were read differently by others, dependent on the race/ethnicity of the performer, and because it is impossible to uncouple these meanings, I use the hyphenated "race-class performances of femininity" as a way to indicate that class performances have race and gender specific meanings. But I could just as well speak of "gender-class performances of race" or "race-gender performances of class." That race, class, gender, and sexual meanings and identities intersect is not simply an abstract theoretical insight. This is a multiplicity "born of history and geography" (Mohanty 1991, 37). Race/ethnicity and class and gender and sexuality are always produced and read in relationship to one another in the social world.

CHAPTER 3

How Working-Class Chicas Get Working-Class Lives

Since I spent my first days at Waretown High in a college-preparatory class (a class that fulfills a requirement for admission to either California State University or University of California institutions), the first students I met were college bound. Later I came to know these girls through the eyes of non-college-preparatory students as "the preps." They were mostly white, but included a handful of Mexican-American girls. Some of the white girls were also known as "the 90210s," after the popular television show about wealthy high schoolers, *Beverly Hills 90210*. The preps eagerly volunteered to help me out with what they saw as my "school project," relating easily to the concept, and they were ready and willing to talk at length about themselves and others. Displaying both social and academic skills, they were, in short, "teacher's pets" (Luttrell 1993) or the "rich and populars" (Lesko 1988).

I soon began wandering the halls of the school in search of a non-prep class where I might find girls who seemed more like I was in high school. The memory of my own gender-specific high school experience led me to the business building, where unthinkingly I looked for a roomful of typewriters and girls with steno pads. Of course, I found neither, but rather rooms full of computers on which some students were practicing their word-processing skills while others were learning computer programming.

Looking for help connecting with non-college-prep girls, I visited the faculty room in the business department, which offers primarily vocational track classes, to recruit the aid of teachers and ask whose class I might visit. When I told these teachers that I wanted to talk to some of their girl students about their aspirations beyond high school, teachers shook their heads and laughed together in a knowing way, one man joking that "They'll all be barefoot and pregnant." While the other teachers expressed discomfort with his way of making the point, they did acknowledge that their students did not have high aspirations and often were "trouble." They told me that one student, Yolanda, would be happy to give me "a piece of her mind," noting further that "if she doesn't like your survey, she'll tell you." They shook their heads about another, Christina, who had recently "told off her employer," and they explained that it would be very difficult to interview any of these girls, because they would fail to show up or I would be able to keep their attention only for a short time. Nonetheless, I was invited to attend their classes and attempt to recruit girls to talk with.

The first day I attended Ms. Parker's business skills class was characteristic of my future visits to non-prep classes. On this particular day, there was a substitute teacher taking her place. The differences between the girls from the college-prep class and these girls were immediately noticeable. The latter wore more makeup and tight-fitting clothing, and seemed to have little interest in the classroom curriculum. In fact, the class was out of the teacher's hands. The girls, mostly Mexican-American, were happy to have me as a distraction. One, whom I came to know later as Lorena, said loudly (Lorena was always loud), "Oh, we heard you might be coming. What do you want to know? I'll tell you." Completely ignoring the substitute, who had clearly given up on having any control over the class, they invited me to play cards. I hesitated, asking what would happen if the vice principal, whom students referred to as "Mr. D," were to come by.

Lorena: Oh, he never does; besides [flirtatiously] he *likes* me.

Becky: He doesn't like me. He's always callin' me into his office for something.

Lorena: He'll just ask me where's the other half of my shirt.

Lorena was referring to the short crop top she was wearing, which was fashionable at the moment, but was against school dress codes because it revealed her bare midriff. Pointing to the man behind the teacher's desk, Lorena went on:

> That's "Mr. H." He's our sub. Don't you think he's attractive? He's from the university too.

She called him over to ask a question, and when he arrived, Lorena opened her book and pointed entirely randomly at a paragraph on the page saying coyly, "I don't understand *this.*" He tried to respond appropriately by explaining the course material, but when it became clear to him that her question was not serious, he turned to me and politely asked about my "study":

> *Mr. H:* What's your focus?
> *Lorena:* [interrupting] You mean what's your *phone number*?

This brought rounds of laughter from the girls. It became obvious to the sub that Lorena was playing, and he wandered away a bit red in the face. She turned to me:

> Did you check him out? You should go on a date with him.

I wasn't sure what to make of this incident for a while, wondering if the girls, whose affectionate self-referent was "las chicas," were "othering" him (as a sub) or me (as the outsider/researcher/white girl) or both of us (as adults) by making one or both of us the target of their humor. As it turned out, this practice of trying to set me up with substitute teachers became almost a hazing ritual. Whenever the girls saw me on a day they knew they were going to have a substitute teacher in class, they asked me to come visit them in class. Not wanting to decline any opportunity to spend time with them, I would always respond to their invitations, stopping in to chat with them for the few minutes before the bell rang and class officially began. Over several weeks, they began to accept and befriend me as I began to respond to the setting-me-up ritual without embarrassment, and I engaged (somewhat reluctantly) in their playful attempts to humiliate the sub, othering him as the sub, as an adult, and as a man; in the process I became less of an other to the girls.

I came to see the ritual of setting me up as one element of a larger theme among las chicas. Bored with their vocational schooling, las chicas often brought heterosexual romance and girl culture into the classroom as a favorite form of distraction. They regularly brought photo albums to look through during class; these contained pictures of a weekend event like homecoming, a prom, a wedding, a quinceañera,[1] or sometimes a new baby. On this day in the business skills class, Imelda had brought a framed collage photo collection of her and Christina, best friends. She had written sentimental words of friendship on the spaces in between the pictures in Spanish. She read them aloud and, then after an awkward moment, read them again, but this time in English for the sake of Blanca, who, wearing a long face, had silently tugged on Christina's sleeve to indicate that she didn't understand.

The conversation turned, and they began talking about a girl they didn't like, one who had been "talking shit about Lorena." They took turns telling whom they would most like to fight. Flor declined her turn, "If I say, I'm afraid her girls will jump me." Bored with this conversation, Christina pulled a folded up newspaper page out of her purse and began reading people's horoscopes out loud. In the background the sub made a useless plea, "Okay, whoever's listening, you need to do chapter five today." On other days the topics of our conversations included fashion, shopping, and recent events on the television soap opera *Days of Our Lives*. Near the end of each period, girls would stop their work early, if they were doing it at all, to pull out compacts, powder their faces, and check their lipstick and liner, reapplying when necessary.

These elements of "girl culture" were notably missing from the college-prep classrooms I had been visiting. It is not, of course, that gender display was altogether absent in prep classrooms, but where las chicas could be found blatantly using class time to primp, applying makeup and adjusting hair, in prep classrooms a girl might secretively slip a powder compact out of her backpack and turn her back away from the teacher to powder her face before the bell rang and the walk between classes, where social life happens, was to begin. For preps the overt use of class time for such an activity was recognized as inappropriate. Moreover, the "natural" look adopted by preps suggests one is not really wearing makeup and to pull this off means application of it must be done in secret.

Las chicas, having "chosen" and/or been tracked into non-college-prep courses, showed little interest in the formal curriculum offered at the school, finding a variety of ways to kill time. They employed rituals of girl culture as an alternative to and refusal of official school activities, including the kind of classroom learning that prep students embraced. Like their male counterparts, las chicas, along with most other students at the school, have had their dignity wounded through exposure to preps who, with the complicity of teachers, routinely and unknowingly inflicted class- and race-based injuries. But, unlike the boys, las chicas' strategy of rejecting schooling, and prep values by association, is usually less violent and less confrontational, and perhaps easily overlooked, often naturalized as heterosexual interest and dismissed.

As Penelope Eckert (1993) explains, middle-class performers embrace adult (and I would add middle-class) norms for the adolescent life stage, and this means preparing to enter another institution similar to high school. Non-preps, on the other hand, violate these norms by laying claims to adult status before middle-class adults think they should. Where middle-class-performing girls (both white and Mexican-American) chose academic performance and the acceptance and praise of teachers' and parents' as signs of achieving adult status, non-prep girls earned and wore different "badges of dignity" (Sennett and Cobb 1972; MacLeod 1995). They rejected school-sanctioned notions of proper femininity. For them, expressions of sexuality, and by extension motherhood, operated as a sign of adult status and served to reject teachers' and parents' methods of keeping them childlike.

There were many occasions on which this difference in orientation between working- and middle-class performers was made clear. When I met Mariana, a Mexican-American middle-class performer and told her I was at the school to study girls, she immediately presumed my interest would be in those "at risk." I sat with her in the library where she worked on a report for her "Transition to College English" class. As she meticulously assembled the planning calendar of her report on the college of her choice, her comments parroted adult and middle-class morality: "There are a lot of teen pregnancies here. It is real sad. Girls whose futures are ruined. It's sad. And there's gang violence." Alternatively, a white working-class performer named Brenda, who approached me from the back of the room at an Future Homemakers of America (FHA) meeting where she had been sitting with a group of friends, asked bluntly, "Who are you?" I began to explain, but she interrupted, "Oh, never mind. We know. We've been talking about you back there." Then jutting out her hip, placing her hand on it, and batting her heavily mascara'd eyes, she said mockingly, "Are you here to study our *promiscuity*?" in full recognition of the fact that adult school personnel perceived her sexualized femininity as a violation of adolescence, and she expected me to do the same.

THE SYMBOLIC ECONOMY OF STYLE

There was, at the school, a symbolic economy of style that was the ground on which class and racial/ethnic relations were played out. A whole array of gender-specific commodities were used as markers of distinction among different groups of girls, who performed race-class-specific versions of femininity. Hairstyles, clothes, shoes, and the colors of lipstick, lip liner, and nail polish, in particular, were key markers in the symbolic economy that were employed to express group membership as the body became a resource and a site on which difference was inscribed.[2] For example, las chicas preferred darker colors for lips and nails in comparison to preps, who either went without or wore clear lip gloss, pastel lip and nail color or French manicures (the natural look). Each group was fully aware of the other's stylistic preference and knew that their own style was in opposition. In short, girls created and maintained symbolic oppositions, where "elements of behavior that come to represent one category [are] rejected by the other, and . . . may be exploited by the other category through the development of a clearly opposed element" (Eckert 1989, 50).

The association of light with prep girls and dark with non-prep girls may be arbitrary, but the association of pastels with "youth, innocence, and gaiety" and darker colors with "somberness, age, and sophistication" does happen to coincide with middle- and working-class life stage trajectories (Eckert 1989, 50). Where middle-class performers experience an extended adolescence by going to college, working-class performers across race/ethnicity begin their adult lives earlier. The importance of colors as a tool of distinction was evident one day before business skills class when I complimented Yolanda on her nail color, and the girls clustered around her desk to compare colors. Bianca felt the need to apologize for hers. Displaying her hand on the table with others, she explained, "Mine is too pink, but it's my grandma's. I was at her house last night and she offered it, and I didn't want to hurt her feelings."

Further, las chicas explained to me that the darker colors they chose and the lighter colors preps wore were not simply related to skin color. As Lorena explained, "It's not that, 'cause some Mexican girls who look kinda white, they wear real dark lip color" so no one will mistake them as white. And when I mentioned that I rarely saw white girls in dark lipstick, Lisa, a white prep, explained, scoffing and rolling her eyes,

> Oh, there are some, but they're girls who are trying to be hardcore [meaning these were white girls who were performing chola identity]. And those hick girls [white working-class], some of them wear that bright pink crap on their lips and like *ba-loo* eye shadow!

The dissident femininity performed by both white and Mexican-American working-class girls were ethnic-specific styles, but nonetheless both sets of girls rejected the school-sanctioned femininity performed by college prep students.[3] Working-class performers across race were perceived similarly by preps as wearing too much makeup.

Girls often expressed disdain for one another's style or at least were perplexed by preferences other than their own. Lorena, describing the difference between las chicas and preps, said:

> Well, those prep girls, they wear their hair real straight and then sometimes just curl it at the end, either this way or that way [motioning a flipped-up or turned-under curl with her hands].

When I asked about makeup, she said:

> Natural! Barely any. Maybe pink or something. Like that ugly girl who got homecoming queen. You know how *we* do our hair right? We put stuff [gel] in it and then scrunch it like this [demonstrating]. Well, some of us wear our hair straight. But then it's real long and no curl at the end.

Leticia gave a lucid accounting of the typography of subculture and style and was very clear in her recognition that preps were the norm from which all others deviated.

> *Leticia:* Well, the preps they usually wear their jeans regular, you know, normal, like how pants are *supposed* to fit. We wear our pants either too big and baggy or at least big at the bottom but tight at the top [bell bottoms], depends on your figure. Those hicks they wear their pants, those ones, umm . . .
>
> *Julie:* Wranglers?
>
> *Leticia:* Yeah, they wear 'em way too tight. And big belts too. I don't know what their shoes are called.
>
> *Julie:* What about the smokers, what do they look like?
>
> *Leticia:* Tore up! They have holes in their pants, and they are all ripped at the bottom. And they wear a lotta black. Heavy metal T-shirts and chains. They dye their hair weird colors.

In spite of the meanings that working-class girls themselves gave to their gender-specific cultural markers—a desire to remain differentiated from preps—their performances were overdetermined by broader cultural meanings that code women in heavy makeup and tight clothes as low class and oversexed, in short, cheap. In other words, class differences are often understood as sexual differences, as Sherry Ortner usefully explains, where "the working class is cast as the bearer of an exaggerated sexuality, against which middle-class respectability is defined" (1991, 177). Among women, "clothing and cosmetic differences are taken to be indexes of the differences in sexual morals" between classes (178).[4] And indeed, this was the case, as middle-class performing prep girls (both white and Mexican-American) perceived las chicas, as well as working-class performing white girls, as overly sexually active. But non-prep Mexican-American girls were seen as especially so because, although there was no evidence that they were more sexually active, they were more likely to keep their babies if they became pregnant, so there was more often a visible indicator of their sexual activity.

BOYS ARE "BUGGIN'"

Las chicas' gender performance and girl culture worked, whether by intent or not, as a strategy to reject the prep version of schooling but, despite appearances, were not necessarily designed to culminate in a heterosexual relationship. Some of the girls whose feminine performance appeared the most sexualized were actually the least interested in heterosexual relations, marriage, or children. Despite what appeared to be an obsession with heterosexual romance, a "men are dogs" theme was prevalent among them. They knew men could not be counted on to support them and any children they might have, and they desired economic independence.

And so their girl culture was less often about boys at all than about sharing in rituals of traditional femininity as a kind of friendship bonding among girls. As Angela McRobbie (1991) describes, although the overt concern in girl culture is with boys and romance, girls often set themselves physically apart from boys. Lorena made this clear one day.

> *Lorena:* Well, when we go out, to the clubs or someplace, we all get a bunch of clothes and makeup and stuff and go to one person's house to get ready. We do each other's hair and makeup and try on each other's clothes. It takes a long time. It's more fun that way. [Thoughtfully, as if it just occurred to her] Sometimes, I think we have more fun getting ready to go out than we do going out—'cause when we go out, we just *sit* there.
>
> *Julie:* So then the clothes and makeup and all aren't for the men or about getting their attention?
>
> *Lorena:* Well, we like to see how many we can *meet*. But, well, *you* know, I don't fall for their lines. We talk to them, but when they start buggin', then we just go.

In short, non-preps had no more or less interest in heterosexual romance than did girls who performed prep or school-sanctioned femininity. Nonetheless, teachers and preps often misread the expression of class and race differences in style among working-class performers as evidence of heterosexual interest. They failed to perceive girls' class and racial/ethnic selves and so unknowingly reproduced the common-sense belief that what is most important about girls, working-class performers in particular, is their girlness. Las chicas' style was not taken as a marker of race/ethnicity and class distinction but was reduced to gender and sexuality.

Not only has girl culture as a method to refuse schooling been missed by androcentric social science, but teachers too tended to naturalize gender and heterosexuality, treating girls' strategies as harmless. Although I once saw a teacher take a magazine away from a boy in class because it was distracting him from the assignment, no teacher ever told the girls to put away their photo albums, although they were at least as much a distraction. Girls across race and class performance were aware of their ability to violate rules without consequence as a result of teachers', and in particular male teachers', view of boys as troublemakers and girls as harmless. Girls told stories of getting out of gym class by faking menstrual cramps, of cheating on laps by doing one and then panting and exclaiming to the coach that they'd done thirteen. Lisa told how a boy who said "fuck" was put in detention all day, but "a girl who was yellin' it in the office, nothin' happened ta her. I counted, and she said it thirteen times!" On our way back to school from a lunchtime birthday party at Yolanda's that had lasted too long, las chicas decided to bring a piece of cake for the teacher they called "Mr. M." so that he wouldn't count them tardy. It worked. When Bianca told me about flirting with a boy in her math class who allowed her to cheat from his paper, I recalled the similar tactics my high school friend Michelle and I used. We were the only two girls in an auto mechanics class, and when the classroom work was over, the boys would work on their cars in the shop while the teacher allowed my friend and me to lounge in his office reading romance novels. One day we discovered a copy of the final course exam on his desk. We scored higher than any of the boys in auto mechanics that year. In a conversation with Mr. Ross about Leticia he said, "It's hard not to like her. I mean she smiles at you the whole time you're chewing her out."

The primacy of gender as the defining characteristic of girls, which I heard from administrators, teachers, and the girls themselves, obscured the ways in which class and race identities informed girls' actions. Evidence of the naturalization of gender, and of heterosexuality in particular, was found in the way physical fights among girls were understood. In my naïveté, I first imagined that there were probably far fewer physical fights among girls than stories told by students and school personnel, as I thought the novelty of a few fights among girls had been sensationalized. So I consulted an administrator, asking about precise statistics. He looked over his chart of violations, which included possession of a chemical substance, truancy, tardiness, and so forth, and found that the rate of violation among boys was higher than girls on every count except fights, on which they were even. Further, these "girl fights" (as well as fights among boys for that matter) were not limited to any particular demographic grouping. When I asked what it was that girls got into fights about, the answer according to administrators, teachers, and girls themselves, was always "boys."

But as I began to ask girls to tell me stories about the specific fights they had been in, it turned out that racial/ethnic and class identities were often center stage in their accounts.[5] In one story, a car full of hick girls laughed at a car full of cholas, who had been pulled over by the police. That night, the cholas showed up, uninvited, at the levee, hick territory, to fight the girls who mocked them. Further, Yolanda explained that the red stain on a soiled maxi pad, the color of which signified *norteño* affiliation and which was stuck on the wall of the bathroom used by *sureño* girls, had nothing to do with boys. I asked Leticia about fights.

> *Leticia:* Yeah, I do. I fought this girl last week. I jus' walked up and smacked her.
>
> *Julie:* Was it about a guy?
>
> *Leticia:* Shit no, I would never fight over no guy. They're not worth it.
>
> *Julie:* Why then? What was it about?
>
> *Leticia:* I don't know, she just thought she was "all that" you know. About color I guess. This *sureño* girl was talking shit to me. She said, "It's all about the south." So I went up and hit her.

And Mariana told me how she and a friend were angered in a classroom discussion where two preps made anti–affirmative action arguments. This, she said, led to a hallway confrontation:

> It was just that they kept saying "they" meaning like either, you know, undocumented citizens or "they" meaning minorities

> or "they" meaning, well, you know. My friend Bianca and her friends went after that girl, went after her and, um, cornered her and asked, "Why are you saying all of this stuff about Mexicans?" They didn't beat her up, they just kinda yelled at her and got her scared and stuff like that.

Mariana and her friends were particularly angered because one of the two preps had a Hispanic surname, so they had presumed her to be Mexican-American and therefore a "coconut."[6] (She was actually biracial and had little attachment to her Mexican-American ethnic heritage.) As a college prep student, Mariana didn't engage in the fight; rather, her non-prep friends initiated it.

While there were many occasions on which jealousies over heterosexual relations with boys were central to fights among girls, this usually occurred *within* racial/ethnic groups since little cross-racial dating occurred. The fact that girls experienced race and class tensions among themselves went essentially unnoticed. School personnel, being privy only to fights that happened at the school, knew less than students about cross-race antagonisms, which occurred primarily off campus. The fact that a color-blind discourse is the most "polite" or school-sanctioned way of talking about race, and that class was largely unavailable as an explanation of social relations, left heterosexual relations as the most readily available way of describing the meaning of "girl fights."

ROUTES TO ADULTHOOD

Sensitive to the fact that girls were aware of the current moral panic over teen pregnancy and anticipated that adults were interested in their sexuality, I generally avoided the topic, letting girls bring it up themselves, then proceeding cautiously with my questions. Often girls preferred to begin talking in the third person about sexuality, describing friends' views and practices, before (sometimes but not always) shifting to their own. Most of the girls I spoke with, across all social groupings, reported that they were sexually active. It was understood that most girls who were in "serious" relationships were probably having sex with their boyfriends, and this was acceptable. Some girls suggested that it was not taboo for girls to have sex outside of relationships, although girls had to be much more careful than boys about their frequency here for fear of being labeled. Girls agreed that there was still a double standard: boys could be sexually active with multiple partners without consequence, while girls were called sluts for the same behavior. What is important to recognize here is that girls' interest in sex was not *always* embedded in a narrative of romance.

In short, there were girls who did and girls who didn't across all group categories, but the race and class injury that occurred was in the perception of who was *too* sexually active. While many prep girls, whose presentation of self was squeaky clean, were sexually active, they were secretive about this violation of adolescence and used birth control pills, often without parents' knowledge (but sometimes with). White middle-class performers were more likely than other girls to have abortions if they became pregnant, as a way of ensuring the life stages that they and their parents had in mind for them. One girl explained, "My friend had an abortion and got her parents' insurance to pay for it without her parents even knowing that was the procedure she had done."

Stories of abortion were almost nonexistent among Mexican-American girls, and Mexican-American girls were less likely than white middle- or working-class girls to use birth control regularly.[7] Girls became pregnant for a variety of reasons. Blanca explained that she lacked information about birth control—"My parents, they didn't tell me nothing about birth control"—and wrongly believed myths like "you can't get pregnant your first time." Mexican-American girls often said they knew about, but didn't believe in, the use of birth control or in abortion. Christina explained, "Having something growing inside you is a spiritual thing. If it happens, then God meant for it to happen. You just have to deal with it." But some were willing to consider birth control, suggesting that abortion was the worse of two evils. The most common explanation given for pregnancies was "it just happened," which seemed most often to mean that girls were unprepared and had no birth control plan, either because they didn't know they were going to have sex or because they were uncomfortable planning ahead to use birth control, as this compromised their belief system or suggested to themselves and others that they were too willing. Sometimes this situation was combined with stories of boys who refused to use condoms:

> *Yolanda:* Well one reason it happens is that guys don't wanna use condoms. And then you just get caught up in the moment.

While girls did too often say they "felt a lotta pressure" and had sex before they were ready, they also often acknowledged their willing participation. But teen sexuality (and pregnancy) cannot be wholly explained either by girls' victimization or by their desire.[8] The most popular discourse at the school among adults was one of female victimization, where girls became pregnant after being pressured by boys to have sex when they were not yet ready. Consequently, in the face of adult authority and public discourse on teen sexuality, the safest narrative for a girl to give is one of victimization, because it evades her responsibility. Less acceptable would be to acknowledge her desire, which is still, it seems, considered taboo for girls even as it is expected among boys. Indeed, any discourse on female desire or recognition that girls may be willing and interested in sex was largely missing among adults with whom I spoke at the school.[9] But the worst possible thing for a girl to admit to is an intentional pregnancy, and only one girl I spoke with suggested this:

> *Leticia:* Well some girls want kids. You go through that phase you know. I did a year or two ago. I wanted one. You want to be a young mother. Don't want to be an old parent 'cause then [if you are young] you'll understand them better.

Regardless of how a girl becomes pregnant (which occurs for a variety of reasons, including the use of birth control that fails), after the fact, having a baby can be a marker of adult status (just as sexuality was), and girls recognize it as such. For non-prep girls who do not have college and career to look forward to as signs of adulthood, motherhood and the responsibility that comes with it can be employed to gain respect, marking adult status. Teachers often expressed surprise at the degree of casualness among students about pregnancies and babies at school, one saying with ambivalence, "Babies are really celebrated here among girls; they are not ashamed. They bring them to class." Another teacher was more clearly sympathetic about babies in class:

> It's a bit awkward because you don't want to seem to support it [teen pregnancy], but the pregnancy and the baby already happened, so it makes no sense to shun them [girls] either. One baby was fussy, so I had to teach while bouncing him on my hip. It's as if the girls are saying, this is my life, this is what happened, don't punish me for it.

In the end, however, girls' overt claim to adulthood startles adult and middle-class sensibility.

Pregnancy and babies became an extension of the girl culture that was present in non-prep classrooms. Talk of baby clothes and the anticipation of delivery were further ways girls overtly expressed their boredom with their vocational schooling and their sense of its irrelevance. About a month before school ended, Elvira gave birth to a baby girl. Either because she had no child-care options or because she was simply excited about her newborn, she brought the baby to school with her several days during the last few weeks of school. The baby became a great distraction in the classroom, and the teacher dealt with it by asking Elvira to move to another room, allowing girls to go visit her there and see the baby two at a time. Eventually she and another girl who were both failing the class, totally uninvested in the work, and distracting other students who did have a chance of passing, were kicked out of the class. Most girls with babies eventually chose to finish their schooling at an alternative community school where they could graduate with fewer credit hours and where classes ended at one o'clock, making day care arrangements less complicated.

Girls' orientation to early maternity is not necessarily linked to an ideology of romance. Girls know from each other's experience that boys should not be relied upon. Sometimes girls believe they are an exception to this rule, one suggesting, for example, that because her boyfriend did not want her to have an abortion, this was a sign that he really loved her. I had this conversation with Yolanda about her friend Bianca.

> *Yolanda:* Well, she should've protected herself. But since she didn't, she should have just had the baby but not get married. It isn't gonna work. He's not gonna stick around. I mean that's the only reason they got married, even though they say they "wanted to anyway." [rolling her eyes]
>
> *Julie:* What would you do?
>
> *Yolanda:* I ain't never gettin' married. But I looove babies!

For the most part, girls were very cynical about boys. They felt that men could not be counted on for economic support or as co-parents, or to meet the girls' ideals of romance and intimacy. One teacher, commenting on conversations among girls that he routinely overheard in his class noted,

> You know, they don't talk about the fathers much. They are pretty irrelevant to them.

In short, working-class performers were more willing to consider parenthood and sometimes marriage as an appropriate next life stage after high school (and sometimes during, which usually meant continuing to live with her parent[s]). While these girls knew that "college" was a necessity to insure a living wage, it was something they would more often consider doing simultaneously with other adult roles. The "going away to college" experience was decidedly a prep one, while working-class performers were likely to attend the local community college and begin their adult lives as workers, parents, and spouses at the same time. They saw no convincing reason to postpone parenthood. Pregnancy is not the cause of their vocational schooling, the cause of their ending up in a low-wage job, or the cause of their poverty, though that myth continues to circulate in public discourse legitimating anti-welfare sentiment and justifying punitive policies (Luker 1996).

For the most part las chicas' girl culture was interpreted as harmless, thought of as natural heterosexual interest, and therefore not negatively sanctioned. But when this girl culture was extended to include maternity, which school personnel saw as too adult and thus found unacceptable, they responded. During a year's end awards ceremony, I sat on the bleachers at the end of the gym near the lunchroom doors among students who were required to attend but had no interest in the ceremony. In the group of Mexican-American students I sat behind, one young mother had a toddler with her who was being passed around, and two young men in particular were competing over who got to hold the child. As one young man made silly faces and got the baby to smile, the group began to laugh, getting louder as they became more and more involved in the baby's play. As the unit administrator and master of the ceremony announced which students had perfect school attendance, had GPAs above 3.5, and were receiving university scholarships, a teacher angrily stomped over to the group of students, chiding them, "You could at least be polite and pay attention when someone is talking." The mother haughtily picked up her toddler and, head held high, walked out of the gym with four girlfriends following in solidarity.

Working-class performers across race shared the resentful view of the ceremony as an imposed glorification of prep students. The teachers and administrators did have some awareness of the way in which celebrating the successes of some made others look and feel like failures. They tried to finesse this by making attendance at such an event optional, where each teacher could decide whether or not to bring her/his class. But if a teacher chose to attend, which most teachers did, every student in that class was required to be either in the gym or in the adjoining lunchroom during this time. Added to the injury of being forced to attend a ceremony celebrating students who were able to achieve "success" by the standards of the institution, adults, and middle-class norms, the teacher's punitive attitude toward the baby's presence was a further insult that put non-prep students "back in their place" by trying to recenter attention on the success of students who could and did follow the institutional ideals.

Although las chicas were no more sexually active than other girls at the school, they suffered the consequences of their sexual activity in ways that middle-class performers did not. (White working-class girls were also more likely to keep babies than their middle-class counterparts, but still not at as high a rate as Mexican-American girls.) The presence of more babies among Mexican-American girls than any other group of girls was wrongly perceived by white preps (and some school personnel) as a difference of sexual morals between racial/ethnic groups. But the deeper injury is that those who have babies will experience the punishment of a gender regime, which blames women who become single moms for their own poverty by suggesting sexual immorality, especially if they are young. This logic fails to recognize that teen pregnancy is highly correlated with class and race: most of these young women were working-class or poor before they became mothers (Luker 1996). Their continued (or increased) impoverishment is a consequence of their vocational curriculum, low-wage jobs, and lack of affordable child care. Further, their potential heterosexual partners are working-class men of color who are also less likely to be able to earn wages that can support families. These young moms don't have and, for good reasons, don't want to rely on male support. They want and need to be able to support themselves and any children they might have. They want economic equality outside of heterosexual relationships.

POST–HIGH SCHOOL TRACKS

Once a year, a nearby vocational business school invited students to come tour their facility, paying the school for the use of a bus and treating the students to a pizza lunch. Most of las chicas signed up to go. We piled into the bus on a rainy December morning. Girls paired off in twos, sets of best friends sharing a seat near the middle of the bus, while boys moved to the back, each occupying a seat by himself, head against the bus window and legs extended to take up the whole space. Given the purpose of the trip, I presumed this would be a good opportunity to talk to girls about their plans beyond high school. But, as usual, this was of little interest. In fact, it was a topic that I saw clearly caused the girls to feel uncertainty and a related stress, so they changed the conversation to music and fashion.

Yolanda had brought along a photo album of Bianca's recent wedding, photos of her reception which was held in the warehouse of her dad's employer. I asked about marriage, and Lorena began:

> I ain't never gettin' married! Or at least not 'til I'm in my 30s. We want to party and kick it and have fun first.

When I pushed further for reasons why, Leticia chimed in:

> Them boys who want to date us are buggin'. They try to control you and tell you what to do.
>
> *Lorena:* Like Omar. We were standing by the business building one day, and he hands me his coat and says, "Watch this." Then he goes off with some friends. I just left the coat on the bench. When he saw me, he said, "Why didn't you watch my coat? It coulda got stolen." Man, that ain't my job!
>
> *Yolanda:* And they tell you you shouldn't wear certain things.
>
> *Lorena:* Yeah, like that white top I had on yesterday. Miguel said I shouldn't wear that. I look like a hoochie [laughing]. I told him *he* looked stupid, like Columbus.

The discussion turned to the prom, and the girls talked amongst themselves about whether or not to go, given the expense, and about all of the pairing up possibilities, making decisions about which of them would go with which boy. They explained, "The boys don't care who they go with. We decide." When our bus arrived at the school, Leticia asked to borrow Lorena's powder. Lorena pulled out her compact, and Leticia closed her eyes and jutted out her chin, waiting for Lorena to powder her face.

At the school we were taken to a classroom and seated in desks. The environment felt school-like and familiar, but in fact this was deceptive, since the woman speaking at the front of the room, a Ms. Laney, was actually giving a sales pitch under the guise of teaching and advising us about the expenses of life and job opportunities. She began by asking how much we thought it cost to live on your own and how much per hour one would need to earn. A boy answered, "About fifteen dollars." This answer clearly was not the one she was looking for, and she kept asking until she got a response of eight dollars. With that she could then follow her routine, which was to list life's expenses on the blackboard and show students how naive they were. In the end she led them (back) to the conclusion that they needed to earn about fifteen dollars per hour and that there was no way they could make this amount with just a high school diploma.

She knew her audience well, asking them rhetorically, "How many of you want to continue to live at home with your parents after graduation?" No one did, of course, and yet these were students who did not have the option of going off to college to escape parental authority. She worked to convince them that their lifestyles would change. She explained that they would want more than Burger King and a movie. They would want weekend trips, concerts, sports events. They would have roommate problems. They would not want to settle for the old Pinto or station wagon grandma was planning to give them. She told them about taxes and insurance, things they might not have thought of before. She joked that for some it was not a problem, because they have rich parents. To the girls she said, "Some of you will marry someone really rich." Addressing the boys in the back of the room, "Some of you will go into crime because you already know it pays more."

She exploited their sense of filial piety, suggesting that the sooner they begin working, the sooner they would stop being an economic burden to their parents. "Wouldn't you like to be able to help your parents out? Maybe even buy them something nice for their anniversary? Send them on a cruise?" She told them there is a difference between education and skills, arguing that going thirty thousand dollars into debt with a student loan for four to six years of college and then coming out with a bachelor's degree in history and therefore no job is impractical. Further, she went on, "Junior college takes twice as long as business school because of crowded classrooms and general education courses which are not necessary." Aware of students' knowledge that junior colleges have open admission and are understood by high schoolers to be the bottom rung, the place for those who can't go anywhere else, she said, "We don't accept just anyone. You have to have a high school diploma. You have to dress professionally here. No jeans. We'll help you understand which clothes are professional clothes and which are not. And you cannot be late. You must be serious about it." But aware of their academic insecurity, she added, "You don't have to have a high GPA, and you don't even have to know how to turn on a computer." She showed them a framed diploma like the one they would receive upon graduation and then brought in Mike, one of their students, a young Latino who had gone to high school in a town near Waretown, to give his personal testimonial.

Mike was wearing a suit and tie and began, "I was a slacker big time in high school."

Ms. Laney chimed in, "You can see the transformation."

Ana asked Mike if it was hard to work a job while he went to school, and he responded, "Yeah, but it's all up to you."

Ms. Laney stated, "The effort you put in here is directly related to the money you earn when you get out. Now he is disciplined and goal oriented."

Ana asked Mike why he didn't go to college, and Ms. Laney interrupted, "That would have taken him seven years."

Mike said, "Yeah, this is a lot more better."

After the sales pitch ended, we were taken to the lounge. The girls rushed to the table where boxes of pizza were waiting, saying, "Hurry, before the guys get there. They'll eat it all." Over pizza the girls discussed the merits of the business school. The tidiness of the package presented to them was quite appealing. In just a year or so one could have accomplished a goal, completed a program quickly, unlike the eternity that four years of high school felt like, and unlike the four or more years college would take. This sounded doable. You could begin in the summer to get schooling out of the way early, and in the end you could have a job where you dressed nicely, maybe sat at your own desk, lived away from parents, did not get married right away. The focus on individual initiative was convincing, causing girls to temporarily believe that they had the power to rise above the constraints against them. When I mentioned to the girls that at no time during the presentation or in any of the written material we had been given were we told how much it would cost to attend, Yolanda immediately put down her pizza and marched across the room to ask a staff member about cost. She returned, "It's kinda a lot—eighteen thousand dollars for a sixteen-month program. But the lady said that in the long run that's cheaper than college. And she said not to worry 'cause they give you scholarships and loans and stuff. And you can pay it back real slow over time, after you get a good job."

Flor wasn't with us that day because she had gone on the tour the year before as a junior and had already made up her mind that she would attend the business school. About two weeks before high school graduation she went to the school to arrange payment, planning to begin her course work in the summer. She came back astounded. "Do you know how much it costs!? They'll give you loans, but you have to pay all that back! What am I gonna do? To apply to junior college now means that I'd have ta pay another fifty dollars for another placement test. My mom is gonna start crying if I tell her that." As we headed toward the counseling office to find applications for junior college, Flor wailed, "I don't know how to do this. No one in my family's ever gone to college." In the end, none of las chicas would attend the business school.

Michelle Fine (1991) provides a critique of proprietary schools (private profit-making institutions) that offer curricula in such areas as business, computing, secretarial skills, travel agent skills, and cosmetology and present themselves as alternatives to the public sector. Such schools advertise far and wide, make appealing promises, and deploy deceptive techniques to recruit the most vulnerable youth. Students in these institutions are disproportionately low-income and from populations of color.[10]

I and many of my Midwestern high school friends attended such an institution after high school, where we chose from impressive programs with titles such as Private Executive Secretarial Science and Fashion Merchandising, then landed jobs doing clerical and retail work. This school indirectly acknowledged that students might be placed in low-level jobs upon graduation, but worked to convince us that the difference between those of us with a certificate and those without was the opportunity for mobility. The fashion merchandising certificate, in particular, held out the promise of mobility at a major department store after "getting one's foot in the door." The brochure and the faculty instilled the hope that after a short time doing retail, one could expect to become a buyer for a department store and have a cosmopolitan life flying about to major world cities, attending fashion shows. Fine names this the "folklore of glamour and success," which students find so compelling in these schools' unethical recruitment techniques.

Most importantly, as Fine found at the high school she studied, I never heard students at Waretown High informed of or protected from the questionable recruitment practices of such schools that disseminate misleading information. When no critique is offered to assist students in their decision making, high schools "perpetuate the prevailing belief in their economic utility" (1991, 93). Though these students think they are making a wise choice in seeking a two-year certificate instead of a four-year degree, since two years is all the time and money they can afford, they will still probably not end up with jobs that pay them enough to support themselves and will quite likely go into debt as a consequence of attending.

HIGH SCHOOL TRACKS

Some girls felt tracked into a vocational curriculum. When I asked Yolanda about tracking, she'd never heard of it. But after I explained the concept to her, she said:

> Oh, yeah. That happened to me. This counselor told me to take all the non-required classes. Now I'm way behind in English and math, so that is why I can't go to a state school. The counselor said I wasn't ready. I heard she got fired for that.

Blanca also hadn't heard of tracking but recognized it upon explanation:

> Oh, is that discrimination? 'Cause then I have experienced discrimination.

When I asked Lorena how she decided which courses to take, she explained:

> Well, the counselor suggests something or sometimes a teacher suggests what you are ready for.

When I pushed for why she had not been encouraged or did not choose prep classes, she explained:

> Well, college-prep classes are harder, and you have to write a letter to get in or something. If the counselor sees you are not smart, then they help you find the right classes. She'll try to find a way for you to get classes and meet requirements to graduate without taking the hard ones.

I asked Flor how she came to be on the vocational business track.

> *Flor:* Well I guess I musta chose the business track 'cause those are the only classes I ever remember taking.
>
> *Julie:* Did your parents encourage you to aim for college?
>
> *Flor:* Oh, yes. It wasn't like "Are you going to college?" It was "Of course you are."
>
> *Julie:* Did they care which kind of college you went to?
>
> *Flor:* No, just as long as I went. I'm planning to go to business school.

Other girls felt they had more actively chosen their course work. Christina explained that her vocational course work began in ninth grade when students were first allowed to choose an elective course. She chose a vocational elective work-experience "class" that allowed her to do clerical work in the attendance office at the junior high for one class period a day, with her aunt, a school employee. Overhearing me ask Celia and Ramona if they recalled how they came to take vocational courses instead of college-prep ones, Lucia asked, "What are prep classes?" When I explained these were the classes that people who want to get into state schools or universities have to take, Ramona chimed in, "Oh, the hard ones, the ones you don't wanna take. Like chemistry," at which all three cringed. Likewise, Marycruz said, "I guess I just always liked business classes. They were something I could do, really easy. I just like the basic stuff."

When I asked Leticia her plan and how she felt about being in the vocational curriculum, she said:

> Well, it's okay, because I just plan to go to the JC for a couple years for general education courses. And then I wanted to go into law. But I found out that law taked too long of schooling. I don't have enough money to go to school that long. So I checked out paralegal, but didn't like that as much. I'll just go to the JC now and decide later.

Now that they were in their senior year, las chicas recognized that it was too late to make up for the consequences of being in the vocational curriculum. Consequently, their primary focus was on graduating from high school, regardless of grades. If it was not necessary to pass a particular class to graduate, then little effort was invested. ("Oh, is there a test in this class today?") Girls experienced class-time assignments as busywork, swapping their papers regularly in class, trading the calculations from each other's cash flow charts in an accounting class and answers on how to select, thaw, and cook meats from a nutrition class assignment, for example. ("It's not copying, it's sharing.") If class was inconvenient, it was skipped. "Well we're packin' 'em in today," the teacher noted during a sixth period class that was half-empty. Blanca had caught a ride home with Yolanda, who, with school permission, left every day after fifth period to go to work. Without a car, Blanca would have had to walk home if she didn't leave early with Yolanda. And Leticia, who hadn't been in school at all the day before, explained, "My mom needed the car yesterday 'cause she had to do something, and I didn't want to walk."

Sometimes girls dealt with their anxiety about the future with a certain denial of the facts, a refusal to believe that things would not work out for them, a tone of self-determination. At one point Vince, a friend, tried to talk Lorena out of going to the business school, saying, "What are you going there for? That won't do you no good. Look at my brother. He went there, and look what he's doin' [warehouse work]. Trying to get out of debt."

Lorena argued back, "Uh uh, they said they place 95 percent of their students. He musta not done well."

Vince argued, "He graduated with an A."

But she replied defiantly, "Then it's his fault for studying the wrong thing. You can't prove me wrong, I'm Lorena."

During other moments when girls stopped the fun to talk about their futures, they became somber, anxious, and depressed. This happened more frequently as graduation approached. Occasionally, girls were able to articulate their dilemma. Yolanda, for example, explained that she had wanted to go into law or international business.

> *Yolanda:* But I know I won't really do that. I mean, the girls and I were talking the other day. We all listed the things we wanted to do. And I said, it's all bullshit. You guys know we ain't really gonna do any a that.
>
> *Julie:* What are you going to do?
>
> *Yolanda:* I don't know. I don't want to work as hard as my aunt [who worked two retail sales jobs] to make enough money. I don't have to have a fancy job like a lawyer. I just want a simple life. An okay car. I want just a pretty good life. No guys, no one controlling me. But [asking sincerely] what kinda job like that is there?

Yolanda implicitly recognized that there is no middle-income, non-college-educated, working-class location for her to occupy, which leaves her in a precarious situation. But given that school culture equates success with college attendance and that failure to do well enough to go to college is readily understood as an individual failure, las chicas were often left with no one to blame but themselves.

Differential skills are learned across academic and vocational curriculums. Where college-prep students learn "critical thinking, problem solving, drawing conclusions, making generalizations, or evaluating or synthesizing knowledge . . . [i]n vocational track classes students are required to learn only simple memory tasks or comprehension" (Oakes 1985, 77; and see Persell 1977). Many of las chicas were, in fact, good students, earning high grades, but in a vocational curriculum. It is working-class students and students of color who are tracked into the vocational curriculum, thus institutionalizing race and class inequalities.

Vocational teachers expressed frustration about their dilemma as non-prep teachers; they feel pressured to encourage their students to go to college, yet this in turn pressures students to feel that they are failures if they do not go—and most of their students will not. Ms. Howard resolved the dilemma by focusing on self-esteem: "No matter what job you have in life, you have to have a sense of positive self. If I can help a kid feel better about him- or herself, then maybe they will do well in an interview and get a job." I also spoke about this with Mr. Young, who genuinely liked and cared about las chicas.

Mr. Young: Those teachers that equate success with college, they make these vocational track kids feel like failures. It's just not realistic. There have to be workers at all levels; not everyone is going to be rich. Not all students have college aspirations. But, of course, if I say that, I get told it is racist. And society has plenty of jobs for people without college degrees. Three of my friends from high school didn't go to college, and they have decent incomes. My buddy Don, he works in construction. He's a contractor now. Steve works for the post office. And Roy works at Sunrise grocery. That's a union job with benefits.

Julie: But what about the girls from your class? They might get lucky and get jobs at Sunrise, but the other grocery stores in town aren't unionized. The jobs most of the girls work now are clerical or retail. Their jobs don't pay as much as the ones you're describing.

Mr. Young: Well, that's true. Most girls don't choose these jobs.

Ms. Lambert, more sensitive to gender, spoke about what she called "the college myth":

> . . . the idea that all kids need to go to college. The problem is there are no alternatives offered for those who can't. There are a lot of warehouse jobs now, but those are jobs held mostly by men, except for maybe a two-or-three-person clerical staff. Some girls can get those jobs. It is just a myth that there are all these jobs out there if people would just get trained. They are not jobs you can live on. And there is no child care at school or work. Girls are crucified. They are told to get off welfare, but they can't live on their wages. I don't tell the girls all this. But I am straight with them. That a job in child care, for example, is a minimum-wage job without much mobility.

Both the school's own internal discourse on race and ethnicity and the wider social discourse on education in general suggest that there are structural reasons why Mexican-American students don't do as well as their white counterparts, but las chicas were not always able to apply this idea to themselves. In comparison to immigrant students who were struggling to learn English and whose parents worked the worst jobs in the community, las chicas seemed well-off. Further injury was inflicted by the occasional poor and/or immigrant Mexican-American student who did particularly well at school and therefore was a mystifying source of confusion. School culture, and society more generally, loves stories of exception, of people who defy the odds. These students are held up as models to which all should aspire, and so much attention is paid to exceptions that it is easy to forget those who make up the rule. At times las chicas were proud that "one of ours" had done well, adding to the collective self-esteem of the community, but at other times the success of such a student was detrimental to the esteem of individuals.

There were also moments, as we will see, when las chicas recognized full well that there were "rich" preps whose lives appeared easy by comparison to their own, giving them a class consciousness of sorts, although always articulated through race. Their race-class consciousness was relational, always shifting in accordance to who it was they were comparing themselves to. These second-generation, settled-living, working-class students did not experience themselves as "poor," were more likely to call themselves "middle," but recognized their difference from the children of the professional middle class. Without a critical discourse on class, they were unable to locate themselves more clearly in relation to their various peers or to locate themselves historically in class terms in relationship to parents and grandparents.

Many of las chicas described parents who were clear that "education is important" and who recognized this for their daughters as much as their sons. It was not the case for these second-generation Mexican-American girls that parents presumed their daughters would fill traditional feminine roles. Families were well aware that dual incomes were requisite. Girls described parents who were adamant that their child attend school every day and finish high school, parents whose focus was on their child not "getting into trouble." But staying out of trouble long enough to be able to finish high school would not guarantee a future better than the one their parents had known. It might have meant that for boys in an earlier industrial context, but for girls, a high school education does not (and never did) guarantee economic security. Parents wanted their children to do better than they themselves had. It appeared from girls' accounts of their parents' views that parents sometimes wrongly assumed that a high school education would mean mobility, compared to parents who had not graduated.

It is not the case that parents did not value education for their children; they clearly did. Rather, the issue is one of social and cultural capital, where working-class parents lack the social networks and skills and knowledge to enable their child. Mariana, for example, was headed for a vocational track when she went to her counselor in ninth grade looking for "a club to join, just some way to meet friends." The counselor decided "that since I was Mexican, maybe I should join MESA [Math, Engineering, and Science Achievement for minority students]." Quite by accident Mariana was tracked upward and was now college-prep. When I asked her about the difference between her parents and the parents of her middle-class peers, she explained,

> Well, they [her parents] can't help me with my homework, 'cause I'm way ahead of them. And they didn't know anything about college applications, SATs, or college-prep courses. They didn't know the difference between the university and a junior college. But they do now.

Further, some working-class parents did not necessarily recognize that junior college and business school function as post–high school working-class tracks in a historical moment when it is widely understood that high school is not enough. Parents tend to blame schools for not doing well by their child, while schools blame parents. As one vocational teacher quipped when he heard from a fellow teacher that a student's parent had called in to ask what she could do to help her daughter pass a class, "You mean there's actually a parent out there who cares?" Girls feel doubly punished, by schools and parents, both of whom blame students for not applying themselves. But no one speaks to the fact of changing labor and declining wages that await this generation of students, a problem that neither schools, parents, nor girls can solve.

Getting a high school diploma, not to mention a year of junior college, deceptively suggests mobility to las chicas and possibly to their parents. But most girls wind up in low-wage clerical or retail jobs. In comparison to mothers (and fathers) whose work was less than glamorous and sometimes dirty (cannery, factory, fields), working in an office or behind a cash register in retail can indeed appear as mobility. It has been suggested that women who work in clean jobs, indoors, near management, wearing "dress up" clothes, have perhaps always been wrongly perceived as middle-class by working-class standards (Willis 1977; Ortner 1991). This confusion was made clear one day when I asked Flor what she wanted to do for work after high school, and she said:

> I don't know. Maybe be a lawyer or a receptionist or something like that. Somethin' in an office.

Given the historic meanings of the category "working class," as predominantly masculine manual labor, postindustrialism does make a U.S. working class hard to locate, especially when so many women fill the ranks.

Girls vacillated between understanding their dilemma, the circumstances of their lives that were resulting in precarious futures, and denial about it. Most of the time they avoided talking about it, distracting themselves with the details of girl culture. The face-saving game non-preps played throughout senior year was to suggest that they were going to business school so they could get done quickly and get a good job, which they would then work while attending college. Or they would say that they would go to the JC, just for a while, and then transfer to college. While JCs are promoted by the school as a route to what students understand as "real" college for those not on the college-prep track in high school, this longer, more circuitous route was a difficult one to follow. There were few to no stories of older siblings or friends who had actually done either route. Going away to college is not a possibility for most of these girls, and attending the local community college is infantalizing, for it means continuing to live at home, continuing to attend school in the town in which they grew up. In short, it doesn't feel much different from high school; hence the expression that "junior college is high school with ashtrays." Most girls told stories of friends and siblings who attended junior college for a year or so before giving it up and settling into a low-wage job.

ON ACTING WHITE

Mexican-American students did have a way in which they simultaneously recognized and displaced class, at times explaining differences among themselves in racial/ethnic terms as "acting white" versus acting "the Mexican role." The class coding of these descriptions is revealed when the categories are pushed only slightly. When I asked Lorena what she meant by "acting white," she gave an animated imitation of a girl she'd met at a Future Business Leaders of America (FBLA) meeting, affecting a stereotypical "valley girl" demeanor and speech pattern:

> Ohmigod, like I can't believe I left my cell phone in my car. It was so nice to meet you girls, do keep in touch.

Lorena perceived this sentiment as quite disingenuous since they had just met. Indeed, part of working-class girls' interpretation of preps was that they were "fake"; their friendships were considered phony and insincere, always working in the interests of social ambition. Lorena went on,

> I'm going to play volleyball for Harvard next year.

Clearly "Harvard" was an exaggeration on Lorena's part, but for her any university may as well have been Harvard, as it was just as distant a possibility. When I pointed out to her that she was using a "valley girl" accent, she explained:

> But it's not just how they talk, it's what they talk about. Like "Let's go shopping at Nordstrom's." They brag about their clothes and cars.

I pushed for whether she thought preps really were purposefully bragging or were just unaware of how their talk affected others around them. She was convinced it was intentional: "They know. They brag."

Erica, a Filipina-American girl who had been befriended by and accepted as one of las chicas confided to me, "There's a lot of trashing of white girls really, and Mexican girls who act white." When I asked her what she meant by "acting white," her answer was straightforward:

> *Erica:* The preps.
> *Julie:* Not the smokers or the hicks or—
> *Erica:* Oh, no, never smokers, basically preps.

At some level, the girls knew that "acting white" didn't refer to whites generally, but to preps specifically (that is, a middle-class version of white), but class as a way of making distinctions among whites was not easily articulated.[11] The whites most visible to them were those who inflicted the most class injuries, the preps. In fact, working-class whites were invisible in their talk, unless I asked specifically about them. The most marginalized, hard-living, working-class whites, known as the smokers, were either unknown or perplexing to most Mexican-

American students. As Mariana, a Mexican-American middle-class performer, said to me, almost exasperated:

> I mean, they're white. They've had the opportunity. What's wrong with them?

The utility or necessity of describing class performances in racial terms as "acting white" is found in the difficulty all students had coming up with a more apt way of describing class differences in a society in which class discourse as such is absent. It is also found in the reality of the lives of Mexican-American students for whom the fact that race and class correlate (that people of color are overrepresented among the poor) was highly visible. This is not to say that there is nothing racial/ethnic-specific that might be named "acting white" outside of middle-classness, but it was not made clear in girls' talk what that might be.[12]

In popular discourse, class is often not a present category of thought at all or is considered temporary (a condition of immigration) and not institutionalized. As a result, categories like race and gender, which appear to be essentially there, fixed, and natural, readily take the place of class in causal reasoning rather than being understood as intertwined with one another (for example, when class difference is read as sexual morality). In other words, class appears in popular discourse, "just not in terms we recognize as 'about class'" (Ortner 1991, 170). Read through gender and through race, class meaning is articulated in other terms.

At times, race/ethnicity was understood and explained by students in performance terms, as when whites were said to act Mexican and Mexicans to act white. Girls were able to delineate the contents of those categories and the characteristics of the performances, which were class coded. But, alternatively, one's race performance was *expected* to correspond to a perceived racial "essence," marked by color and surname. Understandings of race as a performance and as an essence existed simultaneously. Consequently, middle- or working-class performances were perceived and read differently, depending on the race/ethnicity of the performer and the reader. This is because class performances have race-specific meanings linked to notions of "authentic" racial/ethnic identity, where white is high or middle and brown is low. As one Mexican-American girl said, "The cholos play the Mexican role."

The common-sense way class and race codings work together is seen when comparing the styles of working-class performers across race/ethnicity. White working-class youth expressed their overt rejection of prep norms by dressing down. They wore torn-up jeans and anything they could find that seemed to oppositionally confront middle-class performers' ideals of appropriate presentation of oneself, taking the fact that they didn't have the money to meet the ideal to an extreme. In contrast, Mexican-American students employed a different oppositional strategy. Since brown is always already a code for low economic status, dressing down was not part of their defiant style. Cholos' clean look, their crisp and perfectly ironed Dickie brand work clothing and starched white T-shirts, and cholas' perfect hair and makeup represented an effort to defy the color/poverty link at the same time that it refused white middle-class norms by rejecting the prep version.[13]

The notion of racial/ethnic authenticity is a discursive resource mobilized to perform the work of constructing racial/ethnic boundaries, boundaries that are inevitably class coded. In short, race and class are always already mutually implicated and read in relationship to one another. But when class is couched in race and ethnicity, and vice versa, it impairs our understanding of *both* social forces. Not only do we fail to learn something about class as a shaper of identity, but further, because of the conflation, we fail to learn much about the existence of racial/ethnic cultural forms and experience *across* class categories.

MIDDLE-CLASS CHOLA PERFORMANCES

This leads me to the examples of Ana and Rosa and their friends, who were exceptions to the class-origin-equals-class-performance rule. When students perform class identities that do not correspond with those of their families of origin, there is a negotiation between their inherited identity from home and their chosen public identity at school. For Mexican-American girls this negotiation was quite complicated. They struggled with the meanings of and links between class mobility, assimilation, and racial politics or identification where income, what kind of work parents did (such as agricultural or warehouse work), generation of immigration, skin color, and Spanish fluency were key signifiers that then became the weapons of identity politics, used to make claims to authenticity and accusations of inauthenticity.

Friendship groups were clearly shaped by class and race performance. While girls were largely unable to articulate their performances in race-class terms, they knew that each group preferred different styles and that friendships were organized around presentation of physical self. The class origin/class performance correlation existed with few exceptions.

A handful of girls were outliers, third-generation Mexican-American, from professional middle-class families, whose style and presentation of self were consistent with las chicas, even though they attended college-prep classes and planned to go to state schools. They were differentiated from another small group, college-prep Mexican-American girls who, like white preps, wore little or no makeup, whose dress was less gender-coded, and who were heavily involved in school activities. These Mexican-American college-prep girls rejected chola style as "trouble." They perceived las chicas as too allied to boys in gangs; las chicas perceived them as too nerdy and straight.

Ana and Rosa's small crowd were transgressors of a kind. They had each individually struggled to find their place in this race-class meaning system. They had grown up in white neighborhoods and gone to elementary schools that were primarily white and where, as Rosa explained, "I knew I was different, because I was brown." In junior high, which was less segregated, some of them began performing chola style and were "jumped in" to a gang. When I asked Ana why, she explained that she hated her family.

> *Ana:* My mom wanted this picture perfect family, you know. And I just hated it.
>
> *Julie:* What do you mean by a perfect family?
>
> *Ana:* You know, we had dinner at night together, and everything was just okay. She was so *happy.* And I hated that. My life was sad; my friends' lives were sad.
>
> *Julie:* Why were they sad?
>
> *Ana:* One friend's mom was on welfare, the other didn't know who her dad was. Everything was wrong in their families.

As she described class differences between herself and her friends, she struggled for the right words to describe it. And as Lorena sought to describe the difference between herself and her friend Ana, she too searched for words:

> Well, in junior high she was way down kinda low, she got in with the bad crowd. But in high school she is higher up kinda. I mean not as high as Patricia is [another middle-class performer] but she's not as low as she used to be.

Lorena's perception of Ana as high-but-low was shaped by Ana's crossover style and the fact that in some sense she had earned her low status by performing chola identity and gang-banging. Although by the time I had met Ana, Rosa, and Patricia, they had accepted the cultural capital their parents had to give them, were now college-prep, and had been admitted to four-year colleges, they were still friends with las chicas and still dressed and performed the kind of race-class femininity that las chicas did. In this way they distanced themselves from preps and countered potential accusations of acting white. In short, their style confounded the race-class equation and was an intentional strategy. By design, they had middle-class aspirations without assimilation to prep, which for them meant white, style. It went beyond image to politics, as they participated in MEChA (Movimiento Estudiantil Chicano de Aztlán) and tried to recruit las chicas to participate too. In fact, when I went along on the bus ride to tour the business school with las chicas, I was surprised to find that Ana, Rosa, and Patricia came along. I asked why they had come along since they had already been accepted to four-year schools. Rosa responded, "Because we're with the girls, you know; we have to be supportive, do these things together."

Mexican-American girls' friendships crossed class performance boundaries more often than white girls' did because there was a sense of racial alliance that drew them together, both in an oppositional relation to white students at school and through activities outside of the school in the Mexican-American community. Further, Mexican-American girls were also far more pained by the divisions among themselves than white girls ever were (an aspect of whiteness that can seem invisible). There was a recognition among Mexican-American girls of the need to present a united front, and this was particularly acute among girls who were politicized about their racial/ethnic identity and participated in MEChA. For white girls, competition among them (over heterosexual relationships or class performance or whatever issue) did not threaten them as a racial/ethnic minority community; there was (usually) no superordinate goal or outside threat they could see that would necessitate their solidarity on racial grounds. For the most part, their whiteness was invisible to them, though, as we will see, there were times when whiteness, like brownness, functioned as a source of implied solidarity.

In spite of the fact that cross-class friendships were more likely, still class differences were salient among Mexican-American girls, as evidenced in Lorena's description of Ana, and in descriptions working-class performers gave of MEChA, if they knew what it was at all, as "for brainy types," since it was understood as a college-prep activity. Some of las chicas did join MEChA, but they typically played inactive roles. When I asked Yolanda about it, she had this to say:

> Well, we joined, but it's not the same for me as it is for Patricia 'cause her mom is educated and all. She's real enthusiastic about it. You know, she's going to college and will do it there. But like Lorena and me, we can't always make it to the meetings. They're at lunch time, and I have to go to work then, or I want to at least get some lunch before I go to work.

Yolanda and Lorena both had vocational work-experience "class" the last two periods of school, which allowed them to leave school early and receive school credit for working. Patricia expressed some frustration with las chicas' failure to be very involved, as she and the other college-prep MEChA members struggled to find ways to reach *la raza,* to get the people to come to the functions they organized.

Further, the politicized racial/ethnic identity MEChA offered allowed Ana, Rosa, Patricia, and their friends to be middle-class performers and not deracinate. MEChA offers bicultural identity by making it possible for middle-class performers to do well in school and yet maintain a political-cultural racial/ethnic identity. Ironically, although MEChA, at least as it existed at Waretown High, embraced a working-class, community-based agenda, it served middle-class performers, those who were already tracked upward, more than it did a working-class base. It appealed less to working-class performers whose racial identity was more secure and who were less vulnerable to accusations of acting white. Because it was understood as a college-prep activity (originating in the university and promoting higher education), MEChA was therefore intimidating to working-class performers, who experienced class-injury in relationship to it. Class difference stood in the way of the racial alliance MEChA students desired, but it was not understood as such.

If class differences were salient at times among or within Mexican-American student groups, despite cross-class friendships and a sense of racial alliance, those differences were not often articulated as class. Rather, they were expressed as issues of assimilation (who was more or less "traditional"), language fluency, gang antagonism, and acting white. In Ana's and Rosa's attempts to understand their place in a social order where race/ethnicity and poverty correlate more often than not, the salience of color and ethnicity was so integral to their identity formation that they felt compelled to perform working-class identity at school as a marker of racial/ethnic belonging, and to avoid accusations of acting white. As Rosa explained:

> The Mexican Mexicans, they aren't worried about whether they are Mexican or not.

Ironically, while las chicas sometimes explained college-prep Mexican-American students in terms of acting white, las chicas themselves were at times accused of acting white by immigrant students. Lupita, who had immigrated at age thirteen, articulated the sentiments of her peers:

> The immigrants don't get along with the Chicanos sometimes because they come here and they don't feel accepted. It is hard for them to be poor here because in Mexico they maybe weren't. They owned houses. Here they meet people who look like them and who have last names like them, but they act different; it seems like they are trying to be white. Sometimes the Mexicans think they are better because they are pure Mexican, better than the mixing of generations or colors. But I can understand how the Chicanos feel too. They don't know who they really are. They are confused because Mexicans don't accept them, because maybe they don't speak Spanish, and Americans don't accept them because they are Mexican. Sometimes they say they are better because they are American citizens. No one thinks through it logical. They fight instead.

Lupita herself was an "exception," coming from a poor family but performing middle-class school-sanctioned femininity and on her way to a university education. At times her friends were proud of her, "They want to sit next to me 'cause I'm smart, and they think I can help them do well." At other times she had been hurt by their defensive strategy for coping with race-class injury, which was to accuse her of acting white, abandoning her community. This was a weapon they used to heal their own injury by minimizing her achievement.

One afternoon I sat cross-legged on the floor with Rosa in her parents' large home, which was located in a primarily white middle-class neighborhood, and observed the strands of her life. As she described her plans for college, she pulled a box out of her closet, full of *Teen Angel* magazines, her own "prison art" drawings, and a photo of the young man in prison she'd written to for a year. On the wall behind her was a poster of Cesar Chavez and another advertising a PBS special on the Mexican-American Civil Rights Movement. Earlier in the day I had spoken with a teacher who sat on a gang task force in the community. When I asked him what he thought was the reason Waretown students joined gangs, he assumed I meant boys. He admitted he didn't really have a good answer, but then offered a lengthy, contradictory, and dubious explanation that included causal factors such as "family breakdown," "cultural difference," and "oh, racial oppression, too." When I asked him specifically about *girls* in gangs, he responded, "Oh, well, they are just trying to learn how to be young women," and his discussion of them centered on teen pregnancy. There was, of course, so much more to Rosa than that. But he could only see her as gendered; the salience of her race/ethnicity and class identity was left without comment.

Rosa and Ana are only two examples of a handful of middle-class girls whose working-class performance resulted from their struggle over racial/ethnic belonging and the meaning of being Mexican-American. And, unlike Ana and Rosa, those whose non-prep performance included early maternity also suffered the consequence of gender politics, with their potential mobility out of their working-class performance hampered further by their being young mothers.

Yvette and Erica are two girls from middle-class origins whose working-class performance would not be easily escaped. Yvette, whose white mother and Mexican-American father were divorced, had grown up with her mother and white stepfather, who worked in middle-class professional occupations. During junior high she began to resent her stepfather's attempts at parenting her and chose to move to Waretown to live with her settled-living blue-collar father. At this time she reported that she "became Mexican," began speaking in broken-English, and performed chola style. In my first weeks at the school, when I asked teachers to help me locate some of the cholas with the most difficult lives, ironically Yvette was identified by teachers as one who was "very hard" and whom they thought I would not be able to penetrate. She had achieved an authentically believable hard-core chola performance, and teachers knew nothing of her white and middle-class past.

Erica, a Filipina-American girl, told me her family had lived in a middle-class white neighborhood when they first moved to Waretown and she had been grade school friends with many of the girls who were now preps at the high school. After a series of incidents in their neighborhood that the family came to understand as racially motivated, they moved to a primarily Mexican-American and lower-income neighborhood. There were no other Filipinas in her age group at the school she attended, and the white smokers became her new peer group for a short time. But before long the salience of her brown color resulted in her befriending Mexican-American students instead. Erica too "became Mexican," performing chola style, and in the end becoming one of las chicas.

Both Yvette and Erica did finish high school, but on the vocational track. These girls demonstrate both class and *race* as performance and performative. They "chose" from the limited identities made available by cultural discourses on race and class that tend to meld these two together in specific ways. Moreover, racialization and racism pushed the girls in particular directions when they were self-fashioning an identity, and the salience of geography and the demographics of community cannot be underestimated. Erica reported that since no Filipina identity option was available to her within her public peer culture, she traveled from a white middle-class to a white working-class and finally to a Mexican-American working-class identity, stating explicitly that she was most comfortable with friends who understood "just being brown." Even though she began with middle-class cultural capital, explicit racism caused Erica's family to move and instigated her downwardly mobile path. Color shaped her decision to "become Mexican" in a community where to be brown and middle-class was largely incongruous. The fact that these girls made conscious decisions about their racial identities made them aware, on some level, of the malleability (or, more strongly, the falsehood) of racial authenticity and the fact that racial identities can be performed. Their knowledge of this was reflected in their discourse on acting white. What is important to note is that these racial performances were simultaneously class performances, but because of the absence of class discourse the girls' subjective experience was that of performing only a racial identity.

EDUCATED IN ROMANCE?

Overall, las chicas' race-class performance of femininity was read by their peers, and at times by their teachers, as a marker of heterosexual interest and sexual practice. It is an easy equation to assume that las chicas' girl culture, lack of interest in schooling, and poor school performance are a consequence of the fact that as girls they have been "educated in romance," that potentially higher aspirations were sidetracked by girls' socialization in romance and relationship (Holland and Eisenhart 1990).

But this suggested sequence of causality is, once again, a consequence of envisioning girls as only gendered, failing to see their gender performances as race- and class-specific. Rather, their working-class location, informed by racial formation, leads them to a vocational track, and their rejection of middle-class prep norms takes a gender-specific form. Ironically, the tendency to see working-class girls as shaped most by gender may occur precisely because of the particular working-class racialized version of femininity they are performing. We will see that working-class white girls as well are perceived as sexualized; thus class differences, performed in race-specific ways, are often wrongly understood as primarily about gender and a difference of sexual morality between "good girls" and "bad girls." Instead, choices about appearance, girls' use of gender-specific commodities, are one way they negotiate meanings and construct distinctions among themselves in a race- and class-stratified society.

The year I was at the school, the film about the late Tejana music star Selena was being made, and rumor had it that the producers were searching the country for a girl to play the young version of Selena in the film. Las chicas reported stories of younger sisters pleading with their parents to take them to L.A. to try out. The lure that glamorous occupations such as dancers, actresses, pop singers, and models have on teen girls is commonly known (McRobbie 1991, 1994; Walkerdine 1997). But, as Valerie Walkerdine explains, viewing girls' attraction to such stardom only through a gendered lens, which interprets girls as victims of male-dominated culture, misses the class dimension of the draw. In particular, Walkerdine argues against a narrow view that young girls are merely victims, eroticized and exploited, and wants to consider as well (but not instead) their own participation. Aside from what fantasies of sexuality are projected onto them by the male gaze, she asks, what fantasies belong to the girls? Likewise, Angela McRobbie (1984) notes that teenybop culture and the fantasy of fame is far less boring than the menial labor or vocational schooling that working-class girls have to look forward to. Middle-class girls for whom school success is a realistic possibility and who are going on to college and career do have something to look forward to and may be less drawn to the lure of glamour industries as an escape from economic dependency or a crappy job. But for working-class girls, being looked at still presents one of the only ways in which they can escape from the routines of domestic drudgery or poorly paid work (Walkerdine 1997, 142). The body has long been the only raw material or capital with which impoverished and working-class women have to work.[14] When girls reject schooling for glamour, they may resist their class oppression in a very gender-specific way, but—not unlike Paul Willis's (1977) lads—this also works to secure their subordinate place in the class hierarchy, because most of them, of course, will not become stars.

It is far too simple to treat what appears to be a sexualized version of femininity for working-class girls, and girls of color in particular, as a consequence of competitive heterosexuality and gender-subordinate learning in which working-class girls have an "emphasized femininity" (Connell et al. 1982)—especially when narratives of romance were largely missing from girls' accounts of themselves. Such an analysis would suggest that middle-class (school-sanctioned) femininity is "normal."

And while school personnel at times explained working-class Mexican-American girls' gender performance as a consequence of "their" culture, an assumed real ethnic cultural difference in which women are expected to fulfill traditional roles and/or are victims of machismo and a patriarchal culture, the girls' generational status—in two senses—was not taken into account. Firstly, las chicas, are a generation of girls located in a historical context of dual-wage families, and they did not describe parents who had traditional roles in mind for their daughters. All of their mothers worked, and it was clear that dual incomes were requisite for a family economy. Secondly, they are second-generation Mexican-Americans, young women who have no intention of submitting to traditional gender ideologies, although they perceived first-generation girls and their families as "more traditional" in this way.

Las chicas' girl culture worked as a refusal of schooling and of middle-class prep norms. Girls who did not meet prep norms operated in alternative symbolic economies in which they earned and wore different "badges of dignity" that symbolically healed their race and class injuries. Girls like Lorena and her friends, who did not have the cultural (class and ethnic) capital that would enable them to be successful as defined by the institution, rejected the version of femininity performed by preps, the one most sanctioned by the school, and were simultaneously opting out and being tracked out of the game preps could more easily win. And for middle-class girls like Ana and Rosa, whose cultural capital would presumably mean a prep performance would come more easily, the association of school-sanctioned femininity with "whiteness" was a reason to reject it for a racial/ethnic identity that is coded "low." In the end, las chicas' particular race-class gendered performance helps to entrench them in subordinate class futures. Becoming exactly the kind of labor capital cannot refuse, they enter low-paying sex-segregated jobs right out of high school, or enter certificate programs at local community colleges that still land them in low-wage jobs. And, at times, they enter early maternity.

CHAPTER 4

Hard-Living Habitus, Settled-Living Resentment

I went into Waretown High with the by now tired race-class-gender mantra that characterized the scholarship of my generation of graduate education firmly in one hand and my desire to foreground (but not privilege) class and to come to some understanding of class as a cultural identity in relationship to race/ethnicity, gender, and sexuality in the other. I was both pleased and surprised when an event that marked students' understandings of cultural distinctions based on class occurred on one of my first days at the school. At the time, I did not yet have a full understanding of the informal hierarchy among students or of which girls belonged to which clique, but this event was illuminating.

A group of white girls from the college-prep class I'd been visiting were seated at a table in the library talking. I joined them and asked a few questions about the projects they were working on. It was the first class of the morning, and the air smelled of papaya and coconut from girls' hair still damp with the residue of cream rinse. One girl was applying translucent orange-scented lip gloss, which she then offered to others. On the table lay issues of *Seventeen, Glamour, Redbook,* and *Vogue.* The girls were cutting letters of the alphabet out of magazines to decorate the covers of their newly finished assignment. Each girl had researched on the Internet, in the library, and by mail and phone the college she hoped to attend next year and had written a report about that school, its virtues, expenses, and deadlines for admission. I asked Lisa why she had chosen her particular school: "Because I would really like to play soccer for a private Christian college." Another girl had chosen to bypass her undergraduate school of choice altogether and write her report on the institution she planned to attend for graduate school.

A teacher, Ms. Ryan, walked over and sat down, saying, "How are my girls? I don't see you anymore; you never come visit me." She had taught an English literature course these girls took the year before. The girls were happy to have her company at their table, and they engaged in a long conversation with her about her recent dating experiences. Students and teacher interacted informally, much as friends, and it was an interesting moment of cross-generational female culture, as the teacher went on about how a man she'd gone on a first date with left her house late one night only to call her a few hours later to say his car had broken down. She had feared for her safety, refusing to go where he said he was and had called Triple-A to assist him instead. She went on with some prodding by one of the girls to explain why her previous boyfriend didn't work out, because of his lack of desire to be a father to her child. The teacher turned the conversation to one of the girls, asking, "Are you still in love with your guy?" The response was yes, and the girl, Stephanie, explained that he was going to a college in another state on an athletic scholarship, while she would be attending a school here. Ms. Ryan responded, "Well, you better tell him to keep his eyes closed for two years." Another girl, Leslie, responded, "Yeah, you know how men are."

As she told of these episodes in her life and cautioned them, the girls and I all nodded knowingly at appropriate points in recognition of women's vulnerabilities. A girl named Diana pushed for more details about Ms. Ryan's new boyfriend.

Diana: So are you going to see him again? What's he like?

Ms. Ryan: Well, he's real nice. He asked me to go to Monterey with him. He said he'd get a room for himself and a separate one for me so we could just spend the night. He lives between here and there, but said he would come pick me up. Then he asked if I wanted to go for a casual ride in the convertible or more formal in the Mercedes.

Diana: Oh, this sounds too good to be true. He's probably married. You know, you hear these stories on talk shows.

Ms. Ryan: Well, I'm quite a sleuth, and I'm pretty sure he's not married. I'm not sure it could ever work out though. I can't leave Waretown, and I don't think he'd want to move here. He asked if there was anything to do here, and so I had to explain to him that this is [under her breath] a white-trash town. But then given my income, I guess I'm one of them [laughing].

Diana: Yeah, well with my mom's income I guess we are too! [All were laughing and nodding their heads knowingly. I learned later that Diana's parents were now divorced; her father, who was an engineer, had moved to another state, and her mother's computer software business was failing.] But at least one day we won't be.

Ms. Ryan: You guys will be okay. At least you can go home and study. Some of these kids don't have a clue.

The personal nature of the conversation, Ms. Ryan's reference to "my girls," the way they distanced themselves from the category "white trash" and were aided in doing so by the teacher, all confirmed to me that these girls were middle-class performing preps. In short, they were "teacher's pets." In her interviews with working-class white and black women about their school memories, Wendy Luttrell (1993) found that the category "teacher's pet" worked as a common-sense way that women understood class, race, and gender inequalities. The category is an example of just the kind of "displacement" that Sherry Ortner (1991) speaks to. The women knew that teacher's pets were not haphazardly chosen, but were social types, marked by class-specific performances of femininity and the ability to meet normative standards of beauty, including skin color. Teachers' approval of such girls was a "celebration of social injustice" along multiple axes (Luttrell 1993). "Teacher's pet" was not a term used by the girls I spoke with, but the category "preps" served a parallel purpose.

While this episode began as a telling moment of gender culture and socialization, it turned quickly into a study of class meanings and cultural belonging. The distinction between class as an economic category and class as a cultural difference (i.e., cultural capital) was not lost on the girls, as they found humor in the suggestion that Diana and their teacher could be, according to economic criteria, white trash. They knew full well that the teacher and Diana's mother, although they might have been relatively economically poor, were not culturally poor.

"I'M THE ONE WHO DESERVES AN AWARD"

Over the course of the year I came to know well the students who were referred to as trash.[1] During the awards ceremony held at the end of the year to honor high academic achievers (see chapter 3), I watched the event in the gym for a while and then attempted to wander into the adjoining lunchroom. A teacher at the door stopped me, saying, "You'll have to sit down until the ceremony is over." Based on my attire, she perceived me to be a student. I explained that I wasn't, and upon closer inspection she concurred and apologized, letting me pass. As with pep rallies and other school day functions, to ensure control over the student body during such an event, all students were required to be in the building, either in the gym, to watch the event, or in the lunchroom. There the students who had no interest in the activity hung out.

This awards ceremony, along with other ceremonies and pep rallies, was viewed resentfully by working-class performers as a force-fed school celebration of preps. Seated at several of the lunch tables were groups of Mexican-American girls, bored, talking, waiting to be released from this holding facility. Near them in one corner of the room stood a group of cholos. In an opposite corner stood a group of hicks, boys and girls, also waiting for release. And in yet another corner of the room was a group of "smokers," some of the guys passing the time playing Hackey-Sack. From that corner of the room Tara waved me over. I was prepared for her usual routine, which was to gesture from afar that she was happy to see me but to close down once I got near. Tara was flattered by and happy with my attention, yet afraid of it. I began to walk toward her, and surprisingly she met me halfway, saying, "Hey, wha's up?" She was wearing torn-up jeans with long johns poking through and, as usual, her combat boots. Looking out of place in contrast to her black leather biker jacket, a wilting sunflower was stuck in the rubber band that held her hair back. A few others from the crowd clustered around us. Nick, a slight boy wearing a Black Sabbath T-shirt, began explaining animatedly that a couple of hicks wanted to fight him and a friend of his. He went on, "I'm not worried though, [but clearly he was] 'cause all those guys [pointing to his crowd] would back me up." Tara reassured him, "Damn right they would." Again Nick expressed concern, "I don't promote fighting though."

Wendy joined us, saying to Tara, "Hey, I need a loan. My friend needs a cigarette." Tara put her hand in the pocket of her jacket and then craftily passed Wendy a cigarette, keeping it concealed in her hand. Then looking over her shoulder, she feigned concern, "Oh shit, a UA [unit administrator] is right there." She turned to me to say that Lana, a friend of hers whom she had told me about and whom I had been wanting to meet, was at school today after having been absent for a few weeks while her baby was hospitalized. Tara suggested the three of us go find her, and we managed to slip out the door without being noticed by any teachers. As we walked, I turned to Wendy and asked, "So, did you go to the prep awards ceremony?" She appreciated my recognition of what the ceremony was really about and responded, "Yeah. I stood in the door for a minute, but I got bored," then added angrily, "Man, I did bad here until this year. I'm doing good now. I think I'm the one who deserves an award."

Until this year, Wendy had been flunking out of school. In fact, she'd missed almost a whole year. The day I met her she said hesitantly, "My life is unique," and then went on to describe her life in terms of the series of places she had lived since running away from home, pausing and glancing at my face for judgment between describing each episode. Wendy's mother worked the cash register during the night shift at a convenience store. She had been accused of stealing from the store and laid off temporarily, although later she was found innocent and got her job back. During the layoff she brought a stepfather into the house, which Wendy believed was less for love than money. Before his arrival, Wendy said, she and her mother had been like best friends. They were in a bowling league together. They lived in a trailer in the front yard of a relative's rural home and shared its one bedroom: Wendy slept in it at night, and her mom had covered the windows with cardboard so she could sleep during the day. When the stepfather came into their lives, they were able to rent a small house with two bedrooms. But he worked a night job too, and there was a lot of stress around sleep and money. Wendy explained, "He used to come into my room and tell me he was going to leave my mom, 'cause we were all fucked up. Making me cry seemed to make him feel better."

Wendy began flunking her classes and subsequently skipping school. She spent days getting stoned with Lonny, a boy she met at the county fair, who had flunked out of high school after a head injury at his construction job. Wendy's mom came home early from work one morning, at 6:00 A.M., to find Wendy and Lonny sleeping in bed together. "We really were just sleeping. We never had sex. It wasn't that kind of relationship." Over a period of time, her mom came to blame Lonny for Wendy's missing school, smoking dope, and flunking out. The situation came to a head, and her mom threatened him: "Stay out of my daughter's life." Shortly after, Wendy ran away. She lived with Lonny in his camper for a while and then in a friend's closet for a few days until the friend's parents found her and kicked her out. She then planned to live in a fort in some trees near the river, and her friend agreed to bring her food. But she was afraid, and so in desperation she contacted her biological father. He had left her mother when she was pregnant with Wendy, and she had met him for the first and last time four years ago. The father arranged for Wendy to live with his sister, her aunt. Given this life history and the fact that she is now "clean" (stopped smoking pot) and is managing to come to school every day, missing only one class or so a week, Wendy felt she was more deserving of an award than the students who were receiving them.

WHITE WORKING-CLASS INVISIBILITY

The smokers, or rockers, were all but invisible at Waretown High. In fact, I didn't discover them until after I'd been at the school for several weeks. Some students had mentioned them in their description of the peer hierarchy, but I never saw them in classes or hallways or anywhere, it seemed. As one girl described them, "The rockers hang out behind the school. They wear a lotta black. I walk by them on my way to my car at lunch. Sometimes they ask me for a cigarette, and when I say I don't smoke, they look at me like 'Then what are you doing here?' " When I asked her if she knew any of the families they came from and what their parents might do for work, she explained, "I don't think they are really poor, but they are not like regular, in the middle, either," suggesting a category in between for which she did not have a name, while naming her own settled-living working-class family as "regular" and "middle."

The smokers were hard to find because they were the most marginalized geographically at the school. They hung out on the farthest edge of the school grounds, across the softball field near some bleachers that are far from the school buildings. This was, in part, because they smoke, and this location provided them the most protection from the school security officer. If he did show up, they could leave the school grounds and cross the street to where they could legitimately smoke. Where preps carried backpacks to school, las chicas and alternatives carried purses. But smokers, like chola/os, carried nothing at all. Moreover, in class they never took off their coats, which symbolically marked their lack of connection to schooling (Eckert 1989), their desire to be elsewhere, and their anticipation that they might ditch at any moment.

The smokers were marginal discursively as well. When I asked teachers and counselors to direct me toward students from low-income families, they automatically listed special programs for immigrant students as classrooms to visit. I had to explicitly ask for recommendations of white students from low-income families. But school personnel were often incapable of naming who those students might be or where they might be found. When I asked if it was possible that there simply were no or very few white students who were from low-income families, I was quickly assured that this was not the case. "There are plenty of poor white families in Waretown," explained one counselor. But she was still unable to tell me where I might find these students or to name any.

I found that talking about the class differences among students was considered taboo among most adults at the school. In fact, when I asked counselors about particular students' parents, what kind of jobs and income they had, they were very guarded. One counselor immediately referred me to a school administrator. Statistics on the class differences among students, such as parents' income, were not kept and were therefore not correlated with school achievement the way that race/ethnicity and gender were. The only information the school had on parents' income was that which was needed for the free and reduced-cost lunch program. But this information was not used for any other purpose, and no one asked whether there might be some utility in correlating income with school achievement. Talking about a student's racial/ethnic or gender status, on the other hand, was quite acceptable, presumably because those characteristics of a student are considered more obvious and cannot be concealed (though this is not necessarily true). Revealing either the taboo, or perhaps merely the uncertainty of what language to use to talk about class, one counselor made reference to "low-income families," almost whispering the words as if describing someone as low-income was an insult in and of itself. After I used the term "socioeconomic status" in our conversation, she switched to using it as well, appearing to be more comfortable with this more neutral-sounding term.

The smokers were more marginal physically and discursively than the cholo/as, who hung out very near the school buildings, the building that housed the Spanish language courses in particular. The focus in both the media and schools in recent years on "gang problems" meant that cholo/as were considered a potential threat to be kept under control, while the smokers, their white counterpart, for better and/or worse, had far less visibility. It is worth noting, however, that these hard-living whites shared characteristics often labeled typical of gangs, such as reliance on each other as an alternative or surrogate family for solidarity and support, a very age-heterogeneous friendship network based on neighborhoods more than school activities, and strong ties to young adults outside of high school who provide links to working-class jobs and/or a route into the illegal drug economy.

HARD-LIVING HABITUS

At the bottom of the peer hierarchy among white students, the smokers overtly rejected schooling and middle-class norms by association. Penelope Eckert (1989) provides a useful description of the differences between working- and middle-class orientations toward school. For preps, equivalent to the "jock" category in her Midwestern study, being positively evaluated and rewarded at school comes easily, as home matches school, and parents match teachers, in important ways. In both places an orientation toward verbal and literary skills is a key part of middle-class culture. Consequently, for preps school is a home away from home, demonstrated by their being located at the geographic center of the school, as well as by their center-stage role in extracurricular activities and success in the curriculum. Non-preps, or "burnouts" in Eckert's study, are marginal both physically and socially at the school. Where preps focused on school dances, games, and school functions, non-preps organize activities outside.

Most importantly, students learn how to be managers and subordinates. Preps learn to manage others at school, and this occurred at Waretown primarily through prep monopoly of the student government and its activities, but also through their star roles in the arts and sports. In this way preps enjoy an "adult prerogative of autonomy within the school" and are prepared for analogous adult roles (Eckert 1989, 90). Preps defined who it is that extracurricular school functions are by, for, and about. As non-prep students routinely explained, "The preps *are* the school." When I asked, "According to who?," I was told, "According to them, to teachers, to everyone." Preps learn a sense of entitlement from the school, which endorses these power relations among peers by honoring high achievers, making them visible as good examples, and by assuming that students individually *choose* membership in prep or non-prep categories.

Non-preps learn they have a subordinate status and routinely resist their subordination by refusing to participate in those activities organized by preps, like pep rallies, lunchtime lip-sync contests, and the like. As Sam explained when I asked her if she was planning to go to an upcoming school dance:

We aren't the kind of people who go to that stuff. The popular ones go.

Wendy: Yeah, people with names like Harrell and Gaffney [listing well known family names in the community].

Preps were understood as "popular," which was not so much about popularity with the student body as with the school, which meant they were favored by teachers and administrators. Non-prep performers variously viewed preps as unadult and childlike for being involved in school activities or, since such involvement included closer relationships to teachers and administrators, as "goody-goodies" or "suck ups." As Wendy put it, when asked to describe preps:

> Those are the people who try to be in everything. They wear dressy clothes. They are all going to be something great you know.

Viewing preps through her lens rather than "the school's," Starr added:

> Nobody knows or cares what those people do.

Lacking in cultural capital and performing poorly, the smokers had little interest in the academic dimension of school. A spectrum of experience at home and in their neighborhood created a disposition among the smokers, a way of apprehending the world (Bourdieu's "habitus") that did not match the worldview and social skills required to be successful in the middle-class milieu of the school. Their sensibilities, not recognized as a cultural difference of class, were often perceived by school personnel and other students as individual behavioral choices, but were in reality a common culture, evidenced by the fact that these individual students were drawn to one another by the life-world they had in common. The difference between them and other students was that the latter could operate more easily within the normative assumptions suggested by discourse at school of what family life looks like, what parents do for work and leisure, what life trajectory students will have. Key assumptions of this discourse were that parents were confident, articulate, drug-free, warm, and supportive, and had the time and skills to encourage their children's education. Further, it was assumed that their work was "respectable" and legal and their leisure activities morally acceptable to the middle-class and settled-living mainstream.

Sam was the first smoker I met, and when I asked her to introduce me to some of her friends, she explained, "I don't think they'll talk to you. You're kind of an adult figure. They're not willing to tell adults things." Fortunately, Sam was wrong, and I did win the trust of her friends by assuring them that I was not a school official, that I didn't even work for the school, and that everything we talked about was confidential and I would keep their identities anonymous in anything I wrote. I found they were "not willing to tell adults things," not only because of their own illegal activities, but at times because of those of their parents. While they were quite open with me about their own drug use, they were much more cautious about revealing their parents' sometimes illegal income-generating strategies and police records, and stories of "abuse" (although they did not use this term) were carefully told in the past tense or were slips of the tongue quickly retracted. There was a general shame about who their parents were, and they knew that school authorities and preps, both representatives of middle-class respectability, judged their families harshly. These students were surprised and pleased that someone, in this case me, had a genuine interest in their lives, and not for the purpose of imposing judgment and punishment, but simply of understanding life on their terrain.

If students whose categories of perception of social life met the normative ideals of the institution were validated as "normal," the schooling context felt more like culture shock to hard-living students. The same vocational instructor who had told me earlier that she dealt with the dilemma of, on the one hand, wanting to encourage her students to go to college (because she knew it was necessary for an adequate income), but, on the other hand, not wanting to make those students who could not go (whether for financial or academic reasons) feel like failures by focusing on building students' self-esteem told me on this day that she also reconciles the dilemma by trying to teach "general life skills that everyone needs, like good nutrition." She went on, "You know, we talk about the food groups and the importance of fresh fruit and vegetables." Nonetheless, she realized the disparity in her students' experience of even this curriculum and recognized that education is not the great equalizer even when teaching general life skills: "But one of my students came up to me at the end of a class and said to me that her family doesn't buy fruits and vegetables because they are expensive. She said they eat a lot of Top Ramen, and she wanted to know, sincerely, if there was anyway she could make that into a more healthy meal." Shaking her head, she continued, "We talked about how she might use only half a package and add more water to reduce the high sodium content."

In the fall when school began, a common topic of conversation was summer vacation. Students casually swapped stories about their families' summer travels across the country. In private settings I asked girls about leisure, and when I asked Brenda if her family ever went on summer vacation, she responded, "Oh, yes, once a year my mom and I go to Discovery Park." At first, I assumed this was a nearby amusement park, but she clarified when I asked where it was, "You know, the park by the river with the picnic tables. Just on the other side of town." That she named this a "vacation" rather than a picnic was a comment on the disparity between her life-world and the one middle-class students took for granted.

The discourse of other students, teachers, and curriculum material worked persistently to make working-class performers feel marginal and reinforced an ideology of homogeneity that didn't exist in reality. One teacher told me that she had innocently thought she was encouraging students when she told her class that they "need to work hard in school and go to college, so they don't end up on welfare." She received an angry call from a student's mother, who told the teacher that she had "made my kid feel like he is not as good as everyone else, just because we get food stamps." There was often evidence that it was hard for school personnel to understand hard-living students' approach to schooling. One teacher explained, "The information is available to them, you know. The announcements every morning tell them what activities are happening on that day. If you walk down the hall near the counseling offices, there are tables loaded with information about colleges, placement tests, and all. There is a big difference between how much information is available to students and what gets through to them." What she was not taking into account was the life-world of hard-livers, where there are other more pressing worries at hand. Both stresses from home, which were brought to school, and the related marginality smokers felt at school resulted in their rejection of school involvement. Their life-world was one that this teacher did not have access to and found hard to comprehend. For the hard-livers I came to know, even entering the building that housed the counseling and administrative offices was anxiety-inducing.

The teacher's comment about welfare was just one example of numerous offhand remarks I witnessed at the school, though much more often from fellow students than teachers, about people who were "on drugs," whose sexual morality was suspect as a consequence of having too many marriages and divorces ("she's on her third or fourth husband now"), or whose work was low-status ("no one aspires to pumping gas for a living"). The casualness of such comments was made easy by the invisibility and silence of working-class and poor students who sat quietly in the back row or, understandably, skipped class altogether.

Teachers and administrators, trying to be fair and maintain a non-prejudicial learning environment, often seemed like parents managing sibling relations. While many school studies focus on the reproduction of inequality as it occurs through the curriculum or class and racial/ethnic bias of teachers themselves, less is usually said about the hierarchy students learn from each other and the injuries they inflict on each other. It is true that school personnel are complicit in that they informally sanction preps at those times when they are not actively managing tensions and prejudices among students, but my point is that many of the class and racial/ethnic injuries working-class and Mexican-American students felt came from peer relations. Some prep girls explained to me that they, pushed by the student government teacher, attempted to get more people involved in pep rallies by making an announcement to the student body, asking students to sign up to participate in contests and the like, but no one new signed up anyway. This should not have come as a surprise. Prep ownership of school activities was so institutionalized that non-prep students would continue to count themselves out of such activities even when invited and would continue to view those activities with disdain. This was true across race/ethnicity as well as across the class performance divide. Ms. Thomas attempted to involve las chicas in FBLA (Future Business Leaders of America) leadership roles but with little luck. "I think they just see it as another club for white students." Student culture, their sense of belonging and group membership, the ways in which they engage in practices of exclusion, often wins out over school personnel's attempt to impose diversity. There is a hierarchy among students that students themselves police and that school personnel cannot easily remedy.

INDIVIDUALISM: CLASS DISPLACED

Beyond the fact that preps had the cultural capital to thrive in school, the strategies of survival that smokers needed to get by in their world were neither valued at school nor recognized as a set of skills that had a logic and made sense in another context. The disjuncture between middle-class and hard-living cultural lives had a doubly exclusionary effect: working-class performers counted themselves out of mobility by believing that success in school is "not for the likes of us," and practices of exclusion by middle-class performers clearly told the marginalized students that their success is "not for the likes of you." This was evidenced in the pep rally ritual where a popular and comedic prep boy, who was allowed temporary control of the student body, selected, in what appeared to be random fashion, students from the crowd to participate in a variety of contests and games. But the students selected were almost always other preps who were in student government and who had helped organize the activity. Although they knew in advance that they were going to be selected from the crowd, they acted embarrassed and surprised (girls in particular) to have been singled out for such attention. But to students who were not privy to the behind-the-scenes student government management of the event and the network of friends who worked to ensure one another's popularity, it *appeared* that students were chosen based on their individual appeal to the student body as a whole.

Like the exclusionary networks of middle-class society outside of the school, non-prep students were unexposed to and unaware of the amount of inside networking. The event appeared far more fair on the surface than it actually was. In fact, some non-prep students, like Lana, didn't even know there was a student government, or if they knew of it, they had no idea what it was they did. When I told her about the student government, the picture became clearer to her. Less aware of class hierarchy than an economy of beauty, she said, "I always wondered why those girls got chose. They aren't always the prettiest ones." Student government was a privilege of preps that came with enormous perks. Not an extracurricular club, it was an actual class that prep students took for credit. Permission from the instructor was required to get in, and she chose "students who show leadership potential." In this class they learned "leadership" skills, which translated into the management of other students they considered subordinate, a sense of entitlement, and the right of self-promotion informally sanctioned by the school. While non-preps may have attended a pep rally when they entered high school as sophomores, they learned quickly that like the classroom this was another environment that assisted them in feeling like failures.

Like the behind-the-scenes working of student government, the preps' mastery of language and the social world of the school was a mystery to non-preps. Without a language of class difference beyond money, non-preps often internalized that the source of popularity and success was individual attributes, and therefore only personal character flaws remained to be blamed for their own inadequacy. It is far easier for working-class students (as well as teachers and other students) to name the ways in which a lack of money affects them: the fact that they don't have the money for the name-brand clothes and cars that buy social status or the money or time (because of jobs) to participate in extracurricular activities, the fact that college is unaffordable and work necessary. But naming the cultural difference of class is more difficult: the use of nonstandard grammar, parents who cannot help with homework, who may not know about the distinction between college-prep and non-prep courses, who may not know about college entrance exams, who themselves lacked the academic skills to go to college, who might feel they have to devalue themselves and their own lives in the process of encouraging their children to go beyond them, who may wrongly assume that the school will adequately educate their child without their participation, who might desire to avoid the school themselves, because it is a familiar site of failure and intimidation where they are required to interact with middle-class professionals like teachers and administrators. Both economic and cultural capital are the weapons of class struggle. Non-preps had a language of money with which to compare their own life structures with those of the preps, but the cultural differences could only be understood as inherent differences of intelligence, beauty, and social skills.

School-sanctioned routes to success, then, were both unavailable to and rejected by the smokers, and alternative badges of dignity took their place. They created a reverse economy in which they found ways to value self where the institution did not in its daily infliction of injuries. It was cool to not know what was due in class, to be regularly late or skip class, to go to class stoned (on pot) or tweaked (on "crank," that is, speed or methamphetamine), and to receive poor grades that indicated one's indifference—all as if to say, "I cannot fail at your game if I opt out of it." Their cocky attitude and behavior, their refusal to ever let down their guard and reveal the pain of class injury, lent support to the outsider perception that these were kids who chose their lot, didn't care, deserved what they got. Like las chicas, they simultaneously opted out and were tracked out. The girls I knew, like Wendy and her friends, I usually found in non-prep vocational courses like sewing, nutrition, child care, and sometimes business skills. Mary Beth was proudly taking a welding class as well, only one of two girls in it. She found me one day standing in front of "the wall of fame," a wall near the counseling offices on which were copies of letters of acceptance to four-year colleges for seniors who had received them. I was recording who got in to which schools, and she skipped her next class to stand with me and peruse the wall, pointing out which preps were "okay" and which were "assholes." I asked if she had ever wanted to go to college.

> *Mary Beth:* Teachers are always buggin' you about what you're gonna do with your life. I told one once that I wanted to be a journalist, and she said I wasn't good enough at school. I told someone else I wanted to be a psychiatrist, and they said I needed one.

Preps did not consider smokers to have less class privilege than they did themselves, because of course their class privilege was invisible to them. Rather, they considered smokers to be "losers." I asked Lisa, a prep girl, whether she noticed a difference between students whose parents went to college and those whose parents did not.

> *Lisa:* Yeah, those others are just mostly mediocre. Some of them without educated parents, they try really hard and do well because of it, but others just give up. It depends on the person.
>
> *Julie:* What about differences in money? Do you ever have the sense that students from families without much money resent those who have it?
>
> *Lisa:* No, I never heard of that.

In their less judgmental moments, preps described smokers as having "low self-esteem." While it certainly was the case that many of them suffered from low self-esteem, to suggest this as the cause not the consequence of their class location (among other things) helps reproduce the belief in a classless society and suggests an individual rather than societal remedy. This is truly a hidden injury of class: hard-livers experience no dignity in an institution in which preps are celebrated and they themselves are rendered invisible at best and failures at worst. When school personnel held up as models and examples of school achievement those girls whom they admired and considered to have high self-esteem, they helped make institutionalized inequality invisible by implicitly suggesting the differences were merely individual ones. In doing so they failed to see their own role in diminishing the esteem of girls who could not meet the norm. When the accomplishment of middle-class norms is linked to mental health and understood as an individual trait (i.e., this girl has high self-esteem), which is often the case in popular discourse, rather than linked to structural inequalities (i.e., this girl has race and class privileges), it gives cause to question the distinction between having self-esteem and being arrogant. The confidence maintained by occupying a location in our social hierarchy that readily allows the achievement of white and middle-class ideals might be better understood as a feeling of cultural superiority than as high self-esteem. Repeatedly, the prep behavior that teachers, administrators, and preps would positively label high self-esteem was interpreted quite otherwise by working-class girls like Tara and Lorena.

GENDER VICTORIES / CLASS INJURIES

In light of this, I found myself ambivalent about displays of self-confidence among prep girls. I sat with Tara and several other smokers in the lunchroom one day as they skipped P.E. class. A girl named Allison wandered up and sat down to talk with us. Allison was a prep performer in every way with the exception of her style, which was "alternative." In her mind this provided her with an affinity to the smoker crowd, but unknown to her this view was not shared by the smokers. (Many students who believed they were unusual in their ability to cross groups were in fact not as widely accepted as they thought by the groups they crossed into.) I was asking the group questions about "Generation X," if they'd heard of this label, and what they thought about it. They hadn't heard of it, but Allison had. "Oh, yeah, that's the idea that we're all underachievers. It's a bunch of crap." Allison was confident and articulate. She seemed to know something about everything and had an opinion on every topic, which she was happy and able to express. Her verbal presentation of herself was far different from Tara's, and she had no idea, nor did she care, what the conversation was like before her entry into it. She was oblivious to the change her presence created. The conversation shifted to music, and I complimented Allison on her vocal performance in the school musical the past weekend. Everyone agreed Allison had an "awesome" voice. Nick turned to Allison, "Yeah, if you weren't going away to college, you could be in our band." She took this as an opportunity to carry on at length about her plans to perform in college, while the others looked upon her as a curious foreigner, perplexed and injured by her worldview, and annoyed that she wandered onto their turf to begin with.

As representatives of a gender category, preps appeared as young beneficiaries of years of feminist struggle. They were "postfeminist," taking for granted that they would have interesting "careers" (not "jobs"), reveling in the fact that they were not intimidated by boys in the classroom, on the basketball court, or anywhere, it seemed.[2] But they were not only girls, they were also representatives of the middle-class, and the same actions that could be counted as gender victories were also readily interpreted, especially in these rare moments of cross-class interaction, as arrogant and exclusionary. Their sense of place could not be uncoupled from the class privileges they experienced and came at a cost to those who were class-marginalized. As Allison walked away, Tara looked over her shoulder at her and mumbled under her breath, "Don't be so modest." When prep girls are considered not in the context of boys of their own class and racial/ethnic location, but in the context of both girls and boys outside it, their demeanor becomes difficult to celebrate.

Most of my time with the smokers was spent during the lunch hour, by the bleachers. Tara saw me walking across the lawn toward them one day and waved, yelling my name. When I got there, she didn't talk to me, assuming her cool detached identity instead. She only really talked to me when we were alone. Wendy turned to me, "We're goin' to the Quick Mart. Wanna come?" I agreed, and Wendy finished taking requests and money for a variety of things, including generic cigarettes, sodas, and Zig Zags (papers used to roll joints, which she refused to buy: "I'm not supporting your habit") from people sitting along the fence. Five of us piled into Todd's dented 1972 four-door avocado-green Nova. I followed Sam and Wendy into the back seat where Wendy rolled down the back window and waved her hands in the air to try and clear the pot smoke away, a gesture of politeness clearly for my benefit. Tara took the passenger's seat and put in an Eagles tape, fast forwarding it to "Hotel California," a song the group liked for its lyrical reference to pot. Todd got in the driver's seat and slammed the broken door three times. On the third try, it latched but was still ajar.

At the Quick Mart Wendy and I went in, and she collected all the items requested, counting change to make sure she had enough money. Then out of politeness she asked me if she could buy me something, although it was clear she had no extra money. Although it was lunch-time, no food was purchased, and so I bought some gum for myself and offered her a few bucks to help out. She declined the offer and on the way out of the store explained that the clerk at the counter "likes me for some reason, so he gives me the wrong change every day—too much. It helps me out." Wendy's aunt, on a limited income, gave her exactly three dollars for lunch each day. This was the only money Wendy received, so rather than spending it on food, she saved as much as she could so that she could buy a few things she wanted, like a tape here or there or colored pencils for drawing. She hoped to be an artist. With the exception of a few new flannel shirts and a sweatshirt, she wore the same clothes she had worn since the tenth grade. She was not allowed to have a job to earn her own money, as her aunt believed it would interfere with her ability to graduate.

When we returned, we sat in a patchy grass and dirt area littered with cigarette butts under a scrawny tree that provided little shade from the scorching Central Valley sun and played a card game called "bullshit" with Batman cards. The guys in particular seemed to like this game, since it gave them a legitimate reason to shout "bullshit" as loudly as they could, an opportunity to be loud, boisterous, and, they hoped, offensive. Groups of two and three came and went from a nearby port-a-potty, which was used as cover for smoking pot. After one round of cards was over, Wendy and I decided to opt out of the next round and moved away from the group to another small tree. Kate walked up from the street and sat down, pulling a book out of her backpack and handing it to Wendy. "This is for you." Wendy was elated. It was a book on contemporary witchcraft. She turned to me and explained that she had owned the book for a few years and three of them had been practicing witchcraft together, but then the book was stolen. The original had been given to her by a friend who stole it for her from a bookstore where they first found it. She was concerned about the cost that Kate might have incurred and told her, "We'll all pitch in and give you five bucks." Kate said, "Don't worry about it."

Wendy had a knack for turning inherited deficiencies into alternative routes to self-esteem. She was sure that her poverty and emotional pain would make her an artist. Experiencing little control in her life, at home or at school, she employed witchcraft as a creative fantasy route to empowerment.[3] Wendy also talked regularly about a boyfriend, Wayne, who lived in another town and whose initials were carved on her arm, but whom no one had ever seen. She told me that she had stopped practicing witchcraft, not only because she had lost the book, but because "Wayne won't allow me to anymore. Too many weird things were happening." Comments like this about Wayne, which to friends and teachers sounded like subordination, were for Wendy positive demonstrations that she mattered a lot to someone in this world. But this strategy of ego boosting and attempting to gain status was misunderstood by others. One teacher told me that Wendy gave a speech in her class. "All she talked about was this boyfriend of hers. How he won't let her do this or that. How he wants her to do this thing or another. Watching her, the class was just embarrassed for her. It was as if she didn't have a life of her own."

Reading class through gender, this struck me as a somewhat logical (albeit failed) strategy which Wendy employed to deal with class injury. Wayne was not a patriarchal oppressor in her mind but an ally against adults and peers at school who are oppressively judgmental and adults at home who are unaffectionate at best and abusive at worst. A gender analysis is by no means irrelevant to Wendy, but her victim status cannot be reduced to gender outside of her experience of class difference.

Similarly, Tara told me a story that demonstrated the way in which gendered experiences are always inflected by class:

> *Tara:* In junior high, I thought I was fat. So I was throwing up all the time. These two girls, they went and told the school nurse on me. So she calls my house. When I got home my dad was so mad. He started yellin', "What the hell did you do that for? That's stupid!"

Tara had learned early on that her father, who showed little concern for her in this instance, was first and foremost concerned that his kids' behavior could draw unwanted attention to their family and to his own actions since he had "a record" and was on probation, a consequence of dealing in crank. I tried to clarify why she described the girls as "telling on her" by asking if she thought the girls might have actually been concerned about her. She responded, "Oh, no. They were mad at me for some shit. They were trying to get me into trouble." The girls were part of Tara's crowd, but were less friends than acquaintances. And the story revealed her hard-living peers' knowledge that the well-meaning intentions of middle-class do-gooders, agents of the state, the school nurse in this case, can have complicated effects. According to Tara, the girls knew they could get Tara in trouble with her dad by getting the school nurse to call her home. While eating disorders appear to be something girls universally, and unfortunately, share as girls, the experiences of them are always shaped in classed and racialized ways.[4] The nurse, no doubt, did not anticipate that her intervention would result in punishment rather than therapy.

ON FAMILY VALUES

Much as more privileged students described smokers' behavior in terms of self-esteem, so they would also at times attempt to explain a fellow student's behavior empathetically as a consequence of coming from a "bad family." With the aid of contemporary political discourse on "family values," it was no surprise that students understood their own and each others' family lives less in class terms than in terms of family disruption. Routinely, girls and teachers described families as "good families," "close knit," or "valuing family" versus "bad families" or "broken homes," oblivious to the pattern of differential resources among them. For example, when I asked Marla, a middle-class girl, whether her parents had gone to college, what they did for work, and how comfortable they were economically, she gave all the respective answers, explaining, "We're not rich, but we're extremely comfortable. My parents don't drive a Mercedes, because they have four of us kids to put through college." But when I followed up this answer by asking if her friends' families were similar to hers, she responded by naming each of her friends and acquaintances and stating whether their families were "close-knit" or not, neglecting to report on the education and income levels I had asked for, and failing to see the correlation she made between having a "good" family and a middle-class income.

Middle-class girls routinely echoed their parents' and teachers' sense of morality in a hypocritical fashion. In a conversation I had with Amanda and Rochelle on why teenage girls get pregnant, the girls began talking judgmentally about working-class girls they'd known who had become pregnant. Amanda said:

> They're just stupid, ya know. They don't have a good family background.

But both of these girls then went on to acknowledge that they knew of girls in their middle-class circle of friends who had become pregnant but had had abortions.

Ironically, even though having divorced parents is a common experience, it is still stigmatized—or perhaps it is stigmatized anew in light of the contemporary discourse on family values. Even in an era of high divorce rates, divorce was used as an explanation ("She's from a broken home") to explain student failure.[5] The contemporary discourse on family coming from both Republicans and Democrats (and some social scientists)[6] was readily employed by girls to explain differences among them but did not actually adequately explain those differences. When I asked about smokers, commonly both middle-class and settled-living girls would suggest that those students were not from "a good family." I asked some prep girls to define a "good family."

Rhonda: You know, a good family is one that is together. The kids from broken homes are the ones [with problems].

Julie: But Rochelle, your parents are divorced, and you're doing okay, right?

Rochelle: [laughing] Well, yeah.

Julie: And so is Stephanie, and Lisa [college-prep girls who are also from divorced families].

Rhonda: I guess it's different somehow.

Of course, the difference between these middle- and working-class divorced families was the greater economic struggle that was a consequence of divorce for the latter, and the girls failed to recognize this. In focusing on how many parents a family has and blaming divorce for the poverty of women and their children instead of women's low-wage jobs, the intersection of gender and class is easily displaced. The class location of single moms, as heads of wage-poor families, is obscured when they are seen as in an in-between state—in between men, in between "normal" families. These middle-class girls were unable to recognize that their college-educated mothers and fathers had more resources with which to establish two homes and maintain a relatively comfortable standard of living upon a divorce. A discourse on family structure comes at the expense of any mention at all of the differential in resources, both economic and cultural, between these various families, which are salient to meeting middle-class norms. Consequently, the problems in hard-living families are less often perceived as a consequence of poverty (women's poverty in particular) than as "failed" or "bad" family structures.

The inability to talk about families in terms of class difference, displacing this instead with talk about whether or not families met a mythical ideal, was a judgment that came from middle-class girls whose families met the ideal (and even those whose families did not), but was also at times a self-imposed judgment by working-class girls whose families "failed." Working-class students too routinely demonstrated an inability to think of their families in class terms. I asked each girl about her parents, how much education they had, what they did for a living, how "well-off" they were. When I asked Amy, "So how did you think about your family growing up, economically, pretty average or . . . ," she responded, "Well, we fight a lot."

Where middle-class girls often employed family values discourse as a method of distinction between themselves and others, usually in a judgmental way, and settled- and hard-living working-class girls used it to judge themselves on some occasions, the latter's talk was also contradictory, conveying a recognition that something else was at play, that the reasons for the situations they found themselves in were complex.

"HERS IS GOOD. MINE IS BAD."

Liz, a working-class white girl, was unusual in that she hung with the prep crowd and tried as best she could to pass as middle-class. I interviewed her for the first time, along with her friend Amanda. As I explained to them that I was going to ask each of them about their families, Liz forcefully asserted, "Hers is good. Mine is bad," as if to get this embarrassing fact out of the way up front. Amanda lived with her married biological parents, whose income afforded them all the trappings of middle-class life. Liz lived in a trailer with her mother, who worked in retail, and her older brother and his girlfriend, both of whom also worked in retail. All, including Liz, pooled their resources. Her father had left three years before after a series of run-ins with the law for possession of cocaine and domestic violence. Violence and drugs were now gone from her family life, and poverty took their place. I talked to Liz alone the next day.

> *Julie:* When I talked with you and Amanda together yesterday and we started talking about your families, you said that her family is good and yours is bad. What did you mean?
>
> *Liz:* It's kind of like, in my eyes, sometimes people, like, look down on me, you know, because they'll be like, "Hey, let's go to Disneyland" or "Let's go to Monterey" or something. And I can't go because I have to work. And they're like "Well, can't you get out of it?" I'm like, you know, I gotta pay rent, and I gotta pay bills, and I gotta make sure my mom, you know, has a place to live, and I gotta make sure I have groceries. And it's like their parents provide all that. When they [her friends] work, they pocket the money. I don't get to pocket the money. I mean, I like use it to pay all my bills. And, you know, sometimes they're like "You're exaggerating," but I'm not! I mean my mom makes less money an hour than I do, and she works full-time, and I work part-time, and we bring home the same exact amount. And my brother has to help out too. Amanda will try to buy my lunch sometimes, but I won't let her. I don't want to feel like I owe them [her middle-class friends].

Liz showed some recognition of the link between perceiving a family as "good" and the economic resources available to them, demonstrating her awareness of how others place a moral judgment on the two kinds of families. On one occasion, she spoke about her prep boyfriend.

> *Liz:* People say "Oh God, I can't believe Matt would be with a girl like that" and all this stuff, and I'm like, whatever, you know?
>
> *Julie:* What does "a girl like that" mean?
>
> *Liz:* I don't know, like how they look at me. Because, I mean, I'm not from a rich family background or anything, but it's not like I'm like poor and on welfare. My family fends for itself. I mean, we work hard for what we have, and they are just like totally looking down at me.

Moreover, Liz's friends were appalled that Liz's mother accepted the fact that by the spring of her senior year Liz was living almost entirely with her boyfriend. He had graduated from high school the previous year and now had his own apartment, and Liz spent many of her nights there. I asked her what her mom thought about it:

> Well, I don't think she likes it. I mean she'd rather I didn't do that so young, but she's barely supporting herself right now. So I think it's kind of convenient for me to be away. So she doesn't say much.

Clearly, Liz interpreted her mother's acceptance quite differently than her friends did.

This unconscious awareness that having a "good" family was linked to economic resources was evidenced on another occasion by Mandy. As she described her friend Jeff, who had dropped out of high school earlier in the year, I queried her at length about why he was unable to complete high school, given that she had described his family as quite privileged. He had been a prep, and there was no indication he would not complete high school and go on to a college education. I kept pushing for an explanation, and finally she revealed,

> Yeah, he *is* from a really good family. Um, well, I guess I'll just tell you. His brother is dying of AIDS. When he found out his brother was gay and everything else, well, it was really hard for him and stuff. And it is like tearing the whole family apart. This was like a perfect family, you know, a rich family.

Though "good" and "rich" were synonymous adjectives used to describe families, curiously "bad" and "poor" were not used synonymously. While students explained one another's behavior in familial terms ("It's because she's from a bad family"; "It's because her family is all messed up"), they rarely named a family as "poor" or offered this as an explanation for behavior and, in particular, for a student's school performance.

In a hallway conversation with Melanie and Sabrina, two alternatives (settled-living, working-class girls), and Lindsey, a prep (middle-class) acquaintance of theirs, where I asked them to tell me what they thought were the reasons for whether a person did well in school or not, the girls began by arguing that it had much to do with family.

Lindsey: Well all those girls [referring to herself and her prep friends] have intact families.

Melanie: Yeah, divorce is the bad thing.

Julie: Why?

Sabrina: Because then you have rebellious kids who don't like their stepparents and all.

Julie: [Knowing both Melanie and Sabrina were living with stepparents] Are you two rebellious?

Melanie: [laughing] No.

Sabrina: [laughing] No.

In a later conversation with Melanie about whether she was going to college or not she explained, "I don't know. We're kinda poor 'cause my dad [stepdad] just gets disability. Mom's job doesn't really pay much." And Sabrina added, "Yeah, I'd have to pay my own way too." Here their discourse shifted, revealing a recognition that the lack of economic resources, not family structure, was inhibiting their college futures.

FAMILY VALUES, A.K.A. CULTURE OF POVERTY

Settled- and hard-living families are at two ends of a continuum of lifestyles among working-class people. Most settled-living families have relatives who are hard-living and vice versa. Girls could name an aunt and/or an uncle's family, or an older sibling's family, that was at the other end of the continuum from their own. Among whites, the fact that both ends of the continuum were present within a given family or community did not equate to feelings of empathy for hard-livers. Rather, settled-livers, who were often politically and socially conservative, worked to symbolically distance themselves from their relatives and neighbors, considering themselves "good people" and judging hard-livers harshly.

In those empathetic moments where preps suggested that smokers and alternatives might have the misfortune of coming from "bad families," we see the children of such families as without blame, as unfortunate and worthy victims, but not their parents. While the vilification of kids is a current trend in political discourse (Cockburn 1996; Males 1996, 1998), the vilification of their parents is still stronger. As I listened to hard-livers tell me their stories and imagined reproducing them, I pictured their stories being read and interpreted in the context of the compassion fatigue of a nation which mandates that only innocent and truly worthy victims receive sympathy. Fearing the interpretation of stories like Wendy's as a story of kids lost to drugs and poverty as a result of "bad parenting" or a "broken home," I felt it was important to understand the constraints of their parents' hard-living lives as well and the lack of resources they themselves had grown up with.

Family values is a reincarnation of an old theme, namely, the "culture of poverty." This thesis (originally articulated by Oscar Lewis in 1959) suggests that certain personality and value differences among the poor arise out of the very conditions of poverty and then act to perpetuate that poverty. While this logic comes out of a liberal tradition of seeing society as at fault for the problem of poverty, it is too often taken up as the need to change the values of the poor, rather than to change the social organization that causes poverty. In actuality, if poor people behave differently, this does not necessarily mean their values are different than those of the middle class. Indeed, their values and goals may be the same, but they lack the necessary resources to achieve them and must make various adaptations. Pierre Bourdieu's argument that there is a causal relationship between cultural capital and class reproduction, that class culture is determinative of class future, is sometimes misread as a culture of poverty argument. But like Joseph Howell (1973), who suggests that hard-living is not desired, but rather a response to the difficulties of trying to acquire a settled-living life with few resources, we should see hard-living culture not as a "set of *preferences* or *wants*" that are consciously devised, but as "practices" (à la Bourdieu) or "culturally-shaped *skills, habits,* and *styles*" that inform action (Swidler 1986, 275, emphases mine). Culture as values, as consciously held beliefs, is an impoverished understanding of culture; an anthropological conceptualization of culture as the lifeways of a people that are the consequence of the conditions to which they must adjust, is analytically richer. Employing this latter definition of culture, describing cultural capital as causal, differs from a culture of poverty argument, which takes the focus away from social structural constraints on people's lives and puts it on "dysfunctional" or "pathological" values that are presumed to be passed down generationally, so that, once again, the focus is on changing people instead of changing the social organization that produces poverty.[7] Culture, then, might be better understood, not as values and morals, nor merely as ideology or ideas in people's heads, but as the deployment of *cultural competencies* that make sense or have a degree of logic in a given context. A useful corrective to culture of poverty arguments is achieved by focusing on the structures of exclusion (Lamont 1992) that the middle classes engage in rather than on the failure of the poor based on their supposedly inferior beliefs and values.[8]

While among settled-living whites there appeared to be few feelings of empathy for hard-livers, there did seem to be more empathy among settled-living Mexican Americans for hard-living members of the Mexican-American community. There were moments when socially conservative settled-living Mexican-American girls made judgments about the hard-living members of their community, but those judgments were much less harsh, mediated by a discourse on racism as a causal explanation for hard-livers' plight. It may be that these Mexican-American girls were simply more cautious about articulating their judgments in front of me, feeling the need to maintain solidarity in the face of a white person, but nonetheless, "family values" was not a discourse I heard as commonly among Mexican-American students, who seemed much more forgiving and much more likely to associate the problems of hard-livers in the Mexican-American community with racism and poverty than with values.

ON LIES, A.K.A. PASSING

I began to see half-truths, like Wendy's possibly fictional boyfriend, as a strategy of status attainment and class resistance. The teacher who had arranged for me to meet with Starr said, "I've tried to encourage her, you know. And earlier in the year she was receptive. I had her redo some assignments she'd failed, and she did them. I asked her what she planned to do after high school, and she told me she got accepted to the University of California and also one of the California State schools. But I know that can't be. I've looked up her grades and course work, and there is just no way she could've gotten in. But nonetheless, that's what she keeps telling me. 'I'm going to UC.' " The teacher looked to me for a possible interpretation of this. I was in an awkward position when teachers revealed information to me about students, because I could not return the favor, having promised the girls confidentiality. What adults intended as encouragement was more often interpreted as pressure by hard-living students. In Starr's mind, the lie was a way to get this teacher off her back and to save face in front of peers in the classroom.

Over the course of the school year I caught girls in several "lies" and then began making sense of this. One topic on which this happened with some frequency was parents' jobs. I learned of parents' occupations from girls who did not always know exactly what it was that their parents did for a living. They always knew where parents worked, but often no more than that, and generally did not know how much money their parents made. They just knew that they worked, because that's what parents did. Some girls even said they had never really thought about it before I asked. I remember myself, when asked by a teacher at the vocational school I attended what my father did for a living, responding that I didn't really know, and so she asked if he was white-collar or blue-collar. Having never heard of this distinction before, I took it literally: "Well, the shirt he wears everyday is blue, and it has his name on the pocket." Other girls were well aware of what kind of work their parents did and felt an associated stigma. They revealed an awareness in their talk of the prestige scale of occupational titles. When I first met Blanca and asked her what her mom and dad did for work, her head dropped in silence. A few seconds later she lifted it with a big smile and said, "My dad's in sanitation." Esthela scoffed, "He's a garbage man!" Blanca said she did not know what her mom did. Although I asked repeatedly, she always claimed not to know. It wasn't until months later than she finally was willing to tell me her mom did janitorial work in a factory. When it was Yolanda's turn, she said that her single mom "works driving truck. But that is just for now, while she's goin' to school."

Employers often assist us in making jobs sound more important and prestigious than they might otherwise seem by using job titles that sound more desirable than the actual work and pay involved. As Kim proudly told me, "I'm a sales associate at Toys 'R' Us," which meant she ran the cash register. Sam listed her mom's occupation as "photographer." I knew her family was low-income, so I thought perhaps her mom might be an educated starving artist sort. But it turned out that in fact she took family portraits at Sears in the evenings to supplement her full-time job "doing clean up" at the convalescent home. Mexican-American girls described their parents as "farmers," but they were known to white members of the community as "field laborers" or "farmworkers." White students understood a "farmer" to be a landowner who employed farmworkers. Parents who were labeled by students as "managers" and "supervisors" turned out to be folks who had been working at a business since high school (or had even started while still in school) and who through seniority had become working managers. As Yolanda explained her dad's job, "He's a manager." When I asked where, she said, "He manages or heads up a group of farmers." I asked, "So then he tells them what work to do?" Misunderstanding my statement of clarification as a judgment, she said quickly, "Well, yeah, but then he helps them. He doesn't just sit there or anything. He decides what they all should do next."

Awkward moments of cross-class interaction, like the one between Allison and Tara, were most telling. In a conversation with Shelly and Marla, who I mistakenly thought were friends but as it turned out were only acquaintances from a shared class at school, I began asking questions about their respective parents' occupations and education. After Marla listed her parents' occupations as a "special ed. teacher" and "a nurse," Shelly said her dad "drives truck," and her mom has worked various jobs as "a hair stylist" and a "nurse's aide." When we switched to the topic of education, Shelly wasn't sure if her parents had attended any schooling beyond high school. But after Marla listed her parents' college degrees, including her father's graduate degree, Shelly began insisting that her parents, too, had received college degrees, while Marla looked curiously at her and then to me, expecting me to challenge Shelly's account.

CLASS AWARENESS

While differences that manifested as a consequence of class were too often internalized and understood in individualistic ways, there were times when working-class students expressed a rather keen awareness of the class privileges preps took for granted. Working-class students could articulate a sense of unfairness and expressed awareness and hostility toward middle-class cultural difference and assumptions. One example was when Wendy expressed her belief that her accomplishments, albeit very different from preps, deserved an award, an acknowledgment. Sometimes students expressed an awareness of status differences by massaging information about their parents. On one occasion, I asked Starr about the difference between her friends and "preps."

> *Starr:* The rich kids seem to be normal. Into football or whatever. They are treated better 'cause they are into school activities and

stuff. The poorer kids don't get treated bad, but, um, they are not as, um, pub—[hesitating] . . .

Julie: What were you going to say?

Starr: Publicized. But I'm not sure that's the right word.

Starr recognized her own invisibility. Though aware of these differences, and aware of their sense of place in a school and community hierarchy, only occasionally did girls define this in terms of class. Starr explained that many of her friends went to Landon Elementary, which is "the Mexican and lower-class school just 'cause of the neighborhood it's in. It's by Bain Street, where there ain't many white people." She then defined lower-class for me as "people with lower incomes, who only went to high school."

Tara's awareness of class difference was informed not only by her contacts with preps at school but by a boyfriend's family. I asked about the differences between his and her families.

Tara: They're rich. He taught me how to drink high class.

Julie: What does that mean?

Tara: You know, drinking wine with food or something. His dad is a lawyer. His mom don't work, but she's constantly on you about stuff. Like you had to eat right. I ate there sometimes, and she yelled at me for licking my knife. I kept forgetting, and I almost did it again. She looked at me like "Don't you dare, you motherfucker." Her closet was full of shoes. She had so many shoes.

Julie: Can you give me more examples of the differences?

Tara: I don't know. I can't explain it. I just didn't like how they were. I think I just hate rich people.

Following a convention of focus on women's consumption as the most despicable evidence of class difference, women's fashion came up repeatedly in the words of working-class performers as a marker of difference, and women's shoes, in particular, often represented indulgence. I asked Shelly about the difference between her family and Marla's.

Shelly: Well, our house is kinda small. It's three bedrooms but still small. Marla's house is huge, you know, and her mom and dad drive newer cars. When you go over to her house, you have to take your shoes off to walk on the carpet, when the carpet is there to get dirty. I mean you're supposed to walk on it, right? And her mom has in the bathroom all this stuff, Clinique everything, Estee Lauder, and shoes for every outfit. She has Birkenstocks in every color, at least fifteen pairs. When I go to their house, I feel like I can't sit anywhere you know, and her mom makes me feel so scummy, like I'm a loser or I'm dressed all wrong.

Julie: What about your friend Barbara? You said that her family kinda had more money than yours, but I remember you said you liked her mom.

Shelly: Well, yeah, they do have money, but she doesn't *act* like she has money. She's more like my mom. She just dresses casual, you know. Their house looks kinda like ours. And I have another friend whose mom does nails for work. She must have a lotta money 'cause it costs a lot to get your nails done. But she doesn't act rich either. She doesn't say, "Should I talk to you or not." The way preps act is stuck up. They look at you and ignore you based on how you look, what clothes you wear. Kids with money brag about it, that they are going to go home and get money from mom. "Can I have ten dollars?" "Yes." Others can't get any.

Aside from the difference of money, Shelly's words pointed to a cultural difference of class. Marla's professional middle-class mom made her uncomfortable where Barbara's mom, whose income derived from a successful welding shop she and her husband ran, was more familiar to Shelly. The focus in these girls' comments is on mothers, and their description of class difference revolves largely around women's consumption practices (both fashion and home decor). Women, it seems, are more visible targets for class envy because of their association with consumption. The class villain here is not the father who, no doubt, earns the greater part of the money, but the mother whose consumption practices work as status markers.

Likewise, prep girls were an easier target of class antagonism at school, as their concern with fashion and their appearance made them more visible targets than prep boys. Many girls commented that in the economy of style at the school "boys kinda all look the same," which was not entirely true, but the differences among girls were much more noticeable. Preps were hated because, in short, they seemed to have it all. They had romantic capital in the form of nice cars, the expensive versions of the latest fashion trends, and beauty to the extent that money can buy it (professionally manicured nails, trendy haircuts, athletic club memberships for fitness, high-quality cosmetics, etc.). They were pretty in an expensive way, and almost all white boys at school were open to their flirtations because interacting with them was an opportunity to borrow status. At times prep girls, in particular those who easily met normative standards of beauty, were defined by working-class performers as "sluts." While I had expected working-class girls to be defined as overly sexually active, it was at first a surprise to hear preps described as such. But in the preps-as-sluts theme I came to see working-class performers expressing class envy, as they singled out preps for an extra amount of disdain. Preps became the victims of rumor, as class antagonisms were at times displaced and played out in the realm of heterosexual relations.

AUTHENTICS AND POSERS

As Tara, Wendy, Nick, and I walked through the center of the school after leaving the award ceremony, we passed some preps that I knew, who avoided my eye contact as I walked with this crowd of smokers. We stopped uncomfortably (for me) near the preps when we ran into some more friends. Nick, still worried about the hick boys' threat to fight him, exclaimed, "I can't wait to get out of this fuckin' place! And I'm going out with style. I'm gonna wear a bright orange tux to my prom. And my date will wear an orange dress. I don't care how much it costs. I'll find the money. No, I'm going to wear the dress and she can wear the tux." Tara took this discussion of fashion as resistance as an opportunity to brag that although her parents were making her go to a cousin's graduation that weekend,

> I'm going to wear my condom necklace. It's a Catholic school. I spent the whole night figuring out my wardrobe.

The smokers' style was intentionally confrontational and defiant. It was, by their own and others' description, an amalgam or hybrid of punk, grunge, and rocker. While the logic of these styles includes an attempt to present oneself as anti-fashion ("preps are trendy and have to look like everyone else"), in reality much thought went into smokers' intentional attempts to offend the sensibility of middle-class teachers and preps. Nick's plan to wear an orange dress to the prom, Tara's condom necklace, Todd's artistic rendering of two frogs fried together, and Wendy's arm engraved with her boyfriend's initials were badges of dignity within the smokers' economy of style.

This kind of rejection of what is "mainstream" or "popular" (which meant whatever style and music and leisure preps were into) and choice of "alternative" expressions actually existed on a continuum at the school. Within the large mass of students known as "others" were some who also considered themselves as outcasts of a sort, but in a very different way. These were settled-living girls who, though not preps, were still far removed from the cultural life of the smokers. One of these girls, Vicki, explained to me:

> We were preps in junior high. We wore our Keds and Guess jeans. We were in the student government.
>
> *Julie:* Why aren't you anymore?
>
> *Dawn:* When we got to high school, math got hard. And the preps showed up from other junior highs.

These girls explicitly named themselves as "alternative" and "different," and when I asked alternative or different from what, they were very clear: "the preps." Like the smokers, they too recognized their lower place in the hierarchy and embraced it as a fashionable identity. In short, they purchased style that was co-opted, commodified, and marketed for mass consumption by the culture industry as "alternative." In the current moment this was baggy skater style for boys and Seventies retro for girls: hemp necklaces, occasionally inconspicuous tattoos and piercings. Where smokers rejected schooling altogether, skaters were headed for junior colleges with the explicit hope of transferring to four-year schools. This was usually because they were unable to complete all the state school requirements and/or because they could only afford JC tuition. They envied the educational route to class mobility that the preps took for granted at the same time that they rejected it for a stylistic "cool." They distinguished themselves from the Gap fashion of preps. They showed up at events organized by the student government, but then acted too cool to be there. In short, they still had middle-class aspirations. Despite the hostility they sometimes expressed toward the preps, they did not reject prep values wholesale. They were just injured by the fact that they had to compete with preps who had a head start. After the fact of their exclusion from prep circles, they rejected preps and saw themselves as victims of social ambition. Tami, for example, was "sad my friends are all getting letters saying they are going to state schools." And Dawn explained she "really wanted that going-away-to-college experience." Their unabashed desire for it, in spite of the failure to achieve it in the timely way that preps would have, is notably different from the smokers, who are far further down on the continuum of rejecting schooling. In fact, the skaters saw themselves as the mainstream, distinct from both preps and smokers.

As I sat behind the school with a group of smokers who were skipping gym class one day, a group of skater boys walked by, appearing confident and cocky with a sense of entitlement, as if to say "We own the place." They wore oversized baggy shorts, long shirts, baseball caps worn backwards. Immediately annoyed by their presence, Nick started in, "Man, they are such assholes." While skaters wore brand-name skater shoes like Etnies, Airwalks, and Vans, the smokers were more likely to wear Vans-look-alikes from Kmart. Where skaters took their skateboards in their cars to drive to places to skate, smokers were more likely to use skateboards as primary means of transportation. There was a clear class antagonism here, but the smokers didn't articulate it as such. They were more likely to frame it as one of stylistic encroachment by the "others," which they resented, defining themselves as authentic and the others as posers. As Tara explained, rolling her eyes:

> They think they made it up, this way of dressing. Like it's something new. We were doing this a long time ago.
>
> *Julie:* What do you call your style?
>
> *Tara:* I don't know. We used to be the rockers, a long time ago. Then we were the punks, but there's not many punks left. Now I don't know what we're called.

The symbolic economy of style at the school was the ground on which class relations were played out among white students by making claims to stylistic authenticity. Claims to authenticity and accusations of inauthenticity worked to symbolically heal class injury. As it turns out, class displacements and class awareness are really two sides of the same coin; differences in style worked as a way to displace naming the difference of class, but simultaneously were a mechanism through which students recognized class differences. When I asked about class differences among students, one counselor offered, "Well you sure can't tell by the way they dress." In her mind all students dressed poorly, and their choice to dress down was understood as a matter of youth culture, a generational difference. It was easy to miss the subtleties of the distinctions that students took as important in their peer hierarchy, and the availability of cheap versions of high-status commodities did work to hide distinctions for adults at times. But students knew, and they employed fashion to create and solidify distinctions among themselves. The particular symbolic economy at work in Waretown is potentially generalizable to other small-town/rural California communities, but not necessarily beyond. Each setting contains its own set of codes informed by the interaction between its specific geographic location and demographics and the sea of popular culture we all swim in. And while the meaning of signs varies by context, I would suggest that class remains a present, but usually unarticulated element, in all sites.

I recognized one of the skaters who passed by us that day. I had spoken with him early in the school year, before I had met the smokers and fully identified the distinctions that were so important among them. Given his attire I had guessed wrongly and asked him if he was one of the crowd that hung out behind the school. Offended that I mistook him as such, he scoffed, "Who, them? Oh no, they're white trash."

WHITE-TRASH CHOLA

"Poor white trash" was used with surprising frequency to describe the smokers, perhaps reflecting its increased use in popular culture over the past few years.[9] As I have commented elsewhere (Bettie 1995), the category says much about common-sense understandings of race/ethnicity and class. Whiteness is usually an unstated but assumed racial referent (when race is not mentioned, whiteness is assumed), so when it is present, it reveals much. The phrase "poor white trash" suggests that color and poverty and degenerate lifestyle so automatically go together that when white folk are acting this way, their whiteness needs to be named. That is, it is a racially marked category used to describe those who are not performing whiteness (read, normative middle-class whiteness) appropriately. If people of color are, in racist fashion, assumed to always already be trash, either because of innate inferior difference or because of culturally learned difference (i.e., culture of poverty), then hard-living white folks are a failure to the "white race." The presumed inherent superiority of whiteness, as well as the ideology of upward mobility, is challenged by the existence of white trash, and thus the difference of class as class is made visible; poor whites are evidence of the existence of class inequality apart from race. How can one explain white people who behave this way except by acknowledging the existence of class difference per se?

Unlike Mexican-American students, white students, for the most part, did not explain class differences among themselves in racial terms. Rather, class difference was articulated as individual difference (she's "popular" or she's a "loser") and as differences in group membership and corresponding style (hicks, smokers, preps, etc.). Nonetheless, class meaning did at times remain bound to racial signifiers in the logic of white students, as it did among Mexican-American students. This was apparent in the way some white hard-livers worked hard to clarify that they were not Mexican. Tara explained to me in our very first conversation, without any solicitation:

> I'm kinda dark, but I'm not Mexican.

In our conversation about her boyfriend's middle-class parents, she said that his mother had "accused me of being Mexican." She explained to me that she was Italian-American, and her color and features did match this self-description (though it is also certainly possible that there are family secrets she may or may not know). Her father, a poor man, had worked in the fields for a time and drove what she called "a Tex-Mex truck," which was "one of those old beaters like the Mexicans in the fields drive." I couldn't help but think that her defensiveness about her racial status was linked to her class location and further that her class location assisted her boyfriend's mother's assessment of who Tara was, as much as coloring did. In short, Tara seemed to experience herself as "too close for comfort," so to speak, and she made it clear every chance she got that she was not Mexican.

Similarly, Starr, who grew up near Bain Street in a Mexican-American neighborhood and went to the elementary school in town which was largely Mexican-American, also had the sense that some whites, those who were at the bottom of the heap like herself, were almost brown. We were talking in the lunchroom one day about girls and fights when she told me this story:

> *Starr:* Well, the worst one was back in junior high. All of my friends were Mexican, 'cause I went to Landon. So I was too.
>
> *Julie:* You were what?
>
> *Starr:* Mexican. Well, I acted like it, and they thought I was. I wore my hair up high in front you know. And I had an accent. Was in a gang. I banged [gang-banged] red [gang color affiliation].
>
> *Julie:* Were you the only white girl?
>
> *Starr:* Yeah.
>
> *Julie:* What happened? Why aren't you friends with them now?
>
> *Starr:* We got into a fight. I was in the bowling alley one day with my boyfriend. They came in and called him a piece of white trash. That made me mad, and I smacked her. Lucky for her someone called the cops. They came pretty fast.
>
> *Julie:* What did she mean by white trash?
>
> *Starr:* Welfare people. He was a rocker. Had long hair, smoked.

This episode ended her chola performance, and she was part of the white smoker crowd when I met her. Like most other girls, Starr had told me that girls fight primarily about "guys," but her actual story reveals something different. Yes, a boy was central to the story, but the girls were not fighting over him. Rather, her chola friends were bothered by her association with him, which pointed to her violation of the race-class identity she had been performing as a chola. Her friends forced her to make a choice.

Starr's race-class performance was a consequence of the neighborhood in which she grew up, and like Tara, she had absorbed the common-sense notion that white is middle, brown is low, and, most interesting, that low may become brown in certain contexts. Not unlike the experience of middle-class cholas for whom being middle-class Mexican-American felt too close to being white, Starr's working-class version of whiteness felt too close to being Mexican-American in this geographic context. Girls reported that cross-race friendships were more common in grade school, but in junior high a clear sorting out along racial lines emerged (and along class lines too, although with less awareness). Starr's story is about junior high girls working to sort out class and color and ethnicity, about the social policing of racial boundaries, and about her move from a brown to a white racial performance (where both remained working-class). Not insignificantly, her white performance included a racist discourse by which she distanced herself from Mexican Americans with derogatory statements about them.

Understanding Starr's chola performance as a cultural appropriation would be oversimplified. Such an interpretation is suggested by the discourse on "wiggas," which is present both within youth culture (posers, wannabes) and in media accounts, whereby white (and by some accounts middle-class) youth appropriate what is marketed in popular culture as black style. Blackness is currently ubiquitous in pop culture, more present than it has ever been historically, and has become synonymous with hip-hop (Gray 1995). Indeed, in spite of the near absence of black students at Waretown, "blackness" was ever present in their youth culture, represented, for example, in a sign announcing a school dance, which read "Dance da nite away dis Friday afta da game!" Everything youth do occurs in the shadow of popular culture, which glorifies and romanticizes the defiant style of youth of color and black youth in particular. White students' appropriation of black popular culture may be more common, in part, because Spanish-speaking popular culture is less accessible to most white students. In any case, Mexican-American signifiers do not carry the same currency in an economy of "cool" that black (read, hip-hop) ones do, at least not among white students. Starr says she didn't understand her Mexican performance as a choice, an attempt to be cool. Yet in her choice between trash and chola identity, perhaps the latter did have more romantic appeal. Nonetheless, hers wasn't an appropriation of a commodified image, devoid of context. Rather, social geography and the ways in which self is shaped by the degree of class and racial/ethnic homogeneity or diversity in one's community seem salient to Starr's identity options:

> I didn't really think about it. Those were just who my friends were. Who I grew up with. There wasn't really anyone else around.

EXCEPTIONS TO THE RULE

While most of the smokers were from generations of hard-living, working-class families, there were some exceptions. Kate's parents were college-educated middle-class people. Her dad worked as an insurance adjuster and her mom as a nurse. The money and cultural capital that could provide her entry into the prep crowd was available to her. As we sat in the grass talking one day, Kate explained:

> Everyone out here is a reject. But not all for the same reason.
>
> *Julie:* What are the reasons?
>
> *Kate:* Most of 'em are poor and some have family problems. No one's popular.

We had been talking earlier about an anonymous article in the school paper in which a student had written about homophobia in Waretown and about being in the closet. I asked if she knew who it was and if being gay was a reason some of the students were out here on "misfit island." She smiled.

> No, that's just me. Oh, and Mike too. I guess some of the others might be, but just don't know it yet.

I asked Kate if the difference between her parents and her friend's parents ever mattered, if her friends thought she was a poser.

> No, not really. Well, sometimes. When people come over to my house they say "Man this is nice, you're loaded." I don't bring people over much. And then I got the car [nodding her head toward a new, shiny blue, dent-free Honda Accord

> parked on the street behind us], and so that was different from them.

Kate had to negotiate her chosen public identity at school with the inherited sense of place received from her family of origin. She selected a race-class performance that was incongruous with who she "really" was. She reinvented herself early in high school and chose new friends who she anticipated would be less judgmental and who themselves felt as marginal as she did, less than normal, albeit in a variety of ways. She explained that the only rule for membership "out here" was "not to judge." Wendy had indicated this the day I asked if she thought it would be okay for me to come hang out with them, if I would be accepted. "Oh, yeah," she said, "everyone will be okay with it. As long as you don't tell us to put out our cigarettes or criticize us for anything else." These students persistently felt the weight of judgment from the world, and their space out here on the margins was a respite.

Kate's class transgression was not without consequences. Like her new hard-living peers, her class performance meant that she did not take college-prep classes, and consequently she was unsure about her future upon graduation. Not unlike middle-class cholas like Ana and Rosa, Kate began with the cultural and economic capital that could lead her more easily to a secure future than many of her peers, but her working-class performance at school foreshadowed downward mobility. She may or may not receive the economic support of her parents, who she believes "are not homophobic" but "might be when it's their kid." Both Ana and Kate teach us how non-class versions of marginality, in their cases racial/ethnic and sexual identity respectively, can lead to subordinate class futures.

DISSIDENT FEMININITIES

The smokers' terrain was the place where gender performances were most overtly questioned and played with. Girls' friendships at school were clearly organized around the version of femininity they performed. Some of the smokers rejected conventional femininity, and this was manifested in their choice of punk style. Punk, a subcultural style with its roots among white working-class youth in Great Britain, is readily recognized there as an articulation of class consciousness, but it is also a style that signifies a rejection of normative conventions of femininity and masculinity and, at times, heterosexuality. Within this sign system, conventional ideals of feminine beauty are rejected and parodied. Makeup is not used "invisibly" to hide flaws, but rather is worn to be highly visible—on all genders—or not worn at all. Likewise, hair dye is designed to be obvious, intentionally revealing dark roots and bleached blond ends or done in neon colors like orange, blue, and green, or jet black.[10] Given the lack of class awareness in the United States, it is punk's gender transgressions that are perhaps more salient to U.S. youth, and to girls in particular.[11] For all girls, "it is the regimen of dress codes and restrictions on hairstyle and application of makeup that often first exposes girls to gender contradictions. Girls learn that buying and wearing particular clothes is a highly-charged activity that situates one's own desires against a host of social approval ideologies" (L. Lewis 1990, 94). Tara hated what she called "foo-foo girly stuff," and Kate said she'd "die before wearing a dress." Both girls' style worked to mock the conventional trappings of femininity. As Lisa Lewis puts it, "the desire to dress like a boy is an early form of resistance to the physical and mental restraints that gender definitions seek to impose on girls. As girls age and experience physical body changes, they discover relationships between modes of displaying the body and social response" (94).

Sam and Starr on the other hand did follow the conventions of femininity, and their gender performances were highly sexualized. As Lewis notes, "the femininity pigeonhole is opposed symbolically in two usual ways: 1) through affecting an appearance and behavior based on the male adolescent discourse, 2) through exaggeration of the codes of feminine appearance and mannerisms that frequently cross over into sexual display" (1990, 94–95). In short, both these sets of girls rejected school-sanctioned femininity, the kind of femininity that school officials encourage, but also "manage" (Hudson 1984). But their resistance manifested in at least two different kinds of gender performance. While one was dissident in its overt display of feminine sexuality, its goal to subvert adult authority and "send school authorities reeling" (Lewis 1990), the other was dissident in its rejection of both school-sanctioned femininity and femininity per se.

These two manifestations of dissidence existed across the clique structure. Among cholas, for example, some displayed a highly sexual femininity, much like las chicas, but others' style emulated boys', wearing oversized men's pants and loose shirts that did not accentuate breasts, waists, and hips. A less feminine gender performance does not, of course, necessarily signify lesbian sexuality and was not read that way by students. Both appeared to be understood as an acceptable range of heterosexual female gender performance; girls who chose a less feminine style were not subject to the same homophobic commentary that boys whose gender performances fell outside of hegemonic masculinity were.

FUTURES

Both hard-livers and settled-livers came from families with low educational attainment and the related lower income. But whereas the parents of settled-livers had managed to acquire a degree of stability, hard-livers told family stories of hard luck. Recurring themes were illness, disability, and death, and when such hardships occur in the context of making a living on low-wage jobs with few benefits, there is little to cushion the fall. One girl's single mom died in a car accident, which left her children to bounce from relative to relative. Another girl's mom and dad were struggling to support their own family on two low-wage jobs with no benefits when his former wife was injured and confined to a wheelchair and they had to begin supporting her and her children as well. Another girl's parents simultaneously lost jobs in the timber industry when the mill closed, and then both died early of alcoholism, leaving the children to foster care. Many girls had dads who were disabled Vietnam veterans; one who suffered from post–traumatic stress disorder was on and off drugs and was finally murdered in a drug deal gone wrong. One girl told of family hardship that resulted from the unique support required to care for a brother with mental illness; another of a grandpa who moved in and required support after a stroke. Some told stories of generational abuse: "My dad's dad used to beat the shit out of him. It's hard for me to imagine it, 'cause, I mean, I know my grandpa. He's old, and I can't think of him doing it, but I know he did." This girl had suffered in earlier years at the hands of her father in turn.

Smokers had little to look forward to. As Tara succinctly put it, "My life is shit." College was not in their futures, and jobs requiring only high school diplomas (barely achieved) do not pay a living wage and offer no benefits. Their futures were visible in the lives of older siblings and peers. As Lana said, "I don't want to end up like my brothers." One worked in a car wash and the other at The 98 Cent Store. Other peers and siblings worked at convenience stores, the convalescent home, a laundromat, and various other odd jobs about town. Some supplemented their incomes by selling drugs.

As I stood talking in the lunchroom with Starr, she occasionally glanced up at the school janitor across the room and feigned sweeping the floor around the tables with the broom she was holding. She had been given three hours of detention for missing too much school but could earn her way out of it through lunchroom duty. It was the last month of school, and we were talking about her future plans. She was not yet sure if she had completed enough credit hours to graduate and was waiting to hear on this from the counseling office.

> I want to stay in Waretown 'cause I have a friend whose uncle belonged to the carpenter's union, and he said he could get me in as an apprentice 'cause he said they need women. But Mel is gettin' out next week. He's full of jailhouse promises now, but I don't believe him.

Mel, an old boyfriend who had physically abused her and against whom she had a restraining order, was in prison for violating the order but was about to be released. Starr feared him and felt she needed to leave town in order to avoid him. She planned to leave the hour after the graduation ceremony—if she graduated.

Wendy sauntered up. She was waiting to hear whether she'd passed a competency test required to graduate. Near the end of the school year emotions ran high as students suffered the anticipation of the futures ahead of them. The way in which smokers' refusal of schooling helped to symbolically heal their class injuries at the same time it worked to secure their lowly place in the class hierarchy was never more clear. Wendy was surprisingly honest about how she was feeling:

> I hate this place. I want to do something with my life so bad, but I know I never will. Art is the only thing I like. I'm not good at anything else, and everyone here is better than me. I just want some-money and to have the things I like. Fuck school.

On the last day of school, we sat along the sidewalk, our backs against the chain link fence, passing the lunch hour smoking and signing the yearbooks that two or three of them had bothered to "acquire" (but not necessarily buy). Wendy chuckled and read aloud what Todd had written in hers: "See you at the welfare office."

Better off than smokers, settled-living white girls are more likely to find stable futures and even college educations, but if it happens, it will be through a long circuitous route, beginning in community colleges or vocational schools. In high school already many of these girls are struggling to catch up. Vicki, for example, who works a good thirty to thirty-five hours per week combined at two fast food restaurants, described her life.

> *Vicki:* I used to have pretty good grades, you know. I had a kinda high GPA before. But this year I just, I don't know, I guess I'm lazy.
>
> *Julie:* What is a typical day like?
>
> *Vicki:* Well, after school I go home and clean up the house some and find something to eat for me and my little brother—'cause Mom don't get home until 6:30 or so. But then I go to work, and get home around ten. So then I try to do my homework. I probably go to bed around two.
>
> *Julie:* Maybe you're not lazy, but tired.
>
> *Vicki:* Yeah, maybe! I mean before my senior year I didn't work so many hours, but now I'm trying to save for college. But then my GPA started dropping, and I failed this one math class I needed to get into college. And so now I take that math class at the community college two nights a week to make up for flunking it. And then I just found out I didn't get into State anyway. I am kinda feeling bad [embarrassed] 'cause I see other people getting letters saying they got in to state schools. I really wanted to go away to college. I saved really hard and bought a car so I could go, but now it has some problems and isn't running. Doesn't matter now, since I'm stuck here anyway.

Dawn was openly resentful:

> I just don't get it. I thought your senior year was supposed to be so much fun. I'm not having any fun. All I do is work all the time.
>
> *Julie:* What do you do with the money you make?
>
> *Dawn:* I been saving for JC. I didn't apply to the state schools because I didn't want to pay the fifty dollars for the applications. I didn't want to ask mom and dad [a stepfather] for it either. I know they've been trying to save money so they can move, 'cause right now he commutes a long way to work. And my real dad, he's not so good about paying child support, so I didn't even bother asking him.

Several boys and a handful of girls planned to enter the military. For many girls this was not an option because it conflicted too much with their gender identity; Tara, on the other hand, thought it would be great because "I'd get to wear combat boots." Like Dawn, many students routinely revealed an awareness of their parents' financial struggle and made decisions accordingly.

> *Liza:* I'm going to join the army because then they pay for you to go to school.
>
> *Julie:* Could your parents have paid for you to go to college if you wanted to?
>
> *Liza:* Yeah, well, they could've helped. But the thing is, I have two little brothers and a little sister, and so I know that they are going to have to help them out too. So I figured I'd just do this on my own. Hope there's no war.
>
> *Jessica:* I checked that out, going into the navy. But I heard you have to go live in a submarine for two weeks, and there is no way I'm going down there. I saw *The Deep*. That thing is down there! I'm going to business school!

Many settled-living girls were somewhere in between the college-prep and non-prep tracks, taking classes from both. When I asked Tami if she had taken the course work to get into college, she said:

> Well, I started out taking 'em, but we're kinda poor. 'Cause my dad just gets disability and mom's job doesn't really pay much. I'd have to pay my own way. So then I kinda stopped worrying about getting all the courses you need, 'cause I didn't think I could really go anyway. But I did take some of those classes this year, just in case I could get to go somehow.

Settled-livers were the most confused about their class identity. Often quick to distinguish themselves from the smokers, they knew also that they were not quite the same as preps, but were not always clear why. Unlike the smokers, they didn't reject school wholly, yet they were frustrated by the inequality they experienced in relation to preps regarding college and work futures. There are multiple ways in which class remains discursively invisible while its effects are felt. Class is variously displaced, and the injury for both hard- and settled-livers is that without a discourse of class their own lives, and their parents' lives, can only be understood as a consequence of some personal inadequacy, an individual failure.

Like las chicas, both hard- and settled-living white girls had cynical attitudes about family futures. They were full of stories about fathers who had cheated on mothers and ruined marriages, sending moms into spirals of downward mobility; of fathers who failed to pay child support; of fathers who were described as gruff and indifferent at best and abusive at worst. Their own experiences with male peers were too similar and included boys who shirked the responsibility of an unplanned pregnancy. These girls wanted and needed economic equality, whether inside or outside of heterosexual relationships, but sensed this would not come easy.

CHAPTER 5

Border Work between Classes

Many school ethnographies are comparative studies of students across class categories and make generalizations about the experiences of middle-class students and of working-class students.[1] In order to speak about these class categories as if they are two clearly distinct peer groupings, one must ignore many students who are exceptions to the rule that class origin equates to class future. While the correlation is strong between parents' socioeconomic status and a student's membership in a middle- or working-class peer group, tracking experience, academic achievement, and consequent class future, it is imperfect, and there are always at least a handful of working-class students who are college-prep and upwardly mobile and a handful of middle-class students who are on the vocational track and downwardly mobile. Nonetheless, because research generally tends to highlight patterns, such cases are typically ignored, precisely because they are exceptions to the rule.

White girls from middle-class families who were downwardly mobile at school were very rare. Kate was one such girl, and her own account of herself suggests that her sexual identity as a lesbian might have directed her friendship with the most marginalized poor white kids, who construe themselves as misfits of various kinds and who she believed might accept her more readily. Another girl, Leah, was also from a middle-class family but hung with a working-class peer group. She explained her location there in terms of her mother's alcoholism and verbal abuse. The disparity between her family life and that of her high-achieving middle-class counterparts, who she assumed all "have perfect families," was too much to negotiate. She felt more comfortable among a crowd in which difficulties at home (substance abuse, domestic violence, and economic hardship) were not unusual.[2]

Middle-class Mexican-American girls who were downwardly mobile, like Ana and Rosa, were more common. Students' constructions of identity vary by context, meaning that racial/ethnic categories often have different meanings in different settings (Matute-Bianchi 1991; Hemmings 1996). Given the particular racial/ethnic composition of this school, middle-class Mexican-American girls had to negotiate what felt like a contradiction: being simultaneously Mexican-American and middle-class in an environment where such a social location was rare. These girls were vulnerable to accusations of "acting white," to tracking by virtue of color and ethnicity, and to the variety of institutional barriers that impinge on academic achievement for students of color—social forces that increased the likelihood that, in spite of their class advantage (parents' economic and cultural capital), they might become downwardly mobile working-class performers, members of a working-class peer group who were without plans for college and headed instead toward low-wage jobs in the community. The fact that students of color from middle-class origins are more likely to be represented in working-class peer groups than are white students of middle-class origins points to the continued salience of race/ethnicity for academic achievement when holding class constant.

In this chapter I want to focus on those few girls, both white and Mexican-American, who were from working-class origins but who were upwardly mobile middle-class performers in high school, en route to achieving a university education, and to ask what we might learn from their exceptionalism. Foregrounding these exceptions to the rule, I explore what their experience might reveal about the way in which race/ethnicity and gender, as autonomous axes of social inequality, intersect with class.

There are two main questions about these girls that are of interest. The first obvious question is *why* they are exceptional. The answer would be welcomed by educators and policy makers who wish to shape educational and broader social policy to increase the educational success of youth who are typically considered "at risk." I looked for reasons for each girl's exceptionality, why they desired to and were able to perform class identities other than their own. In fact, the reasons seemed multiple and varied, but some patterns can be identified, which I offer here as tentative explanations for why these girls are upwardly mobile, as I have done for the downwardly mobile middle-class girls we've met like Ana, Rosa, and Kate.

The other question is *how* they do it. How do they negotiate the disparity between the working-class identity acquired from home and the performance of a middle-class identity at school, the disparity between their family lives and the family lives of their middle-class peers? What is the subjective experience of class passing, of "choosing" upward mobility and all that comes with it? While the question of causality is difficult to answer and my analysis should be considered exploratory and limited, given my small sample, this second question is more readily answered given my ethnographic methodology.

WHITE GIRLS: CONTINGENT ROUTES TO MOBILITY

I met Staci during a slow day in the yearbook class. Most of the students were working on various aspects of pulling that year's annual together, but Staci felt she needed to put her energy elsewhere on this day and was headed to the library to look up some information for a history paper due at the end of the week. Staci's membership in the prep crowd was unusual, given her parents' economic and cultural capital. Her father worked "doing maintenance" at a retirement community. But the fact that her mother worked for a time in the kitchen at the private elementary school in town enabled Staci to receive a subsidized private school education, and she ran with the most academically elite crowd of girls at the school.

Like Staci, Heather had also attended private school but not with a subsidy, and it was difficult to understand how her parents could have afforded it. Her father worked as a mechanic and her mother as a nurse's aide. Between them they were nearing middle-income, but most Waretown families in this category were not sending their kids to private schools. As I pushed for a clearer explanation, she indicated that her parents experienced great financial sacrifice in order to send her to school, even borrowing money from relatives, but they felt it was worth it. According to her, her parents wanted to segregate her from "bad influences." This turned out to be a euphemism for Mexican-American students.

Likewise, Jennifer told me that while her parents had been able to afford to send her to private elementary school, they could not afford to send her brother too. Instead, they arranged for him to attend school in a neighboring town, and, once again, the reason was to avoid "bad influences." When I pressed her for the meaning of this, she hesitated before describing her brother.

> *Jennifer:* He's, um, he won't admit to being prejudiced, but he doesn't like Mexicans. He thinks they should all go back to their own country, and he's very, like, I don't know, he's just very opinionated, very traditional like my dad, he just, I don't know.
>
> *Julie:* So he doesn't like going to school in Waretown because there is . . .
>
> *Jennifer:* Mexicans, and he doesn't, and I know he'd get in a lot of trouble if he was here. And, plus he swims, and the swim team at the other school is better. And it is just a better education there.

The neighboring town was composed of primarily white residents and was mostly middle-class. Many working-class whites with jobs in the town could not afford to live there and commuted from other, more working-class towns nearby, like Waretown.

Mandy was also college-prep, although her membership among these girls was even more difficult to explain. She had not attended private elementary school yet did reasonably well academically in junior high and managed to get in with the prep crowd by high school. When I asked her why she was not friends with the kids from her neighborhood and what motivated her academically, she readily articulated a self defined in opposition to her older brother. As she explained,

> My brother, um, actually had his first child before he graduated from high school. After he graduated, they got married, and he joined the navy to support them. I can remember being at my aunts' and uncles' houses, and they're all talkin' about my brother and me and what's gonna happen to us. And even my cousins, they used to have bets on if I was gonna get pregnant by fifteen or sixteen. I was kind of destined to fall into my brother's footsteps, and so I think that ever since I was ten years old, my goal was to prove everyone wrong. I was gonna graduate, I was gonna go to college, I was gonna make something big, and then I was gonna come back and say, "Well, look what I did." When I entered high school, my family started realizing that I was gonna do something whether they wanted me to or not. All of the sudden I started getting this support, and it was like, you know, "You might be the first one of the family to actually do something."

Heather had a similar story:

> My brother, Ray, he's a hoodlum. He dropped out of high school. He had lots of problems with drugs and alcohol, and after he dropped out of school, he had a really rough time. My mom, when he left the house, she just cried. It was, it was something that you just did not talk about. She rolled with the punches the best she could. I just saw them [my parents] in so much agony about him the whole time. He was such a rebel. I felt bad for them. He put them through so much.

Later, she added,

> I'm an angel. I do my schoolwork, don't get into trouble. My parents have had enough of that.

At times, then, an individual girl's academic motivation seemed to come from defining herself in opposition to older bothers who were labeled delinquent and who, as the girls had witnessed, caused their parent(s) angst. It seemed that feminine norms sometimes allowed girls to forgo the delinquent paths their brothers might have felt compelled to follow as working-class boys, the need to engage in rituals of proving masculinity. I heard this story frequently enough, among both white and Mexican-American girls, that I began to suspect that working-class girls might experience a certain advantage over their male counterparts as a consequence of being girls. The social pressure for girls to conform and follow rules as part of the definition of femininity makes it a possibility that they might do better in school than working-class boys, for whom defining manhood includes more pressure to engage in risk-taking behavior and overt resistance to control. Girls may not only be less likely to engage in such activities but are relatively less likely to be labeled and punished as delinquents if they do (although this was somewhat less true for Mexican-American girls). That working-class girls might actually do better academically than working-class boys is a possibility easily missed by those taking an additive analytical approach to race, class, and gender as social forces. Such an approach would simply presume that girls' educational experiences and opportunities are in all cases "worse" than boys', rather than exploring the unique set of challenges girls face. Even if working-class girls do have higher academic achievement than their male counterparts (and this is unknown), the possibility of pregnancy and the fact that jobs for women with only a high school degree pay less than those for men with the same degree mediates and inhibits girls' mobility in the long run.[3]

Liz articulated yet another route to mobility. When I asked how it was that she came to be a part of her college-prep friendship circle, she explained that early on she discovered that she was good at basketball, and it was through this sport that she met and began to spend time with girls who were far more privileged than she was. Through association with high achievers, she was exposed to information that helped her get ahead. Overhearing conversations about college requirements and college-prep courses made her aware of the existence of two tracks of schooling and what she was missing out on. She clung to a middle-class girl, Amber, her best friend, hoping, it seemed, that she might "catch" the middle-classness Amber took for granted. Unable to name her desire as class envy, she simply said, "I'd like to be in a situation like that."

But I would expect that sports as a route to mobility was more common for boys than girls, given that high schools tend to offer more support for male athletics and that boys are more likely to choose athletics than girls. For some girls, being athletic still conflicts with a feminine gender identity, just as did the military option, which has historically worked as a route out of poverty for working-class boys.

WHITE GIRLS: BECOMING UPWARDLY MOBILE

Common among those girls whose families were much more working-class than the families of their closest friends was their nascent awareness of the difference between these class cultures. Class is a relational identity; awareness of class difference is dependent upon the class and race geography of the environment in which one lives and moves. While the community of one's formative years and schooling experiences, in particular, may be key shapers of one's perceptions of class difference, awareness of one's location in a class hierarchy is an ongoing and context-specific process. Beverley Skeggs (1997), in her semi-autobiographical book, explains that because her childhood was spent in a class-segregated community, "My first real recognition that I could be categorized by others as working-class happened when I went to university. . . . For the first time in my life I started to feel insecure. All the prior cultural knowledge [capital] in which I had taken pride lost its value, and I entered a world where I knew little and felt I could communicate even less." The working-class, upwardly mobile girls I met, by virtue of their location in mixed-class peer groups, had an earlier awareness of class distinctions, although they did not often name those differences as such.

In other words, upward mobility might occur at various points in life. As they acquire cultural and economic capital at different ages, upwardly mobiles begin passing in middle-class contexts at different times. Where Skeggs only began passing upon entry into college, some of the girls I knew began in junior high, and those with private school educations, in elementary school. Given that Staci has been part of a middle-class peer group since her private elementary school education, even though she is from a working-class family, her experience of college will likely be far different than the one Skeggs describes for herself. How comfortable one is performing a middle-class identity might in part depend on how long one has been doing it and how much time has passed for advantages to be gained from upward mobility, thus making the experience of working-class upwardly mobiles difficult to generalize about.

Another factor in the variability of class experience is geographic location. Most people tend to believe that school curricula are fairly standard across the country. While we know that not all students will *learn* the same things, we too often assume that everyone is *exposed* to the same set of knowledges (Oakes 1985). As Jeannie Oakes shows in her 1985 study of tracking, this is clearly not the case. Students are exposed to very different knowledges, not only as a result of which track they are assigned to, but also as a result of the geographic location of their school. In working-class communities where the majority of the student body is not expected to attend college, a school may offer a stronger vocational than academic curriculum. In Waretown, the children of farmworkers attended the same high school as the children of landowners, but the latter were, of course, a smaller population. The majority of high school graduates (70 percent) did not go on to attend four-year institutions, and Waretown did offer a strong vocational curriculum.[4]

Geographic variability shapes the likelihood of class mobility. Being working-class and attending a well-funded school with a middle-class clientele where a curriculum of knowledge that is highly valued by society is made available is a far different experience than attending school in an isolated working-class community where the mere exposure to a college-prep curriculum is limited. Upwardly mobile girls from Waretown will likely develop an even greater awareness of class difference when they leave this agricultural community behind.

Due to their location in a college-prep rather than a vocational curriculum, these upwardly mobile working-class girls at times showed a clearer understanding of the fact of class differences than did their vocational counterparts. Liz was one of very few students I met who actually named herself as "working-class."

> *Julie:* You said you were "working-class" earlier. Where did you get that term, what does it mean?
>
> *Liz:* I learned it in a social science class or maybe in history. Working-class is like the serfs you know, the working-class are the majority, blue-collar versus the college-educated.

It is ironic that Liz learned this in her college-prep curriculum, and this raises the question of what it might mean for working-class students (especially those located in the vocational track who will continue to be working class) to become conscious of themselves as class subjects, to learn labor history, for example. Even the smallest exposure to knowledge of class as a structural inequality might aid those students who can only see their status as linked to their own and their parents' individual inadequacies, because this is all the U.S. ideology of individualism offers as an explanation for economic inequality. As we've seen, working-class vocational students were obscurely aware of their difference from college-prep students, but never articulated it as clearly as Liz did.

Unlike working-class girls who were segregated in vocational tracks and so were rarely in mixed-class settings or peer groups, those working-class girls who were middle-class performers were not *as* mystified by the success of preps. By virtue of crossing, they could see the advantages and privileges their middle-class friends experienced. They were more acutely aware of the cultural differences based on class, as they found themselves exposed to the children of middle-class professionals in the college-prep curriculum, on the basketball court, in student government, and in middle-class homes. They could see the reasons why they had to work harder, and they were less likely to attribute friends' success to some innate difference between them.

Unlike vocational-track working-class girls, who were often unclear about the differences among community college, state university, and UC (including prestige differences), and unclear on the distinctions between various kinds of certificates and degrees available, these working-class girls who were early middle-class performers had come to understand these distinctions through exposure to the college-prep curriculum and friends who took such knowledge for granted. When I asked Mandy if her mom and dad had gone to college, she said:

> No. Dad was in the army, Vietnam. Now he works as a postal clerk. My mom, well, I argue this with my mom all the time. She's convinced she went to college. And I'm not convinced she did. She went to junior college and got an associate degree. She calls this college, but I don't. I mean it's just a certificate, she's a secretary. I'll be the first one in my family that's ever gone to a four-year college.

These girls also perceived that they had to work exceptionally hard to earn their high school diploma and to get into college relative to their middle-class friends. As Staci said,

> They've always been kind of handed everything, that they've never really had to think about their future, and I was always, like, I don't want my future to be like my parents. And, I mean, that was like a big influence on me, I mean, my goal is I don't ever want to have to worry about money, like we have all my life. My friends never had to deal with that or anything and, it's just like everything has always been handed to them, and they, I mean, they never knew anything else.
>
> I want to go to college and get a good education so I can have a better life, and they have always had a good life. I work my butt off, but it just seems easier for them. It's just always everything has always kinda been there for them.

When I asked Liz (working-class) and Amanda (middle-class) whether they considered themselves good at school, Amanda modestly offered "pretty good," while Liz shook her head "no."

> *Amanda:* No, you are too.
>
> *Liz:* Well, I'm not. She is an amazing writer, and I mean sometimes she'll have a lot of fun in class, but she, I mean, she's an A student all the way. Everything she does is—
>
> *Amanda:* When I do my work, I do okay, but I'm a procrastinator, and I don't apply myself.
>
> *Liz:* When she applies herself, she is like great.
>
> *Amanda:* But Liz's good. She works hard at it.

In a later private conversation, Liz expanded on her perception that Amanda could afford to be a bit reckless about school, procrastinate, and still do alright. She felt that Amanda took much for granted that she does not. Liz, working incredibly hard to stay on top, feels she has no room for occasional slip-ups the way she believes her peers do.

Moreover, these girls were aware of the fact that they exceeded their parents' educational level early on, and they perceived the fact that their parents were unable to help them with school as a handicap. As Mandy explained,

> Ever since I've been in honors classes, I've always been around these people, you know, their parents have advanced degrees and everything else. My parents were never able to help me out with math. Once I entered algebra, that was it, that was as far as they could help me. I remember one time in this one class we had this project, we had to build something. One girl's father was an architect, and her father designed and basically built the entire project for her. We all had these dinky little things, and she's got this palace!

Later, however, she attempted to define her parents' lack of education as an asset.

> I mean, I was never mad at my parents because they couldn't help me. I was actually happy, because once we get to college, you're not gonna call your parents up and say "Hey, Dad, can you design this for me?" You're on your own then. And so I've always had to work on my own with my schoolwork, it was always on my own, whereas other students, they always had their parents standing right there, you know?

Simultaneously distancing from and connecting to parents was a common theme in the discourse of these upwardly mobile working-class students. On the one hand, they wanted to point to the importance of mobility, while on the other hand they did not want to degrade their parents by suggesting they sought to become someone other than who their parents were. Such a desire to distance themselves from elements of working-class community while remaining close to and respecting their parents was a difficult process to navigate and often left them speaking in contradictions. They experienced some confusion and ambivalence when they realized that their own desire for mobility implicitly might mean that something was wrong with who they and their parents are now.

These middle-class-performing working-class girls were also readily able to see the differences between their own parents and those of their friends. They were painfully aware of the fact that their friends' parents viewed their own parents with indifference at best, disdain at worst.

When I asked Liz, whose mother works in retail, if she and Amanda's parents knew each other, she said they did and then went on,

> Well, but my mom is not *friends* with her mom. They [Amanda's parents] are not rich snobs, like in New York or something, but her mom would see someone who helps her in a store as, well, just a clerk in the store. My mom would be [willing to be] friends with her mom, but I think her mom would be less accepting.

When I asked Mandy about what differences she perceived between herself and most of the students she takes courses with, she noted,

> In an honors class once, the teacher asked how many of us had parents who went to college. All but me and two others raised our hand. I know people think differently of me, [shrugging] but oh well.

I sat next to Heather at a girls' basketball game one evening. She was sitting on the bleachers with the rest of her prep friends, front and center, cheering on the team, many of whom were part of their peer group. She kept glancing at the corner of the gym where several adults were standing, people who had come after halftime (when admission was free) to watch for a few minutes but weren't committed enough to staying to take a spot on the bleachers. I asked her if she was expecting someone, and she whispered, "My dad said he might stop by and check the score. I hope he doesn't." In a later conversation she said,

> Well, just, um, my family is a lot different than my other, my friends' families. Just because my friends' families are real formal, and they are, like, a lot, I don't know, a lot different. Like my best friend's dad owns the bank, and they always have nice things, and it's like, I don't know. I've been embarrassed, especially of my dad, a lot, just 'cause he's a real hick-like kind of guy, wears those kind of clothes, I don't know. All growing up, I was embarrassed of him, and I didn't want to take him anywhere. They are just different from a lot of other people's parents.

Where I first thought the idea of her father attending the game represented the standard embarrassment teens experience in relationship to having their parents near them at social events, I recognized later that its meaning went beyond this for her. In the middle-class milieu of the school, some parents are more embarrassing than others.

MEXICAN-AMERICAN GIRLS: CONTINGENT ROUTES TO MOBILITY

There was a small group of Mexican-American girls, mostly second-generation but also including two girls who had immigrated, who were from poor and working-class families and who were exceptional in that they did not identify with the cholas or las chicas but rather were middle-class performers on the college-prep track.

Like their white college-prep counterparts, they performed school-sanctioned femininity, wearing little or no makeup and less sexualized or dissident clothing than working-class performers. Teachers perceived them as modest and tasteful, their demeanor as "nice," not "hard," and they were very involved in school activities, although different ones than white preps. Although cholas and las chicas were distinct peer groups, these Mexican-American college-prep girls linked the two in their minds because both enacted dissident versions of femininity and a race-class performance that represented being in or at least allied to gangs. They participated in and took leadership roles in other activities like MESA (Math, Engineering, and Science Achievement program for minority students), EOP (Early Outreach Program), AVID (Advancement via Individual Determination program), Ballet Folklorico, the organizing of the annual Cinco de Mayo dance, and similar programs and activities.

As with the white girls, it is difficult to account for upwardly mobile Mexican-American girls' exceptional status, but there are a variety of enabling conditions for each of these individual girls' mobility. Although the experience of exceptionalism that these girls articulated in some ways paralleled white working-class girls' accounts, in other ways the two groups' experiences diverged, revealing the racial/ethnic specificity of their early mobility experiences.

Like Liz, Adriana's location in the college-prep curriculum seemed in part to be linked to organized sports. She showed a talent for soccer early on and received much support for it from home, because her father was a big fan. ("Soccer is always on our TV," she said. "He gets cable just for the soccer.") Adriana's friendship group in junior high thus included many of the college-prep girls who tend to dominate organized sports. Like Liz, through association with preps, she experienced the benefit of the privileged treatment by teachers and counselors that is often reserved for college-prep students. But while she was friendly with these girls in the classroom and on the playing field, she primarily located herself in a peer group of other working-class Mexican-American girls who were middle-class performers.

Like the white working-class girls, these girls at times told stories of defining self in opposition to delinquent brothers. When I asked if she was going to go to college, Adriana said,

> Yeah. That is my hope, because all my brothers have let my dad down. My dad was like, he really like was hoping that, he thought they would, you know, be somebody, you know. It's like a lot of pressure on me to be someone, you know, not like my brothers. And I know I can do it. I mean, I want to do it, but you never know what's going to happen.

But more often they told stories of older siblings as the source of help and inspiration to go to college. Usually, but not always, these older siblings were sisters, generally an older sister who had finally managed, through a long and circuitous route that included junior college and many part-time and full-time jobs, to attend a four-year school. The older sisters sought to help their younger sibling manage more easily by advising them on the importance of getting the courses required for state university or UC admission done in high school (rather than in junior college), on taking SAT tests, and on filling out applications for financial aid and admissions on time. Luisa had two older sisters attending state schools, and she had been accepted to three university campuses. I asked her if her mother had encouraged her to go to college early on.

> *Luisa:* No, my sister did. She kind of like, she's the one who encouraged me.
>
> *Julie:* Your mom didn't?
>
> *Luisa:* She doesn't really want me to go away. She's not really educational. She doesn't really, I don't know, I guess, understand what college, you know, is all about.

When I asked her if she had understood the differences between attending a junior college versus a state university or UC school, she said,

> Yeah, just from my sister. She always taught me what, you know, she's the one who told me what the differences were, and she helped me figure out that I wanted to go to UC, because I didn't want to go spend two years at a JC and [then] like go for four more years, because I thought that was like a waste of two years."

Although Angela did not have older siblings guiding her, she clearly saw it as her job to help her five younger siblings. When I asked her about her social life, she said,

> Well, I don't spend time like I used to, with friends so much. My family, my little brothers and sister are more important than friends. They need to get ahead. And I don't want them to get behind or something. I want to help them do well.

Because she had so many younger siblings to help, who took energy away from her own schooling and who would need to use the family's economic resources, I had doubts that Angela's college dream would be realized, but it seemed likely that her siblings would benefit from her sacrifices. Indeed, this was a factor for Victoria, whose mobility was fostered by having older siblings—much older, in fact, since her mother was forty-two when Victoria was born. Not only were these older siblings able to advise her, but by the time she was ready to go to college many of them were established and could help her financially.

In short, older siblings who were the first in the family to go to college turned out to be important sources of insider information already known to students whose parents were college-educated, providing cultural and social capital not available from parents, and at times economic capital as well.

Two of the girls in this middle-class performing group were immigrants, and explaining their exceptionalism requires other considerations. These two girls were fluent enough in English to be able to complete college-prep courses. The remainder of immigrant girls in the senior class were on the vocational track. Many authors have noted the greater educational success of immigrant students compared to their second- and third-generation counterparts.[5] It was Waretown school counselors' subjective impression that immigrant students "do better" in school. However, precise statistics were not kept, and there are so many variables to account for that it is impossible to say if this is true for certain. For example, does saying immigrant students "do better" mean that they have a higher rate of graduation and/or higher grades? Are those grades and graduation rates linked to an academic or vocational curriculum?

A limitation of my own study is that, since I am a monolingual English speaker, I only studied fully bilingual and English-speaking girls, which meant they were almost entirely second- and third-generation. With only two immigrant girls in my study, I am unable to make generalizing comparisons between the experiences of these two college-prep immigrant girls and their vocational-track counterparts. But the fact that I met only two college-prep immigrant girls in a senior class of nearly five hundred is telling. If immigrant students in general were doing well at Waretown, they were doing so in the vocational, not the college-prep, curriculum.

One explanation for the achievement of these two immigrant girls is that their parents had some other benefits and resources that enabled them to be more mobile than their vocational track counterparts. In her work on the educational mobility of low-income Chicana/os, Patricia Gándara (1995) asks not why low-income Chicana/os fail, but why those who experience class mobility succeed. She suggests that "family stories" can work as a kind of cultural capital for these students. The people in her study told stories of coming from families that were well-to-do or had achieved high levels of education in Mexico, or of families that had lost their fortunes—and so their status and financial well-being—in fleeing Mexico because they were on the losing side in the Mexican revolution.

When I asked Lupita, who had immigrated at thirteen, had quickly learned English, was an academic star at the school, and had been admitted to several University of California campuses, why she was different from the other students in her neighborhood, she explained that while their families had immigrated from rural areas of Mexico, her family had come from an urban environment where there was greater access to education. In fact, she had an older sibling who had received a college degree in Mexico.

> The majority of the immigrant families, they are totally farmworkers. In Mexico they used to work on farms, they used to work in the fields, so they came, and they are having the same work they used to do, right? So it's like their lives, they didn't change as dramatically, because they came to the same work they were doing. They used to live in little towns where they didn't have high schools there. If their kids wanted to go to high school, they would have to go to another town where they have high schools. So, I mean, they're used to that, you know, they're used to saying, "Okay, high school is the top thing that you're going to get because we have no more way to get any more education for you." And I think the difference is that we [her family] used to live in a big city where we had all the facilities. And, I mean, my brother, he's a college graduate. So it's been like a tradition in my family to go to school.

And Angela reported that her family had been well-to-do in the United States before they were deported:

> My grandparents owned property here. They were well off. After the war, my grandfather had to come back across the border and start from scratch all over again.

Employing Bourdieu, Gándara suggests that in telling these stories to their children, mothers, in particular, transmitted a disposition toward schooling and the future that worked as cultural capital for their children. In other words, having a structural rather than an individual explanation for one's class location, such as the history of colonialism and institutionalized racism, assisted some working-class students' success. Family stories "represented the creation of a history that would break the links between the parents' current occupational status and their children's future academic attainment" (1995, 55).

Gándara also speculates that some of the family stories may not be true, or are embellished, but points out that their truth or falsity is at some level irrelevant to the purpose that they serve, which is to create a positive perception of oneself and one's family and engender in children a sense of hopefulness and deservedness that might otherwise be absent. The stories establish individual and family worth by suggesting that "We don't really belong in these circumstances, it is a mistake, and in fact we do have intrinsic worth despite appearances." Consistent with this, Lupita described grandparents who were property owners in Mexico and explained that there was a family dispute over this property when the grandparents died. In her mind, her family's current state of poverty was only because of this dispute.

In part Gándara is engaging the same questions as does Jay MacLeod (1987) who, while in no way diminishing the importance of structural variables, also considers the role of aspirations in either enabling or restricting mobility. In some cases, working-class black boys in MacLeod's study had higher aspirations than did their white working-class counterparts. This was, in part, because black students believed that while things were especially difficult for their parents' generation, they themselves would reap the benefits of being educated in a post–civil rights era.

MacLeod's research was done in the early 1980s, but in the 1995 edition of his book he finds that these black students' aspirations were dashed by their experience in the job market after high school, suggesting that a latter generation of black students may be less naive about the effects of the civil rights movement, as their lives clearly represent to them that the status of black Americans is characterized not by a linear progression upward but by peaks and valleys. Likewise, the girls I studied were fully aware of the fact that the status of Mexican-Americans was not on a linear progression upward and that their lives might not be any easier, even given the Mexican-American civil rights movement. In just the past five years, they had witnessed the passage of three ballot measures in California that put clear brakes on the possibility of mobility for Mexican Americans. Proposition 187, passed in 1994, took social services such as public health care and public school education away from undocumented immigrants. Proposition 209, passed in 1996, eliminated affirmative action and thus encouraged other states to do the same. Proposition 227, passed in 1998, formally ended bilingual education in the state of California, re-igniting an English-only movement that spread throughout the country.

I began to identify an "immigrant orientation" (Ogbu and Matute-Bianchi 1986) that existed among some girls, regardless of whether they were immigrants or not, meaning they employed as a mobility strategy the belief in the classical immigrant story of using education as a route to the American dream of upward mobility.[6] As Gándara explains, some of the people in her study, even some who were second- and third-generation Chicana/o, "behaved very much like recent immigrants in their transmission of a hard work / education-as-a-mobility-strategy ethic" (1995, 112). This group of working-class college-prep students engaged this strategy, holding out hope for education as their route to mobility, more than did vocational students (cholas and las chicas), who were far more cynical about their ability to achieve success via education. However, these college-prep girls were not blind to the barriers that exist or to new ones that were currently being created by the state legislature. They were in fact, neither duped by achievement ideology or blindly assimilated, but rather were able to hold both hope and a practical cynicism in their minds simultaneously.

If, as MacLeod suggests, working-class students of color at times have higher aspirations than white working-class students, this does not mean that those higher aspirations result in higher achievement; a variety of structural barriers remain in place that inhibit their mobility. In the cases of Lupita and Angela, while family benefits, whether real or imagined, shape student aspirations, they do not dictate outcomes. Lupita did appear to come from an educated extended family in Mexico, and her college-educated sibling provided her with cultural capital that would possibly benefit her. But with five younger siblings, no health care, and a sick mother, Angela remains less likely to reap the benefits of her higher aspirations. Even though she was admitted to a UC campus, she was hoping to attend a nearby junior college:

> That's the only place I can go, because I can't afford to go away.

And when I asked Lupita about her family's income, she explained,

> Oh, you know how Mexican families are, a little bit from here, a little bit from there. My dad pays the rent, mom buys the food, my little brother pays the phone bill, and I'm responsible for the gas bill. My uncles fill in whatever else is needed.

Adriana cannot afford not to live at home, and her family cannot spare her economic contribution to the household.

MEXICAN-AMERICAN GIRLS: BECOMING UPWARDLY MOBILE

As with white working-class upwardly mobiles, these Mexican-American middle-class performers could see the differences between themselves and middle-class preps (mostly white) somewhat more clearly than their vocational counterparts could. But where whites articulated their difference from preps in veiled class terms, Mexican-American girls articulated their difference clearly in terms of race. For example, Luisa commented:

> I think it is harder for Mexican-American students, because I think most white people have, like, money, like their parents, they went to college, and they have money. They have an education. But, you know, I'm not saying, well, you know, it's my mom's fault that she didn't go to college. She could have, you know, but I don't know, it's just, like, that's just what it is, kind of. The white students don't understand because, you know, their parents got to go to college, you know, had an education, they all have jobs.

Like white girls, Mexican-American girls wanted to point to the importance of mobility, yet did not want this to mean that their parents' lives were without value. They thus expressed a certain amount of ambivalence toward mobility and/or the acquisition of the middle-class cultural forms that accompany mobility. This can be seen in Luisa's comment above, where she identifies her mother's limited education but then notes her mother is not to blame for this. Similarly, Adriana said,

> Well, I'm proud of my parents. I'm proud of my dad, because, like, if anybody says anything about their parents, you know, like that, like an expression, "Oh, they went to college," you know, or "They have a business degree," or something like that. Like I'm proud of my dad, you know, he learned just from doing, from life. Being as poor as we were, he, you know, we're like doing good, you know.

Mobility experiences can never be understood outside of their racial/ethnic specificity. Like white working-class girls, these girls were well aware of having exceeded their parents' abilities. But for them the acquisition of middle-class cultural forms also meant becoming bilingual, while their parents remained primarily Spanish speakers.[7]

Where white working-class girls would say generally that they didn't want to struggle for money the way their parents did, Mexican-American girls were cognizant of the correlation between being Mexican-American and being poor and were more likely to name the specific occupations that the poorest people in their community worked and identified their motivation to escape these kinds of work. Angela declared:

> I don't want to be like everyone else, I want to, I want something better. I hate working in the fields, that's not for me, and I don't want to do that. It is minimum wage and I don't want to work for that.

And Adriana said,

> When I think about havin' to work in the fields or cannery, then I get back to studying real hard.

Unlike third-generation girls of middle-class origin who struggled hard in this particular context with being at once Mexican-American and middle-class and who tended at times to buy into the idea that to be authentically Mexican one must adopt working-class cultural forms, the college-prep working-class girls discussed here refused to interpret mobility as assimilation to whiteness and were not apologetic about their mobility; they did not feel any "less Mexican" for being college bound. John Ogbu and Maria Eugenia Matute-Bianchi (1986) suggest there is a difference between students who adopt an immigrant orientation toward schooling and those who adopt a caste-like orientation. A caste-like orientation equates schooling with a loss of racial/ethnic identity (i.e., "acting white") and leads to an adaptive strategy of resistance (often resulting in school failure). Ogbu and Matute-Bianchi argue that this orientation is prevalent among involuntary immigrants or indigenous minorities, while an immigrant orientation is prevalent among voluntary immigrants. Mexican-Americans pose a challenge to this formulation, given that their status as voluntary or involuntary immigrants is ambiguous. The exact reason why some students of color equate educational mobility with acting white while others do not and instead formulate a bicultural identity is unclear. Consistent with my findings here, Matute-Bianchi (1991) found *both* a caste-like orientation and immigrant orientation within the native-born group of Mexican-American students she studied, and she usefully names these as among a number of competing "ethnic strategies."

As Matute-Bianchi explains, this focus on strategies is an alternative to conventional theories that explain achievement in terms of students' levels of acculturation or assimilation. These different strategies each "reflect a different accommodation to the sociocultural context" (1991, 240). This handful of working-class college-prep girls enacted a different strategy than students who experienced or feared school success as assimilation. The former saw themselves as disproving white stereotypes about Mexican-Americans through their hard work and success, and they took pleasure from that. They adopted a strategy of "accommodation without assimilation," meaning that in the face of racial conflict and inequality, they made accommodations "for the purpose of reducing conflict," yet at the same time allowed their "separate group [identity and culture] to be maintained" (Gibson 1988, 24–25). In this formulation it is indeed possible to do well in school and not objectively be assimilated or "acting white." In short, they found ways to reject assimilation without resisting educational mobility.[8] The identities they negotiated for themselves might also be understood as what Gloria Anzaldúa (1987) has described as "mestiza consciousness" and Chela Sandoval (1991) as "differential consciousness," whereby a person copes within a given context, not by abandoning parts of the self, but "by developing a tolerance for contradictions, a tolerance for ambiguity . . . [an ability] to juggle cultures" (Anzaldúa 1987, 79).

The correlation of race and poverty promotes the common-sense belief that middle-class and whiteness are one and the same; as a result Mexican-American students must negotiate educational mobility with the broader social perception that this mobility represents assimilation to whiteness. This assimilation is resisted and gets played out as intra-ethnic tension, as vocational Mexican-American students accuse college-preps of "acting white." These working-class upwardly mobiles did occasionally receive such accusations from their working-class peers, but they interpreted this as a joke, which though painful at times, was not taken as a real challenge, and their racial/ethnic identity remained unthreatened by their college-prep status. Secure in her working-class, Mexican-American identity, Mariana explained,

> I'm not really acting white because look at where I live and who my friends are and what I do.

Mariana lived in a Mexican-American neighborhood, hung out socially with other working-class, but college-prep, Mexican-American girls, and was heavily involved in school and church activities that focused on her community.

What I mean to point to here is the possible salience of class on the formation of a bicultural racial/ethnic minority identity. Research that refuses a class reductionist analysis and gives autonomy to race/ethnicity as a distinct axis of inequality has lent much to our understanding of minority achievement by usefully exploring school success or failure in terms of students' perception of schooling as an additive or subtractive mode of acculturation (Gibson 1988; Matute-Bianchi 1991; Ogbu 1991; Fordham and Ogbu 1999; Valenzuela 1999b). These studies, however, do not address or explore the meaning of class difference between and among students of color as it is experienced in the peer culture, and too often fail to give continued attention to the possible effects on achievement of class difference across race/ethnicity. I don't mean to suggest that class is causal of a student's orientation (caste or immigrant), because I found no clear pattern of class origin correlating with orientation, but I would nonetheless like to suggest that it is worth exploring further whether class meaning might inform students' racial/ethnic-class performances and strategies and shape the experience of racial/ethnic identity. The fact that upwardly mobile students grew up working-class meant that their identity as Mexican-American was consistent with the common understanding of race and class as correlated. Their Mexican identity appeared less challenged (both internally and externally) than was the case for some middle-class Mexican-American girls, whose middle-class status made them appear to themselves and to others as acculturated. This, even though they were not so far removed from Mexican-American cultural forms. Some of their grandparents, with whom they had much contact, were immigrants; their parents were fluent in Spanish; and parents' work (as an ethnic studies professor, a labor lawyer, and a university administrator of minority programs, for example) promoted or at least made available a cultural and political racial/ethnic identity. Perhaps they were not "actually" or "really" more acculturated, but they were more middle-class, and this affected their view of themselves and others' view of them.

Like the role MEChA eventually played for Ana and her friends, the existence of school activities that were specifically linked to the concerns of the Mexican-American community simultaneously taught upwardly mobile students the skills they need to go to college and yet enabled them to maintain their racial/ethnic identity while doing so.[9] Because students were not compelled to interpret their mobility as evidence of assimilation, these programs were experienced as less colonizing. They made it possible for racial/ethnic belonging not to be automatically lost with class mobility. Becoming middle-class requires doing well in school, and for Mexican-American students, doing well in school too often means learning a colonialist history, English, and the suppression of one's own culture (Darder 1991). Schools routinely fail to provide genuine bicultural education, and consequently the curriculum makes it difficult to embrace an identity that is middle-class and Mexican-American at the same time. As Angela Valenzuela (1999b) explains, Mexican-American students go through a "subtractive schooling experience," whereby schools subtract cultural identifications from students rather than adding to them and thus fail to promote bicultural identity as an option: schools offer either/or instead of both/and.[10] Schooling experiences that are not subtractive and colonizing can assist by offering a bicultural identity, the possibility of being middle-class and maintaining a racial/ethnic identity of color simultaneously. Although I have focused here primarily on students' constructions of identity within the peer culture, this, of course, occurs within an institutional context. The influence of the structure of schooling on student identity formation and the responsibility of schools to provide the context for mobility should not be underestimated or ignored. These identity negotiations occur in a society which largely denies both that there is class inequality and that it is correlated with race/ethnicity and gender, and they occur in schooling contexts which often fail to offer the kinds of bicultural identity options that make achievement more likely.[11]

RACE MATTERS

While all of these girls, across race/ethnicity, have not articulated their early mobility as particularly painful, it is likely to become more so as they (if they) proceed into college, which will take them much further away culturally from family and community than mere high school mobility could. Many have written of the pain that working-class upwardly mobile people experience when leaving their community behind and/or the difficulty of finding ways to reconcile the discord between class background and present status due to mobility.[12] This experience differs, of course, for whites and people of color, as racial/ethnic groups of color are more consciously aware of themselves as a community of people because of a common history of colonization and oppression that results from being historically defined as a racial group. Alternatively, an aspect of whiteness is that whites often do not immediately experience themselves as members of the racial/ethnic category "white," but as individuals, and, without a cultural discourse of class identity, they do not readily experience themselves as members of a class community either. Evidence of this can be seen in the way white working-class college-prep girls expressed their experience of and concern over how education was distancing themselves from their parents. They did not articulate this as a distancing from their working-class *community;* their pain was more often articulated in relationship to an *individual* family, not a people. In short, these white working-class girls were not routinely accused of acting "too bourgeois" the way that middle-class performing Mexican-American girls were accused of acting "too white," because such clear language for class difference was unavailable. Their mobility appears less complicated because they are not made to feel that they are giving up racial/ethnic belonging in the process. And while a sense of loss, an unarticulated class longing, may remain, precisely because it is unarticulated, it may be a less salient force. In a way, the lack of class discourse may be either a hindrance or a help for white working-class students. On the one hand, because class is unarticulated, they have only individual characteristics to blame for their class location: their status is a consequence of the fact that they and/or their parents are just "losers." On the other hand, their mobility may be made easier since they did not experience the same intra-ethnic tension or antagonism within their community over the link between mobility and assimilation that Mexican-American girls did.

As we have seen, being brown or black tends to signify working-class in the United States, given the high correlation between race and class. Consequently, for white working-class upwardly mobiles, the class referent is escapable precisely because of their whiteness. For whites, class does not as easily appear encoded onto the body (although it certainly can be and often is).[13] White working-class upwardly mobiles can pass as middle-class more readily. At school, where no one necessarily knew where working-class white students lived or what their parents looked like, their classed identities could be invisible if they worked at it and learned how to pass, as many do. The possibility of, and perhaps ease of, upward mobility for white working-class students may also be greater, given that Mexican-American girls were more likely to experience tracking as a consequence of counselors' perceptions and stereotypes. The correlation between race/ethnicity and class means that counselors are likely to assume that brown students are from low-income families (even when they are not) and therefore to make assumptions about what educational resources they need and can handle. White working-class students can escape tracking more easily because their color does not stand in for or signify lowness.

As I sat with las chicas one day, perusing an old yearbook, they laughed at their sophomore pictures, noting how much more "hard core" they looked then. These photos would have been taken just after junior high, when counselors help guide students into vocational or academic tracks. Because of an inability on the part of the school personnel to recognize the racial/ethnic specific meanings of their dissident femininity (which included darker makeup and clothes that overtly displayed sexuality), these girls, who were in many ways no different from their middle-class performing counterparts, were assumed to be going "nowhere." It is no surprise that they ended up on the vocational track.

The experiences of these girls reveals that, in order not to be vulnerable to tracking, a Mexican-American student has to be phenomenally good academically, perform a school-sanctioned femininity that signifies middle-classness to school personnel, and have no transgressions or slip-ups along the way.

EXCEPTIONS PROVE THE RULE

I have pointed to various reasons for the exceptionality of upwardly mobile working-class girls, noting the racial/ethnic specificity of their experiences. Much of what I found about Mexican-American girls is consistent with previous work done by Gándara (1995). She points to several contingencies that lead to Chicana/o mobility, such as students working extra hard to get themselves de-tracked from the vocational curriculum, the geographic location of schools (attending a predominately white and/or middle-class school where there was greater access to a college-preparatory curriculum), positive peer group influences, positive sibling influences, social isolation as a consequence of an illness or some stigma, phenotypical differences,[14] the ability to maintain a dual identity, parental encouragement (especially from mothers), and parents' preserving children's study time by forgoing the children's economic contributions to the family.

I found some similarities between working-class white and Mexican-American girls' experiences in relationship to both questions I posed: Why does mobility occur, and how is it experienced? Both white and Mexican-American girls defined themselves in opposition to an older male sibling. Sports as a route to mobility seemed to exist as a possibility for those girls whose gender performance did not conflict with athleticism. There is some evidence that working-class girls, across race, may be more academically oriented than their male peers. Both sets of girls were aware of having exceeded their parents' academic abilities early on. Both experienced some confusion and pain around the distance between themselves and their parents on account of this, although this was experienced in a far more dramatic way for Mexican-American girls. As a consequence of their location in a college-prep curriculum, both sets of girls seemed to have a greater understanding of class differences compared to their vocational counterparts, although this was articulated obscurely in class terms among white girls and almost solely in racial terms among Mexican-American girls.

As expected, I found important differences between white and Mexican-American girls' experiences as well. Not surprisingly, racism informed white working-class mobility; two white girls articulated their parents' desire for them to be segregated from Mexican-American students. The greater salience of race over class in a society that lacks a discourse on class means that white girls' mobility is less encumbered in some ways than for Mexican-American girls. Mexican-American girls, in contrast, are pressured (though not necessarily successfully) to sacrifice racial/ethnic identity by educational curriculums that routinely work to colonize their Mexican identities, but at the same time, the girls may be pressured from their peer group not to "act white."

Comparing white and Mexican-American upwardly mobile girls' exceptionalism instructs us on how class intersects with other social forces and how this intersection informs the reproduction of inequality. My comparative approach has enabled me to point to similarities and differences between white and Mexican-American working-class possibilities for mobility and thus to demonstrate how gender and race/ethnicity as autonomous axes of social inequality inform class formation and to expose how class is lived out in gendered and racialized ways.

The differences between the experiences of working-class white students and working-class students of color are especially important to point to in a moment when, in a most peculiar fashion, conservatives have, through California's Proposition 209, appropriated a discourse on class and used it to help dismantle the need for affirmative action based on race/ethnicity (a topic I will return to in chapter 6). Alternatively, I would argue that we need an analytical and political focus on class, but not at the *expense* of gender, sexuality, and race/ethnicity. Indeed, attention to these other social forces and axes of inequality is key to an enduring and successful class-based politics, a global class politics that is sorely needed as we enter the twenty-first century. Although affirmative action without attention to class is *liberal* policy that is of little help to the mass of working-class students (white and of color) who are tracked out of a college-prep curriculum in junior high and earlier high school years, affirmative action based on race/ethnicity *can* help this handful of exceptions, upwardly mobile working-class girls of color, making sure that these qualified students meet with educational opportunity. But affirmative action based on *both* race/ethnicity and class could help create both racial/ethnic and class (across race/ethnicity) diversity in higher education and produce some mobility.

Both middle-class girls who were working-class performers and working-class girls who were middle-class performers show how class can be conceptualized as a performance, as something that can be put on and accomplished. At some level these girls were consciously choosing to pass, to perform an identity which they did not see as their own. Certainly the working-class girls knew that, based on who their parents were, they were not expected by the school to be college-preparatory.

But, of course, class-passing down is far different than class-passing up. And there is a great difference between middle-class girls who rejected middle-class cultural forms, like Kate and Ana, and their working-class counterparts who did not have parents' middle-class cultural and economic capital to reject in the first place. That is, it is one thing to "perform" working-class identity if you have middle-class cultural capital and quite another to be working class and trying to acquire the cultural capital that even allows you to pass as middle-class. These are not parallel experiences. I was struck by how incredibly hard these working-class girls were working. Their desire for mobility came at a cost. They did not have the social life that is considered to typify the high school experience. Mariana had been very involved in putting together the Cinco de Mayo dance, an extracurricular leadership activity that is an advantage in packaging oneself for college admissions, but she was not there for the dance itself. The next day in school I asked her why, and she explained that she was behind in her school work and couldn't afford the time. These girls' lack of leisure time paralleled their parents' working lives. They worked extra hard to catch up for all they had missed out on compared to their middle-class counterparts. And of course this difference in experience will matter in later years, when they share the same college classrooms with and are evaluated by the same standards as middle-class students.

Aside from conscious passing, or class as a performance, at another level these class identities were performative: the girls were in the process of acquiring cultural capital and a middle-class habitus and *displaying* that outside of a conscious *choice* to pass. On the one hand, these upwardly mobile working-class girls were on occasions passing as middle-class. But, on the other hand, the experience of a college-prep curriculum really did give them academic skills that helped them refashion a class identity and enable their mobility. In short, they displayed a bicultural class identity as they inhabited a space in-between, a state of becoming; class performance/passing *becoming* class performative. But they also lived in a state of longing: longing for both class mobility and a return to the familiar comfort of their class "home." That home is, of course, experienced differently across race/ethnicity, as it is also an ethnic home.

In the end, although these girls, as upwardly mobile working-class students, represent exceptions to the rule that there is a correlation between class of origin and educational attainment, this does not mean that class can be dismissed or rendered insignificant as a social force. The fact that these girls are exceptions, that there is a variety of individual contingencies that resulted in their mobility, serves to prove the rule. These girls represent a small fraction of the working-class girls at the school, the majority of whom were vocational-track students who will not escape a working-class future. Gándara reminds us of the necessary link between these individual circumstances and structural opportunities. Any of the contingencies that were in play for these girls "would not have been sufficient if these subjects had not also met with opportunity" (1995, 113).

Finally, these working-class girls' acquisition of cultural resources is no guarantee that upward mobility is an automatic outcome for them. Their high school mobility buys only a limited degree of certainty about entrance into the middle class. Outside of the most exceptional academic performers who could win scholarship money, family income and a willingness to accept the burden of student loans ultimately shaped the decision on which college to attend or whether to go to college at all.

CHAPTER 6

Sameness, Difference, and Alliance

I began my relationship with Waretown girls seeking to understand the ways in which class subjectivity is constructed in relationship to gender and racial/ethnic identity in historical context. As I traveled among the various groups of girls at Waretown High, there were days on which similarities among them seemed ever present and days on which difference abounded.

Apart from the handful of upwardly mobile working-class girls, the exceptions to the rule, it was hard not to notice that the mass of vocational-track working-class students across the difference of race/ethnicity—las chicas, skaters, hicks, cholas, and smokers—had something in common. This was their use of gender-specific commodities to negotiate and construct differences between themselves and college-prep students. Through these commodities they created styles and practices that worked as alternative badges of dignity; they made overt claims to adult status; and they invoked various kinds of claims to authenticity (racial, subcultural) as a strategy to heal various injuries of inequality. Though narratives of romance were routinely absent from the accounts that those girls who performed a sexualized version of dissident femininity gave of themselves, their styles were routinely interpreted by others as a preoccupation with heterosexual romance. Both school discourse and social science discourse narrowly interpret these girls' trajectories to be a consequence of gender-subordinate learning when, in fact, their racial/ethnic and class locations shape their lives as profoundly. In the end, their very rejection of prep femininity helped entrench them in their class futures.

Across their differences, girls revealed an inarticulate awareness of class at the same time that they displaced class onto other discourses of difference. Because they lacked a discourse of class, they often invoked a discourse of individualism, blaming themselves for their lot in life. They could see the difference that money made, but differences in cultural capital were more obscure to them: their parents valued education but lacked the cultural capital to assist them; talk of their futures made them anxious and depressed, as they were aware that middle-income working-class jobs were unavailable. Settled-livers, more likely to view themselves as middle-class, were more confused about how class shaped their lives than hard-livers, and they were all cynical about boys and family futures as a method of ensuring economic stability, expressing a nascent desire for economic autonomy. They suffered from their institutionalized exclusion via tracking. For Mexican-American girls tracking was, of course, shaped dramatically by color and ethnicity. Moreover, they experienced yet another sense of exclusion: a curriculum that routinely rendered their culture, language, and history invisible.

"YOUTH IN CONFLICT"

But these working-class girls' shared marginalization across race did not result in any kind of awareness of their similarity to one another. These groups of girls, who usually spent their time in the lunchroom during pep rallies and other prep celebratory functions and whose names were missing from the "wall of fame," viewed one another as "others," and a would-be lunchroom alliance was unlikely. There was, however, at least one occasion on which a dialogue among these various groups resulted in a momentary sense of commonality. It was during a non-prep English class, one that was often taken by students who had failed other English classes and that was unfortunately titled Youth in Conflict. The class had read the book and then watched the movie of *The Outsiders,* and this spawned a discussion of social groups at Waretown High. Representing all non-prep groups at the school, these students jointly realized that what they shared was the part of their self-definition that was in opposition to middle-class performing prep students.

The opportunity to politicize issues of inequality, which occurred in the discussion that day, was a rare occasion for vocational-track students. Among working-class performers, the awareness of "place" and the cultural and economic differences linked to it did not often result in a political consciousness, and this was in part due to tracking. Given their vocational course work, non-preps across race had little opportunity to learn, in a schooling context, about a variety of political issues or to be encouraged to judge and compare them and articulate a position. Over the school year, as I wandered from college-prep courses to vocational courses, I saw that middle-class-performing students were routinely expected to learn about social and political issues (albeit uncritically) in college-prep courses in government, English, speech, and social science, while this was simply not a key part of the vocational curriculum. Further, middle-class students much more often described parents who read newspapers, watched the news, and discussed politics. I noted the sad irony that middle-class students who had an "interest" in a more conservative political position were more politically articulate. So when I asked preps their opinion on affirmative action or welfare, they happily and confidently argued their point. When I asked non-prep students, their response was less sure. Regarding affirmative action, for example, Tara said, "What is that again? Is that the thing where you have to hire certain races?" And Blanca, whom I found one day frosting the carrot cakes made by her home economics class that she would later take to an elementary school for an after-school program, responded, "I think we talked about that in a class once; I didn't really get it. But I think I'm probably for it."

In spite of the fact that the diverse Youth in Conflict students demonstrated their shared experience of being subordinate to a minority of middle-class-performing prep students, the important differences among them were not left unnoticed, and it was often white students' racism and sense of entitlement that kept the distance intact. I asked students about relationships between whites and Mexican Americans at Waretown High. Diana, a white prep girl, explained, "There are a lot of tensions here, but they are kinda hidden. Except for last year." My question often invoked from students stories about an incident that had happened on Cinco de Mayo the previous year, when some Mexican-American students brought the Mexican flag to school as part of the celebration. According to various accounts, some hick students took offense and went home to retrieve Confederate flags to display. Symbolic oppositions between hicks and chola/os were ever present. The rising tension resulted in one major and several minor fights at school that day. As Diana explained:

> During lunch hour on that day, the hard-cores, they were circling the school in their low cars [low-riders], driving real slow like they do, waving their flags. And the hicks, they were driving around the school too in their big trucks with the huge tires, going real fast, and carrying their flags.

As we will see, white students across groups shared similar views about Mexican Americans in Waretown, but the political economy of agriculture produced the ongoing spectacle of hicks, white students interested in agriculture, versus Mexican-American students, whose grandparents, parents, and/or themselves had worked in the fields, making it easiest to locate racial tensions between these groups. These inequalities were especially salient in Waretown where Mexican-American students who, along with their parents, worked as field laborers might at times sit in the same classrooms with students whose parents were the wealthy landowners who employed them.

When I first began to learn the group categories students used to describe themselves and others, I imagined that "hick" was a derogatory label used to describe white working-class rural kids. Hicks were looked down upon by other students at the school, preps in particular, stigmatized as backward and strange even in this town built on agriculture. As Rhonda, a prep girl, described them,

> They wear their hats and drive big trucks. And the girls sit right next to the guy in the truck, like not in the passenger seat. It's so stupid. And they wear like these huge belt buckles. It's like they are having an identity crisis or something.

But along with students fitting that description, the sons and daughters of rather well-to-do farming families or parents who held relatively high positions in agribusiness also participated in FFA (Future Farmers of America) and took courses in agriculture. Given that the hicks appeared to be white students from both landowning farm families who employed migrant labor and students from low-income families (farming and not), who all shared in common an interest in agriculture, I momentarily considered that the concept "status group" was a more appropriate descriptor of the category "hicks," since class did not seem to be a determinant of group membership.

But shortly after I had recorded this observation and analysis, I came to learn that a finer distinction was made by students, which indeed did sort hicks out along class lines. As two prep girls explained to me:

Lisa: Well, like Joey, he's not really a hick, he's a farmer.

Julie: What is the difference?

Diana: Well, farmers drive nice Chevy pickups with tool boxes in the back. They dress nicer and they smell good [referring to the use of cologne].

In short, farmers were datable in the eyes of prep girls. On the other hand, Lisa and Diana laughed as they described hicks who were "missing teeth," who "dress strange" and "drive them old clunkers with the bumper or door falling off."

Not only did preps make this distinction, but so too did working-class students who self-defined as hicks. As I stood with Bonnie, watching the hay-bucking contest on FFA Family Day, she scoffed that Ryan, one of the participants, had missed an FFA event last week because he was "too busy golfing."

Julie: Do the other guys [hicks] golf?

Bonnie: [laughing] No. Well, he's not really a hick. I mean look at the way he dresses. He wears Mossimo [designer-brand clothes], and he's on the tennis team and is going to college and all. He's more like a prep. It's like there are some hicks who are kinda preppy hicks, you know?

Likewise, Molly scoffed at two girls who passed us by in the parking lot. When I asked if they were hicks, she said, "Well, they like to think they are, just 'cause they listen to country music. But they are not *real* hicks." Working-class hicks never named their claim to hick authenticity as about class, but they sorted it out as such.

Those students who self-defined as hicks were working to reclaim the label, as I learned in a conversation with Molly.

Molly: Well, it just seemed like we needed to have a name you know, something to be called. And people were callin' us that, and so we just started using it too. It used to be people called us Okies or something, but we're not all from Oklahoma.

Julie: But do you think people use it in a bad way?

Molly: Well, they did, but so what? I mean it used to kinda be like that, like "stupid hicks," but I don't know, I guess if you just speak to them in their language [shrugging her shoulders] . . .

Some teachers had noticed that the meaning of the term and category had appeared to change over time. As Ms. Wyett explained to me, "It used to be that 'hick' was a kind of derogatory name, but now they claim it. Like a 'gay and proud of it' sort of thing. Now it's a category that they seem to be okay with calling themselves." Mr. Hill, an ag teacher, however, expressed concern, "I don't think these students understand that people use that term negatively. They use it to describe themselves, but they don't know that people are laughing at them."

The reclaiming of the hick label and the use of the Confederate flag both provided evidence of the presence of a white identity. That is, whiteness appeared as a conscious part of hick identity rather than as a category that was invisible to them, normative and unstated. The Confederate flag, as opposed to the American flag, represented the desire to conflate national identity with whiteness and demonstrated that students were acting based on a *racial* identity. Mr. Hill suggested to me that the students who brought the Confederate flag to school didn't fully understand its meaning, and there was some evidence for this. When I asked Molly and Heidi what the Confederate flag meant, Molly made a guess, "I don't know, I think it has something to do with blacks and the south." Heidi nodded, "Yeah, somethin' like that."

But the fact that students were unable to articulate well the historical meaning of the flag does not mean they didn't understand the racial sentiments linked to it. When I pushed Molly for further meaning, she explained, "It means that whites are just as good as anybody else." White students, and hicks in particular, felt that chola/os believed "Mexicans are better than whites." They persistently misread the chola/os proud demeanor as a claim to racial superiority, since the race-class injury that resulted in the chola/os' defensive defiant attitude was not apparent to them. But sometimes when I asked what the Confederate flag meant, I was told "white pride." It was a slippery divide between white students' attempt to suggest they were "as good as," which connotes equality, and their sentiment of white entitlement and superiority. Ironically, in contrast, Mexican-American students I spoke with were sensitive to the negative connotation of the hick label and hesitated to use it. When I asked Lorena how she felt about hicks, she said, "I call 'em the cowboy class. Some of them are pretty nice." When I asked her about the flag incident, she hung her head and said sadly, "Yeah, well they shouldn't have done that."

Although, as we've seen, class distinctions were routinely (if obscurely) made by white students among themselves, at times those were forgone, and a shared white identity emerged. The flag incident on Cinco de Mayo provided one opportunity for this. While the most common version of the story was one in which the hicks were blamed for having brought the flag to school, all white prep students I spoke with were sympathetic. In fact, the year of the incident white preps in the student government demonstrated their ideological alliance with white working-class students—albeit in their middle-class performing way—by writing editorials for the school newspaper on the meaning of being an American and the inappropriateness in their minds of the Mexican flag at school. Similarly, Mexican-American middle-class performers rushed to produce opposing editorials. Thus, despite the difference in ideology by race/ethnicity, class remained salient, as Mexican-American and white middle-class performers alike wrote editorials while chola/os and hicks fought it out in the school parking lot.

Some versions of the story suggested it was farmers (read middle class) who brought the Confederate flag to school, while hicks received the blame. Although almost all white students shared the same attitudes toward Mexican Americans, the accusation of crude racism (the Confederate flag) was projected onto the hicks, pointing to the way in which class differences among whites are, at times, played out around race and racism. Joanna Kadi (1996) keenly describes the negative perception by urban and suburban middle classes of hillbillies and rednecks, white rural working-class people, as a kind of classism that comes from conservatives and liberals alike. In liberal circles, one marker of having progressive politics is displaying oneself as antiracist, and this can, at times, unfortunately manifest as a demeaning of and distancing from white working-class people, who are constructed as stupid and racist. But white racism is not limited to the working-class; it is merely that middle-class expressions are interpreted as less vulgar or crude. Conservative middle-class students at Waretown perceived themselves as superior to rural working-class students, though they shared the same political sentiments. And some of these college-preps, though politically not liberal, fancied themselves "aware" or "enlightened" about race.

This was evidenced one day in a conversation between Shelly (vocational-track working-class performer) and Marla (college-prep), both self-defined hicks, when they told me their version of the Cinco de Mayo event. As Shelly spoke, she pronounced poorly various Spanish words like Cinco de Mayo and Mexican-American students' names. Each time, Marla shot critical glances at her and rolled her eyes at me. When Marla told the story, her pronunciations were correct, and she embellished a bit on the meaning of Cinco de Mayo for Mexican Americans. Learning a second language was required as a part of her college preparatory curriculum, and a small bit of cultural history had been a part of that. Although she judged Shelly as ignorant, their political views of the event were completely in sync, both arguing that the Mexican-American students should not have brought their flag to school, that immigrants should not receive public education, and that Mexican Americans receive unfair advantages as a result of affirmative action.

The similarity of attitudes among working-class and middle-class white students was not lost on Mexican-American students. As Ana explained, "The preps, they think the same way, they are just more p.c. [politically correct] about it." Likewise, Mexican-American students were in ideological union across their differences and suggested that on this day the Mexican flag represented not a national celebration so much as a cultural/political one, marking racial/ethnic pride. As Mariana explained, "Oh, everybody got together, all the Mexicans, north, south, immigrants, Chicanos. Nobody cared about those differences on that day."

PROPOSITION 209: A RACIAL PROJECT

Beyond the alliance created on Cinco de Mayo, racial/ethnic alliance across class was also manifested in attitudes toward California's Proposition 209 (strategically and misleadingly called the California Civil Rights Initiative, or CCRI), passed in 1996, which eliminated state affirmative action programs, including admissions policies in the California State University and University of California systems.[1] To the pleasure of white conservatives, University of California Regent Ward Connerly, a black man, became the measure's leading spokesperson and argued for income instead of race as a fairer criterion for admission. In this conservative community, all of the white students I spoke to, without exception, supported Proposition 209. Both working- and middle-class white students were easily swayed by Proposition 209's "class instead of race" logic, which both groups interpreted as white instead of brown, where "class" stands in for white and "race" stands in for brown (and black).

For working-class performers it was less college admission than job competition that concerned them, since the deciding moment for whether or not a student is going to a four-year institution occurred for them two to three years before, when they "chose" the vocational over the college-prep track. Consequently, by their senior year these students lacked the course work for admission to four-year schools. Although white working-class students experienced a feeling of unfairness in relationship to preps regarding educational achievement and college, they lacked a discourse of class that could explain their own and their parents' "failure" and that would allow them to articulate the class antagonism they felt toward middle-class students. In its absence, a discourse of individualism and meritocracy helped render institutionalized class inequality invisible and reinforced the feeling of white working-class students that they were individually flawed "losers." And while Proposition 209 pointed to class inequality and provided the potential for white working-class students to name class as a disadvantage they could identify with, this possibility was usually derailed by the fact of a readily available racist discourse on "reverse discrimination," which scapegoats people of color for white working-class pain. In the end Proposition 209 added fuel to this fire. The fact that Mexican Americans were overrepresented among the poor and that this is unjust was usually unapparent to whites, and when it was made apparent, it was perceived as natural and normal because they had the psychological wage of whiteness and conflated being American with being white (DuBois 1935; Roediger 1991). Unfortunately, working-class students were less likely to see themselves as victims of class inequality than as victims of "reverse discrimination."

My findings parallel those of Jay MacLeod (1995) in his study of white and black working-class boys. Unlike black students, who understood their parents' class location as a consequence of racial discrimination (but not necessarily *institutionalized* racism), the white working-class boys in MacLeod's study had no clear way to explain their own and their parents' lot in life. Looking for a reason other than individual deficiencies (lazy, stupid) to explain their location, and without a discourse on institutionalized class inequality and a corresponding class identity, they decided to blame students of color, operating from a white (and in their case male) identity. The moment where class insight and political identification might have occurred was derailed by a political discourse that scapegoats people of color and usurps class awareness. Without class to blame and without a way to explain who they are both economically and culturally, white working-class students are vulnerable to racist discourses which blame people of color for white working-class lack of mobility.

Somewhat curiously, white middle-class students in Waretown were also swayed by the color-blind "class" logic of Proposition 209. Preps' sense of racial competition was based in who was and who wasn't getting into which college. And the students of color most visible to them were the handful who sat next to them in college-prep classes. Preps' own class privilege was unapparent to them, so much so that the mass of working-class whites and working-class Mexican Americans were so "othered" as to be invisible. The only Mexican-American students whom preps could imagine going to college were already very much like them, in that they were middle-class performers (whether they were from middle-class origins or were working-class exceptions to the rule). At times, these college-prep Mexican-American students were resented as "box checkers" who were perceived to be unfairly benefiting from their "minority" status, such that middle-class white students also constructed themselves as victims of "reverse discrimination." These college-prep Mexican-American students were highly visible, to the disadvantage of their vocational-track peers. Since the large body of working-class vocational students were not in the running for college admission anyway, among college-prep students, *class* in the discussion of college admissions was taken as a code for *white*.

And perhaps rightly so. Class inequality is not adequately addressed by eliminating race/ethnicity as a criterion for student admission, since the vast majority of working-class students of all colors are tracked out early in high school. When liberal educational policy attempts to deal with social inequality by trying to get everyone into college, it fails to address the fundamental fact that global capital needs uneducated, unskilled workers, and that workers need living wages. White students did not support Proposition 209 because they understood institutionalized class inequality; rather it was because they were aware that race was being eliminated as a criterion, which benefited them regardless. Ironically, because it offered class instead of race, not in addition to race, the discourse surrounding Proposition 209 encouraged students to understand inequality *solely* in racial terms and in the end worked as a racial project that created an alliance among whites across class and among Mexican Americans across class. Because any clear understanding of institutionalized class inequality is missing from U.S. popular and political discourse, *class* was read as racial code and used to rearticulate white privilege.

The salience of *both* race and class to school achievement is reflected in correlations to SAT (Scholastic Assessment Test) scores. While it is the case that there is a direct correlation between income level and SAT scores within every racial/ethnic group and across gender (Sturm and Guinier 1996), it is also the case that SAT scores and college completion rates among black and Latino students across all economic categories remain lower than those of whites (Takagi 1992). So even if we set the mass of working-class vocational students aside and look solely at those college-preparatory-track students who have completed the requirement for admission to state university and UC schools (which includes those few exceptions to the rule), a shift away from race/ethnicity and toward admissions based on class fails to acknowledge the need for and benefits of racial diversity in higher education for all students. After finding out she had been denied admission to one of the five University of California schools she'd applied to, Rhonda, a white prep, said to me, while rolling her eyes, "They don't want me, being I don't have any cultural diversity." Oblivious to how the presence of people who are "other" to her might benefit and broaden her own education, she could see no legitimacy to diversifying the student body for its own sake. The class primacy discourse of CCRI worked to delegitimate progressive arguments for a university student body that is representative of the diversity of the state and, related, for a curriculum that meets the needs of the total population it serves and reflects the history and experience of all Americans.[2] Indeed, though Waretown High had made efforts to establish a multicultural curriculum, Mexican-American students' experience remained oddly invisible, in spite of the fact that they made up nearly 40 percent of the student body.

WHOSE HISTORY?

In a general education course I visited on American government, the teacher, Mr. Baldwin, lectured casually on early American history, "as far as our country starting out and everything," and his talk was peppered with phrases like "we had to pay taxes to the British," "we didn't like it," "our colonies wanted independence," and "later we won Mexico." Querying the meaning of the words of the Declaration of Independence, that "all men are created equal" and have the unalienable rights to "life, liberty, and the pursuit of happiness," he called on one of the school's "best and brightest," a white prep boy, son of a lawyer, for the meaning of the word liberty. "Freedom," came the answer. The teacher went on, "What did the founders mean by the 'pursuit of happiness'? What was the pot at the end of the rainbow?" No one provided an answer, giggling instead, whispering over his use of the word "pot" and forcing Mr. Baldwin to answer his own question: "Land. The pursuit of property." He then asked, "How politically correct were the founders?" and when he got no response, again answered his own question: "Well, they said all men are created equal, but freedom was not extended to slaves or women. They did not have freedom because they could not own property."

Toward the end of the period, he told the students to take out a blank piece of paper for a pop quiz. He asked the questions out loud, and when he reached the third question, "When was the Declaration of Independence signed?" a Mexican-American boy near the front row muttered, "I don't know. *We* weren't there." Mr. Baldwin responded, "You weren't there?" appearing to search his mind for a way to handle this challenge, when a white boy in the class added, "Yeah, I wasn't born yet." The teacher chose to interpret the former student's comment not with the political meaning the student possibly intended, but as consistent with the smart-aleck response from the white student. Mr. Baldwin quipped back to the white student, "Yeah, well you need to know these dates anyway, don't you," ignoring the opportunity to make visible the vast difference between the brown and white students in his class, the racialized political history between the United States and Mexico.

The Mexican-American student's comment pointed to the fact that the ancestors of the Mexican-heritage students in the class were not a part of the early political origin of the United States under study in today's class, and they had a different story to tell. Theirs was, of course, a story of Spanish colonization and the creation of "mestizo" or "racially mixed" identity through voluntary and involuntary sexual relationships between Native Americans and white Spaniards. When the Declaration of Independence was signed, Mexican-heritage people were not U.S. citizens, were not part of the referent group, the "we" that the teacher had named, though they were already at work building ranches in the west, unaware that later the United States government would conquer their territory in a quest for land during the U.S.-Mexican War and turn them into foreigners on their own land. Many would then be displaced, cheated out of their land, and eventually become a source of cheap labor as the U.S. labor force became segmented along racial/ethnic lines. This is not a history parallel to that of white ethnics.

Episodes like this reveal that too often schools, like the larger society, routinely fail to acknowledge these differences in "American" experience. All Mexican-American students, across class, generation, and citizenship status, are rendered invisible and recolonized in such moments when the curriculum subtracts cultural identifications from students (Valenzuela 1999b). It is no wonder that school success is viewed by students of color as acting white when it means learning and regurgitating a colonizing curriculum that erases one's racial/ethnic self. Here acting white is not only about acting middle-class, but is about holding one's tongue and identifying with the white "we" in a colonialist curriculum. Here becoming middle-class via education and becoming white are made to be one and the same. And such invisibility fosters ignorance among us all. Shopping in Waretown one day, I saw a toddler, a brown girl, crying at the front of the store; clearly she'd been separated from her parent(s). The white working-class woman who tried to ask the girl her name, but only got a louder cry and more tears, announced on the microphone, "Attention Kmart shoppers. We have a little Spanish girl up here who has lost her mother." It's hard to know whether by invoking "Spanish" she meant to indicate Spanish-speaking, though the child didn't speak, or if her use of the label "Spanish" reflected a kind of white discomfort with applying the label "Mexican" to someone's face, because within a racist culture, to be labeled Mexican is an insult in and of itself.

WHOSE PRESENT?

At the annual FFA banquet near the end of the school year, hicks and farmers celebrated the year's achievements, inviting their families to eat tri-tip steak and baked potatoes. Girls who normally appeared in school every day in practical work clothes were on this night all gussied up. The scene was characterized by elements of rural culture: one girl appeared in an American flag T-shirt; a couple of boys wore camouflage; the room was a sea of cowboy boots and hats; and the event was punctuated by country-western music.

These largely white students stood on stage receiving scholarships from agribusinesses in the community. Weston and Sons awarded a scholarship to Ben, the handsome, smart, confident son of a landowning farm family, who told the crowd of his plans to attend California Polytechnic Institute for a master's and doctorate degree and his hope to become the CEO of an agribusiness firm. In turn, local businesses were given plaques in appreciation of the support they had given the FFA program throughout the year, in the form of money and supplies. Though boys dominated, girls were a large presence, and they too received scholarships and outstanding projects awards, one for research on alfalfa breeding and another for raising six steers. One girl received a comical award, a pair of stilts from boys who remembered that she was "always too short to reach" in welding class. And one girl gave an award to a boy, a tube of lipstick, in appreciation for the day he wore makeup to help her fit in, as she was the only girl in the hay-bucking contest.

As the ceremony proceeded, the FFA officers moved onto the stage, each naming his/her title and role in the tradition of the organization: "As the historian, I keep the scroll and document events"; "As the treasurer, I keep a record of receipts and disbursements just as Washington kept his accounts . . . and was financially independent." The vice president explained, "The plow is the symbol of labor and the tillage of the soil," and the president continued, "The rising sun is the token of a new era in agriculture. If we will follow the leadership of our president, we shall be led out of the darkness of selfishness and into the glorious sunlight of brotherhood and cooperation." These officers, all white, mostly boys, performed a ceremony that ironically invokes eighteenth- and nineteenth-century images (the scroll) of early American farming (the plow) and an early nation (Washington) and claimed for themselves "the dignity of labor without which neither knowledge or wisdom can accomplish much" to an audience almost void of the Mexican Americans who are the twenty-first century farm labor in this community.

There were, in fact, a handful of students with Spanish surnames among the crowd. According to one agriculture teacher, these students have developed strategies for dealing with the covert and overt racism found amongst the farmer/hick peer group. Most of them, he explained, claim a white Spanish heritage. While their claim that they are the descendants of white Spaniards and therefore "pure" Europeans may be true, it is also quite possible that they are mestizos whose nineteenth-century ancestors chose to disassociate from Mexicanness, preferring to identify instead with the higher status Spanish conquerors when white (and racist) settlers from the east began moving into the west. These white immigrants to the west "made racial distinctions among the Mexican population on the basis of the clearly perceptible class and somatic differences" (Almaguer 1994, 55), reluctantly viewing those who were wealthier, fairer, and who claimed Spanish ancestry as white. Those Mexicans who were poorer and darker-complected were racialized as nonwhite, demonstrating again the inextricability of race and class signifiers. Wealthy Mexicans were both displaced by and absorbed into white society after the war, and the immigration of thousands of poorer peasants from Mexico into the United States has "led to a metaphorical 'darkening' of the Mexican image in the minds of whites" (72). Given the strength of anti-immigrant sentiment today, Spanish-surname families might continue or begin anew a conscious rejection of any indigenous background that would associate them with contemporary poor brown people. But given the Eurocentric history found in school curricula and national cultural discourses, their claim to white Spanish ancestry may be meaningless to many. Molly, the white girl we met earlier, contemplated out loud why her crowd, which included some of these Spanish-surname students, received the label "hicks." At one point she said, "Well, we can't be called rednecks, 'cause we aren't all white." Whether she was invoking phenotype (to be a redneck requires white skin, with the back of the neck often burned by the sun when laboring outdoors) or reflecting a common-sense assumption that the term "redneck" refers to white racists, Mexican-American students did not logically fit into the category "redneck" for her. Apparently the distinction that some students with Spanish surnames made between being Spanish or Mexican was lost on her and no doubt many other white students.

Clearly white working-class students in Waretown would benefit from a political and cultural discourse on class that would sort out class differences among whites, making class subjectivity less obscure and less conflated with race, but so too would working-class Mexican Americans like las chicas. While these girls had a way of explaining school "failure" in terms of racial inequality, this only worked in relationship to white students. Again, leaving the exceptions to the rule aside, it didn't help them understand why some of their own succeed while others don't, why Ana and Patricia, for example, were en route to college in spite of their early working-class performances, in spite of their having hung with "a bad crowd," a commonly accepted explanation for school failure. The fact is that middle-class students' working-class performances can sometimes be "corrected": parents' money and cultural capital can help buy them out of trouble if needed and aid them in the long run. The accusation of acting white, leveled at middle-class performers, was, at least in part, a defensive strategy that healed class injury. It was a way of saying, "I don't understand your success and my failure, so I'll minimize your achievement by accusing you of acting white." Without class as a dimension of subjectivity with which to understand themselves, las chicas, too, were sometimes left with individual inadequacies as the only thing to blame school failure on. Moreover, had institutionalized class differences among Mexican Americans been recognized, this might have helped the MEChA students achieve the racial alliance across generations they desired. In failing to negotiate class differences within and among the Mexican-American student body, they lost their constituency, because working-class students perceived MEChA as for middle-class performers or "brainy types."

In earlier chapters we saw ways in which class difference was salient, although not articulated as such, *within* racial/ethnic groups, both white and Mexican-American, played out on the terrain of style and manifesting as different gender performances. But here we see that in relationships *across* racial/ethnic groups, race/ethnicity often trumps class. The salience of class difference was at times forgone for racial alliances, both among white and Mexican-American students. Race and class political positions are situational and relationally defined, such that race and class alliances are potentially always shifting. But the possibility of a class alliance across race seems to be eternally defeated, both by the absence of a fully articulated political discourse on class and by the presence of a racist discourse that naturalizes racial/ethnic inequality, conflating whiteness with citizenship and blaming people of color for white working-class pain and white middle-class fear of downward mobility.

But a cultural and political discourse on class would not be useful if it completely displaces one on race, offering up instead a colorblind imaginary, as if we can erase the history of racialization by fiat. This history of racial politics remains salient outside of class formation and shapes whether people's subjective identifications, and related political actions, are likely to be along class or racial/ethnic lines. Moreover, the current state of racial inequality is not merely the historical residue of past injustices. Legislation like Proposition 209, in purporting to end the salience of racial categories by declaration, ends up working as a contemporary racial project, recreating racial injustice anew.[3] Proposition 187, whose supporters had ambiguous motives ("to save state resources or to save the state's racial identity from becoming increasingly nonwhite" [R. J. Garcia 1998, 118]), reflects the state's and the nation's sense of entitlement to cheap nonwhite labor while denying that labor full participation in society and denying any U.S. responsibility for undocumented immigration. Thus it too can be readily understood as a racial project that reinscribes economic racial injustice. In short, when cultural discourse renders the political history of differences between white and nonwhite experiences invisible, this affects the citizenship status of *all* students of color, regardless of class differences within and among them. Located in an environment that marginalizes them at best and reflects hostility at worst, such students read signs that make it clear they are unwelcome to participate as full citizens.

EN-GENDERING RACE-CLASS RELATIONS

On Cinco de Mayo during the year I spent at Waretown, I sat talking with Molly and Bonnie at the cement tables outside the ag building. Molly told me that, much to her embarrassment, her boyfriend, Rick, had brought a Confederate flag with him to school that day and his friend Jaye had brought a Border Patrol hat, though both had left the items in their trucks. Molly's embarrassment was a consequence of Rick's willingness to be overt about his opinions and potentially confrontational. This was a theme that repeated itself as I spoke with white girls, trying to discern if girls "do" race relations differently than their male counterparts. Girls' comments suggested that the gendered difference in expression was at least in part related to differing rituals of gender performance. In fact, girls across race-class locations believed that boys' fights were different from girls' because boys are willing to "fight over nothin'." They believed that girls fought only when there was "a really good reason," while boys would "look for anything to fight about," "they make up reasons, excuses." Girls' views suggested that race relations, and in fact all relations, among boys were shaped by boys' need to ritually demonstrate masculinity through conflict.

White girls recounted this same gender difference among their parents. Descriptions included: "My dad's kinda loud about his opinions"; "My dad's kinda racist, but only at home"; "My mom gets mad at dad 'cause he uses words like nigger and spic and stuff." Although these girls routinely described mothers who attempted to monitor men's crass expressions of racism, when I asked if their mothers agreed with their fathers on political issues like affirmative action and immigration, they said yes. Likewise, while white girls said that they were "embarrassed" by boys' racism, when I pushed them for whether or not they agreed with the sentiments expressed by their male counterparts, they said they did. When I asked Molly if she agreed or not with Rick's views, she responded defensively,

> Well, I don't really understand it either, why they [Mexicans/ Mexican Americans] bring the flags. I mean they're *here* now! If they think Mexico is so great, why are they here?

While gender often made a difference in the way students' practices manifested, with girls' racism more subtly expressed, the similarity in attitude and practice across gender points to the salience of white girls' race and class identities and interests.

MacLeod (1995) suggests that although white working-class boys have race and gender assets on the job market, and class as a disadvantage, their location in a society convinced it is classless ensures that it is not a class identity they embrace. Rather, they embrace a white and male identity and, with the help of contemporary political discourse, complain about reverse discrimination against them as white men. Not unlike Paul Willis's (1997) working-class lads, they embrace both racist and sexist discourses, which provide a sense of superiority and help soften the blow of their class futures. Likewise, Lois Weis (1990) suggests in her study of white working-class students across gender, that boys are especially vulnerable to the rhetoric of the New Right with its coded racism and promotion of a normative male-dominated family form.

But white girls, Weis suggests, given their experience of gender subordination, exhibit the *potential* for feminist critique and gender alliance. To what extent are girls' race and class identity politics mediated by their experience of gender inequality? Like Waretown girls across race and class, the girls Weis studied are not geared toward domestic futures, but toward furthering their education and/or securing a job and avoiding exploitative relationships with men. Although Waretown girls demonstrate an awareness of gender inequality, like the girls in Weis's study, they don't "see their identity as shared or collective, much less as feminist" (179), since their solutions are individual and private, and they do not think of themselves as women with a collective political gender interest. They were, as we have seen, more likely to identify collectively along race and, more obscurely, class axes.

When girls did collectively complain about gender inequality, they did not understand it as institutionalized in class, for example, via occupational segregation. Rather, their nascent feminism was limited to an annoyance with boys' controlling tendencies and various double standards regarding sexuality and beauty norms. Moreover, girls made their complaints *within* their own race-class groupings. So even though all girls, across race-class groups, shared the similar experience of this kind of gender injustice, they seemed rather unaware of the fact. In part, this was precisely because their gender performances varied along race-class lines, and they made wrong assumptions about the heterosexual practices of others, based on those performances. How could they have gender solidarity when they played out their race-class differences in terms of heterosexual relations, as, for example, when they accused one another of promiscuity?

The salience of girls' race and, obscurely, class selves should come as no surprise. Perhaps more now than ever before, girls are aware that they are directly competing with one another over societal resources. They are cognizant of race and, less clearly, class competition between each other as racialized (though exaggerated in the minds of whites) and classed (less clearly understood) subjects in relationship to both jobs and college admission, while a feminist political discourse that might assist them in politicizing their gender identities remains unheard. They were, for example, largely oblivious to gender as at all relevant to changes in affirmative action. And this race-class struggle over social goods like jobs and education becomes less and less obscure as heterosexual girls attempt to, and working-class girls are forced to, reject economic dependency on men.

Feminists have historically argued that girls' low aspirations are the consequence of the fact that they are, as girls, instructed that the key part of their lives is heterosexual relationship.[4] This causal argument suggests that low achievement among girls is a consequence primarily of gender socialization and institutionalized gender inequality. But it is not at all clear that a culture of romance and competitive heterosexuality is what *results in* girls' low aspirations. Such a gender-centered analysis fails to explain the academic success of college-prep girls and to tell us why girls "choose" from a variety of gender performances available to them. It also fails to consider that working-class and racial/ethnic girls of color, like their male counterparts, usually "choose"—or are simply tracked into—a vocational curriculum. Why would we assume that girls' "leveled aspirations" (MacLeod 1995) are due primarily to gender while boys are due to class and race locations?

In failing to see the way in which gender identity is inflected by other subjectivities and the way in which the "gender order" (Connell 1987) is informed by other social forces, it is deceptively easy to read the non-academic non-college-prep performances of femininity among most working-class girls as a consequence of their gender victimization only. When doing so, inevitably, it seems, working-class white girls and girls of color appear, in a somewhat patronizing gesture, as more duped by the trappings of patriarchy than middle-class white girls, who appear in individualistic terms as more astute and consequently as having higher "self-esteem." While gender inequality has a logic of its own, and is reproduced for all girls across other social differences, it is nonetheless important to analyze gender subordination in the context of women's own race-class groupings. If a non-prep identity is one that girls construct less (or not only) in relationship to boys than one that is enacted in relationship and opposition to one another as girls, then the different versions of femininity performed would be better understood as racial/ethnic and class variances among girls themselves.

GENERATION

Girls today grow up in the shadow of postfeminist popular culture where certain, albeit distorted and contained, feminist ideas have been absorbed, while others have not. By *postfeminist* I mean an attitude in which young women take certain feminist gains for granted but fail to see them as the achievements of a political struggle (Stacey 1990). All girls, across race/ethnic and class identities, are still subjected to and feel the burden of the "sexual auction block," where they are put into competition over sexual attractiveness as a form of symbolic capital (Holland and Eisenhart 1990). But postfeminist popular culture at times suggests to girls that the terms of heterosexual courtship and sexual politics are uneven, that independence is psychologically rewarding, and that women have a right to it.

Popular culture is not "a seamless text of oppressive meanings"; there are "disruptions and inconsistencies and spaces for negotiation" (McRobbie 1994, 163). While the girls I knew too often felt inadequate when they did not meet the normative standards of beauty projected by the film, television, and music industries, they also took pleasure in the oppositional moments found therein. Lyrics of female musicians, for example, at times told stories that resonated. Girls felt validated by themes of gender injustice, even as the lyrics were sung primarily by women who met the unreasonable standards of female beauty required for star status in music videos. But Waretown girls failed to understand feminism as a tool for collectively confronting this kind of sexual politics. Their understanding of feminism was limited, and postfeminist ideology is one reason for the absence of a collective feminist voice, the sentiment of gender injustice having been appeased by limited gains. Feminism as a social movement appears to many as passé. In the end, the oppositional moments found in popular culture pose a limited challenge, and gender inequality, as it exists inside and outside of economic inequality, is reproduced, but it is important to recognize that girls "do not mechanically accept it" (McRobbie 1994). They are not passive victims of mass culture, and the complexity of their practices should be recognized.

Moreover, while historically all girls may have been (however unevenly) "educated in romance" (Holland and Eisenhart 1990), schools, parents, and girls across all racial/ethnic and class categories now acknowledge that girls will work, whether in "jobs" or "careers." They know this perhaps less because of the success of feminist ideology than because women's paid labor has become, and for some always has been, an economic requisite for families (Stacey 1990). Taking historical circumstances into account, Angela McRobbie (1991) has suggested that the "absence of a prince" might produce "changing modes of femininity." While the "prince" was always less a real possibility than part of an unattainable middle-class nuclear family ideology for working-class women, and for women of color in particular, perhaps he is increasingly absent as an ideal at all. We need to consider that we now see a generation of young women most of whom at no point expected or hoped to be economically supported by men. This is more true for working-class girls than middle-class ones. Employing family values discourse, some middle-class girls said they desired to stay at home and raise children later in life because they believed that was best for children. They expected male support to do so, but feared this dependency as well. Consequently, they naively imagined they would have fantasy careers that would allow them the ultimate flexibility of working at home and/or taking time off from a career without damaging it and expecting to return to it after kids were grown.

While it may not always be apparent to them, gender projects do work to secure the class futures of Waretown girls. The dismantling of affirmative action threatens to perpetuate a gender-shaped class hierarchy. So too do challenges to women's reproductive rights and welfare reform, which has meant that mothers with children and victims of domestic violence no longer have this cushion, small as it was, thereby reproducing women's economic dependence on men and an imbalance of power within families.[5] Such gender projects occlude women's economic autonomy and naturalize their dependency on men while simultaneously punishing them for their dependence on the state via a moral discourse on "welfare mothers."

In short, young women's class futures are ensured by a stalled gender revolution, but it is one that has been *uneven* in its effects. All girls I talked to across all social categories expressed a desire to be economically independent. They all wanted to go to college (which meant anything from university to community colleges to vocational schools) to get better jobs or careers. Gender identity was not subordinate to work identity for either middle- or working-class performers, but for different reasons and with different assumptions. Among this generation, middle-class girls, who are mostly white, appear as young beneficiaries of feminist struggle (but fail to credit it), as they look forward to careers (not jobs) and *relative* economic independence. But working-class girls more often think of work in relationship to family instability. They are aware of the dangers of economic dependency and divorce-induced poverty for themselves and any children they might have. Aside from postfeminist ideology, working-class girls' desire for female autonomy is enhanced by their witnessing an employment crisis among men in their communities, true for white working-class men, but even more so for men of color. They see the men in their communities are often unemployed or underemployed and are all too likely to deal with this hardship by abandoning their obligation and responsibilities to the women in their lives and the children they helped create.

Working-class girls know from experience in their own families of origin that male wages alone cannot support families, and they also know, both from experience and from postfeminist popular culture, that men cannot be counted on to meet their ideals for intimacy and egalitarianism in relationships. So they will not have and do not want male breadwinners to rely on at the same time that they will not have wages that allow the economic autonomy they desire. Their class futures are secured by the historical context in which they live, where a deindustrializing economy offers them only low-wage service-sector jobs, largely without labor union protection, and where a middle-income, blue-collar breadwinner "family-wage" job after high school is *still* not an option for women and no longer a real possibility for men. The fact that economic equality has not occurred for women inside or outside of heterosexual families, in combination with the poor job opportunities offered by a postindustrial economy, leaves these working-class girls in precarious circumstances.

But Mexican-American working-class girls face the specific impact of racial projects like the persisting anti-immigrant sentiment endorsed by the successful passage of Proposition 227, which ended bilingual education in California, and Proposition 187, which intended to eliminate public health care and public school education for undocumented immigrants.[6] While this social policy was directed at immigrants, because in everyday life these "others" were painted with a broad brush, second- and third-generation Mexican Americans felt the injury simply by virtue of being brown. Moreover, second- and third-generation Mexican Americans in Waretown often had extended family members who were directly affected by immigration policy. And Proposition 209, by refusing to acknowledge the overrepresentation of women and men of color among the poor and working class and thereby failing to challenge white entitlement across class, recreates and exaggerates a race-shaped class hierarchy, perpetuating institutionalized racial inequality for Mexican-American women *and* men in Waretown. This not only makes Mexican-American girls' economic autonomy apart from men unlikely, but, given the lower earning power of the men who are their likely potential partners, they will be poorer and more dependent than white working-class women, even in the context of heterosexual relationships.

That gender and racial projects manifest with uneven effects on girls across social locations is apparent in the demographic composition of the senior class at Waretown High. The settled-living Mexican-American girls we met in chapter 3 and the hard-living white girls we met in chapter 4 were not from parallel locations. Hard-living Mexican-American students, girls in particular, had few representatives among the senior class, having already left Waretown High to work and/or to attend alternative education programs.

In sum, we can locate similarities among girls across race/ethnicity and class, but of course profound differences exist as well. Class alliances remain unlikely because of the absence of a discourse of class, and gender alliances are often absent because of the pervasiveness of both postfeminist and antifeminist discourses. While racial/ethnic alliances among people of color are necessary to illuminate and deter ongoing racial projects, dangerous and powerful white alliances across class are working to maintain white privilege.

CHAPTER 7

Conclusion

Great social and historical changes . . . altered not only outward forms—institutions and landscapes—but also inward feelings, experiences, self-definitions.

Raymond Williams,
The English Novel from Dickens to Lawrence

In junior high and early high school, multiple social forces conspired simultaneously to shape Waretown girls' lives: a more difficult curriculum, tracking, talk of college and adult futures, an awareness of what parents can and can't afford and expect, and the push toward compulsory heterosexuality. Girls sorted through all this and began drawing conclusions about what is or is not "for the likes of me and my kind," as friendships were increasingly organized by race/ethnicity and class and as girls began to formulate identities based on the possible futures they imagined for themselves.

Working-class performers, across race/ethnicity, had their dignity wounded through exposure to middle-class performers who routinely, and often unknowingly, inflicted class and race-based injuries in their practices of exclusion. Differing race-class performances of femininity took hold as girls defined themselves relationally in opposition to multiple others and as working-class girls adopted alternative badges of dignity that worked, at times, as a kind of resistance to symbolically heal class and race injuries. In short, girls began constructing future class positions for themselves without the awareness that they were engaged in doing so, and future class positions were constructed for them as their limited economic and cultural resources ensured that the vast majority of working-class girls would both opt out and be tracked out of a middle-class trajectory.

I have tried to model one way of thinking about class in relationship to other axes of identity by exploring what utility might come from thinking through class as a performance and as performative and by exploring how the various gestures of class performance never exist outside of race and gender meanings. Thinking through class as a *performance* is useful for understanding those who cross borders, those exceptions to the rule who are consciously passing (whether it be up or down, and both occurred). The correlation between class origins and class performances is not a perfect one, and the exceptions are telling, informing us in important ways about how the forces of race/ethnicity, color, gender, and sexuality intersect with class. Rather than ignoring exceptions, I pursued them and pushed for reasons why a given student was an exception to the pattern of class-origin-equals-class-performance.

For example, we saw the conflation of race and class meanings (where brown signifies poor and white signifies middle-class) result in working-class performances among middle-class Mexican-American students like Ana and Rosa, who felt compelled early on to perform a chola identity as a marker of racial/ethnic belonging in an effort to avoid accusations of acting white and to maintain a Mexican-American cultural identity at school. The fact of an uneven distribution of material resources across race, representations in popular culture that persistently link color and poverty (e.g., the overrepresentation of low-income people of color on television news and fiction), and the lack of a bicultural curriculum at school, all work to make color and middle-classness seem to be mutually exclusive, a seemingly unavailable identity for these girls. However, through the discourse of empowerment provided by MEChA (and various other programs for students of color), which offered a strategy for resisting a colonizing education while acquiring skills for mobility, students did find a way to construct for themselves a middle-class version of Mexican-American identity.

Similarly, while homophobia obviously can work to keep gay and lesbian students closeted, we saw that it might also work to push those students to marginalized working-class-performing groups. This appeared to be true for Kate, who had both economic and cultural resources available to her, but sought friends who also felt marginal, albeit in a variety of ways.

In addition to working-class performers of middle-class origin, there were middle-class performers of working-class origin, whom we met in chapter 5. These girls, located in a college-prep curriculum and exposed to middle-class cultural forms, easily saw the differences between themselves and their middle-class friends' lives and consequently became aware of the structures of exclusion at work in ways that vocational track students did not. They learned the cultural content of middle-classness, began to acquire cultural capital by association, and learned to perform a class identity they did not originally perceive as their own.

Thinking through class as a performance enables us to acknowledge exceptions to the rule, to understand that while economic and cultural resources often determine class futures, this is not inevitable. It allows us to explore the experience of negotiating an inherited and a chosen identity. It helps demonstrate the ways in which other axes of identity (like gender, sexuality, ethnicity, whiteness or color) intersect with and inform class identity and consequently shape class futures (sometimes in spite of class origin). That is, class performance is shaped by factors other than class.

Useful in these respects, the concept of performance is, however, potentially weak if it is taken to imply more individual agency than is warranted. My use of *performance* should not be misunderstood as a negation of the autonomy of social structures which have "historical weight" and "formidable inertia" (Winant 1995, 504) and which are the context for and preexist individuals, producing and regulating various kinds of historically specific subjects in the first place. Hence the utility of theorizing the other side of performance, *performativity,* which points to the fact that girls were enacting class scripts (and race and gender and sexual ones) of which they were unaware or only obscurely aware. Social actors largely display the cultural capital that is a consequence of the material and cultural resources to which they have had access. Structural, institutionalized inequalities preexist and for the most part produce girls' race-class-gender performances. While these structures are not automatically or inevitably *re*produced, but rather are constantly constituted and historically contingent, by and large structures of inequality reappear over time, albeit with new veneer. With few exceptions, it appeared that working-class girls would have working-class futures, and middle-class girls, middle-class futures. The concept of performativity points to the ways in which we are produced by the weighty structures (at once material and ideal) that preexist us, and highlights the extent to which the reproduction of inequality does indeed happen behind our backs.

DECONSTRUCTING CLASS

I have argued that one's class self is shaped by the economic and cultural resources found at home, that is, parents' socioeconomic status, which individuals then bring to mixed-class settings. Somewhat reluctantly I have employed a categorical notion of class, naming each girl's class origin based on the socioeconomic status of both of her parents, her grandparents, and other key adults who provide economic and cultural resources, thus leaving the notion of class "origin" relatively unproblematic. Even though class is not best conceived as a static demographic variable, but as a process always changing and in formation, there is, of course, analytic utility to considering its temporal fixity and identifying individual class locations within the long arm of history.

But I hope, in fact, to make the notion of a fixed class taxonomy problematic. Understandings of class origin must be analyzed in ways that are informed by the structure of gender, racial/ethnic, and sexual inequality. For example, women of color, men of color, and white women all often experience a disparity between educational attainment and economic reward. It is useful then to think about economic and cultural capital as somewhat independent of each other, and to understand that their separability often has to do with institutionalized race, gender, and sexual inequality.

Beyond this, the tenacious ideology of "the family" (found in popular, political, and social science discourse) shapes assumptions of what a middle-class or working-class family looks like, when in reality the fluidity of economic and cultural capital within any given family often makes its "class" hard to name. Frequently, the class status of women, their husbands or partners, and their children may not all be the same. The family and gender revolutions of the second half of the twentieth century, generated in part by women's higher participation in paid labor, has made marriage more voluntary than it has ever been. Consequently, divorce and the subsequent coming and going of parents and stepparents (usually fathers and stepfathers) from children's lives means women's economic resources are often quite fluid (even in the lives of middle-class women, whose income drops substantially upon divorce).[1]

On the other hand, women are still not likely to pair with men outside of their *social* class; thus, cultural capital is less fluid in children's lives, as their parents are usually not too disparate from each other in educational achievement. But being "mixed-class" in this cultural sense does occur. What class was Bev, whose high-school-educated mother works for minimum wage in retail but whose part-time father, with whom she spends weekends, went on after the divorce to acquire a bachelor's and a master's degree, becoming a member of the professional middle class? At least one prep student, Staci, had attended a private elementary school because her mother worked in the school's kitchen and so was able to enroll her child at reduced cost. By high school, this student had acquired middle-class cultural capital of her own, beyond that of her parents. Older siblings, who were the first in the family to go to college, brought middle-class cultural capital to younger siblings, acting as important sources of information already known to students whose parents were college educated. Such mixed experiences complicate one's sense of class location and identity.

These examples, along with the fact that class is experienced in racial/ethnic- and gender-specific ways, suggest that it is important to recognize *contrasts* in working-class experience rather than to affirm a normative, monolithic, or authentic image. Diverse class experiences derive from many factors, not the least of which is social geography, the ways in which a class self is shaped by the degree of class and racial/ethnic homogeneity or diversity in one's community. Class is a relational identity, and we must always contextualize it in communities, for it is from communities that "young people draw conclusions about what sort of people they are, what society has in store for them, and what they can therefore hope for" (Steinitz and Solomon 1986, 135).

In short, class is not a categorical given, but is historically composed. Though it is a structure, it is a fluid one, not simply reproduced but constantly recreated and cocreated with processes of racialization and gender and sexual formation.

A DISCURSIVE ABSENCE

Because of the ways in which race, class, gender, and sexuality are historically constructed and performed in relationship to each other, class subjectivity varies not only across race/ethnicity, gender, and sexual groupings, but differs generationally as well. Recognizing that all these axes of social organization are always changing and in formation, it is important to see young women as historically situated and to ask what "cultural forms and expressions . . . seem to suggest new or emergent 'structures of feeling' . . . among girls" (McRobbie 1991, 72).

Returning to some of the theory problematics discussed in chapter 2, I take it as a given that identity and experience are always discursively mediated. Consequently, I take girls' common-sense understandings of self-identity and "experience" (in particular, the presence/absence of class as an articulated identity) less as *truths* than as *windows* into the "complicated working of ideology," the webs of power and meaning that make such experiences and subjectivities possible (Fuss 1989, 118).[2] Experience is mediated by the discursive frameworks for understanding ourselves that are made available to us.

Examining the process of identity formation, the ways in which girls construct themselves in and are constructed by discourse, was in part a process of discovering what preexisting cultural discourses girls tap into to narrate their identities. Through their self-narrations they presented the intersection of those contradictory discourses that construct their subjectivity. Identities are fashioned from the limited repertoire of understanding ourselves and our lives made available to us in public discourse. Significantly, these discourses routinely offer depoliticized identities and work to naturalize hierarchies of inequality.

Class is largely missing as a category of identity offered by popular culture and political discourse in the early-twenty-first-century United States. Class is not a central category of thought, making it difficult to have a cultural or political class identity. Class is often conceptually displaced onto or read through other categories of difference like gender and race in such a way that class itself is rendered invisible. While it is not a more fundamental axis of identity or mechanism of social organization, it is perhaps more often obscure. Given the U.S. ideology of upward mobility, class is either not a present category of thought at all or is present but understood only as a difference of money and therefore as temporary. Consequently, categories like race and gender, which *appear* to be essentially there, fixed, and natural, readily take the place of class in causal reasoning, rather than being understood as mediated by or inextricably intertwined with class and one another. Thus, common-sense discourses on race and gender can work to preclude class visibility.

We saw ways in which girls both did and did not recognize class difference. Understanding group differences as differences of style was a way of simultaneously displacing and recognizing class difference. White working-class students (such as hicks and smokers) made claims to stylistic authenticity (which turned out to be class-coded) and dismissed those who were "posers." Among Mexican-American students, such authenticity claims included accusations of acting white, which obscured class at the same time it provided a way of talking about class differences, both those between white middle-class preps and working-class Mexican Americans and among Mexican-American students themselves. The symbolic oppositions students employed were linked to the use of gender-specific commodities, as when girls understood group membership as related to preferences in clothes, makeup color, and hairstyle. These emblems of class-race membership among girls were often misunderstood, interpreted as "moral" differences in sexual practices, as when working-class performers rejected school-sanctioned femininity for various racially specific dissident femininities. Thus, school-sanctioned femininity and dissident femininity were symbolic markers of class and racial/ethnic difference. But class and race difference was displaced and made invisible among girls, as their preferences were understood as solely linked to heterosexual relations: girls in gangs "are just trying to learn how to become young women," and girls' fights are "about boys." Girls routinely demonstrated that class antagonism and injustice were felt ("I think I deserve an award"), but they were rarely articulated as the difference of class.

This is not to say that race and gender were understood *accurately* while class was left obscure. In fact, it was the *essentialized* conceptualizations of race and gender that helped to keep the difference of class invisible. Race and gender were more readily perceived as natural and inevitable causal social forces, while class was left unnamed altogether, invisible as a category of belonging or causality. It was left unnamed because of the lack of a fully articulated cultural or political discourse on class as such. In short, the girls and school personnel were constructing many social identities, but were only aware of some; those most visible were race and gender. Empirically, institutionalized class inequality, the difference that economic and cultural resources make, structured girls' lives, but class meaning was routinely articulated through other categories of difference (race, gender, sexuality) and in other terms (family values, individualism, self-esteem). This is a trick the ethnographer can easily miss.

It is not the case that race and gender are mere ideologies that mask the reproduction of class inequality. Racial and gender formation are organizing principles in their own right. In the end, inequalities along multiple axes are reproduced, meeting the demands of capital, white supremacy, male dominance, and heterosexual privilege, but the *invisibility* of class is also reproduced, as race, gender, and sexuality often entirely take its place in girls' understandings of who they are, and in schools' and broader society's perception of who girls are in general.

Moreover, economic restructuring further obscures class, as working-class jobs in the United States have become less industrial and therefore less easily perceived as working-class. In addition, in political discourse a working-class constituency goes unrecognized as class difference is downplayed and the myth is maintained that we are all part of a great "middle class" (sometimes described ambiguously as "working families"). All of this aids youth in defining their families' and their parents' and their own service-sector occupations as middle-class. As Lois Weis (1990) points out, one flaw in the idea of reproduction theory,[3] which argues that schools function to reproduce class inequality, is that the *precise* reproduction of classes cannot occur (or at least is not perceived to occur) when working-class youth do not follow in parents' footsteps by obtaining the same kinds of jobs. With factory closings and other changes, their parents' occupations are not available, and newer service sector jobs carry different meanings. If we refuse to essentialize class and instead focus on class as a formation, not an invariant structure but a dynamic historical process, then the changing demographics of labor must be—and can be—taken into account.

The social organization of race, gender, and family are key to these shifts in class formation. In the second half of the twentieth century employers were drawn to inexpensive female labor, made cheap precisely because of the male struggle for the breadwinner wage that was itself informed by an ideology of "the family" (Stacey 1990, 1996), in which a nuclear structure that fostered women's dependency was naturalized. Consequently, that women are now (and increasingly) the majority of "workers" is, ironically, what may make class seem less salient as a social force, a cultural identity, and a potential political identity.[4] Likewise, that people of color are overrepresented among workers is rendered inconsequential by a historical discourse on race that naturalizes a racial division of labor and conflates whiteness with citizenship and national identity.

The continued naturalization of gender and family, and of white supremacy, can be witnessed in the contemporary political rhetoric of "family values" and "youth crisis," both of which draw attention away from the fact of downward mobility among working-class people and especially among those of color. The problems that working-class girls face are not limited to their age grouping, are not a condition of youth or a consequence of a crisis among youth, but are the same problems that plague adult working-class women in twenty-first-century capitalism—low-wage jobs, lack of affordable child care, and limited access to higher education. This goes unrecognized, while working-class women, and Latinas and black women in particular, are targeted as the culprits responsible for passing on poor values to children and perpetuating welfare dependency. Despite thirty years of second-wave feminist critique, the fact that our wealthy nation fails to provide living wages and affordable housing, health care, child care, and reproductive control for its workers (read: women) remains unaddressed.

Workers need unions to make jobs more profitable and need a return to middle-income "working-class" jobs for men *and women*. Unlike the historic working-class struggle for the family wage, this time around women's economic autonomy is imperative. Gender must be an organizing principle of labor, as must a vigilant attentiveness to the ways in which discourses on the family work to negate the individual worker's rights to a living wage that meets her own (and her children's) basic necessities. A cultural and political discourse that naturalizes "the family" works in reality to recruit people into relationships of exchange (Rapp 1978), which often become involuntary relationships of dependency (usually women's). Through various policies that focus on family/work interchanges (too often conceptualized as women's issues) the state, complicit with capital, asks "the family" to do all that it cannot do or refuses to do in terms of making sure the basic needs of the citizenry are met.

While the shift from industrial to service work (where the latter is often coded feminine and middle-class) poses a general challenge to the (re)creation of a U.S. working-class identity and to the anachronistic language of class itself, this begs the question of whether the kind of sex-segregated, often service-oriented, labor that women have historically performed has ever been perceived as working-class. Paul Willis (1977) explained long ago that working-class boys tended to see schooling and schoolboys as passive and effeminate, and these associations were key to the logic they used to reject schooling as they romanticized manual labor as masculine.[5] Further, the service-based work women performed was often not perceived by working-class men as *real* work (because it is sometimes clean and non-manual, and may be located in offices near management), in spite of the fact that it is low-paying, low-prestige, and routine (Halle 1984), not to mention nonunion and increasingly temporary and without benefits. The signifiers femininity, passivity, conformity, middle-classness, and consumption (versus production) meld together in such a way that women, it seems, cannot be or authentically represent a working class. It is, most certainly, a hidden injury of class when working-class women's lives are coded "middle" because of their gender. These same injuries are repeated in social theory when it fails to envision women as class subjects. Working-class women have never starred as the romantic revolutionary subject, suffering instead the injury of invisibility, and performing "feminine" work which received little dignity or respect in a symbolic economy of class that construed masculine manual labor as more authentically working-class. This could only happen by ignoring women's reproductive labor within families and by coding women's paid work as supplemental to the family economy, which was never true of working-class women's work, and is increasingly untrue of middle-class women's work (Stacey 1990).

There is a parallel here to the way in which women have been absent as racial subjects in ethnic nationalist discourses.[6] As Rosa Linda Fregoso explains, women have not been perceived as historical representatives of Chicano nationalism, wherein the authentic Chicano nationalist subject has been portrayed as a masculine antihero: "the pachuco as urban warrior" (1995, 322). Class and race signifiers meld together in such a way that the authentic ethnic nationalist subject is imagined as working-class, and, as we have seen, feminine codes can work to preclude women's belonging. Class, race, and gender codes are mutually implicated in such a way as to render women of color invisible as either race or class political subjects. Stuart Cosgrove provides a telling historical example in his analysis of the zoot suit riots of the early 1940s. The female counterparts of male zoot suiters were "ridiculed in the press" for their "black drape jackets, tight skirts, fish-net stockings and heavily emphasized makeup" (1989, 14). But, as Cosgrove explains, their very existence suggests a more radical reading of pachuco subculture than media accounts provided. Women's participation and gender-specific "emblem of ethnicity" point to the fact that the tensions of the time were at once racial/ethnic, generational, and class-based and could not accurately be portrayed as boys-will-be-boys fights between white servicemen and Mexican-American men.

The invisibility of women as class subjects was made apparent during one of my last conversations at Waretown High with Mr. Scott, a white teacher who was trying to convey to me the economic struggle of most Waretown families. He explained that many Waretown students have to work jobs while they are attending high school. With pride he added, "Some of the Latino boys, they just take their paycheck right home to their mother." While his statement linked race and class, revealing an awareness of Mexican Americans' higher rate of poverty in the community, it also linked masculinity and class; he remained unaware that there were many girls, a handful of them white, but more of them Mexican-American, who were doing the same, bringing paychecks home to assist the family economy. Girls too are class subjects with identities and futures in relationship to work and income. In failing to perceive girls' class and race selves, the teacher unwittingly reproduced the commonsense belief that what is most important about girls is their girlness. When girls' identities and futures are imagined only in gendered and familial terms, whether by social policy, schools, or girls themselves, class futures are constructed for young women without any visible recognition that this is occurring.

When we look to the multiple discursive sites and practices in which women are and are not constructed as, and do and do not experience themselves as, class subjects, we can see that there are "classifying projects" (Skeggs 1997) at work, but they are rarely named as such. Those classifying projects are found in the discourses of popular culture (where working-class people are represented, but not defined as class subjects), social science (where too often working-class authenticity has been imagined as white, male, and industrial), politics (where talk of family values and youth crisis displaces talk of real economic differences), and schooling (where discourses on individualism, meritocracy, and an immigrant ideology reign). Through an analysis of these discourses and through attending ethnographically to the ways in which these discourses enter girls' lives, I have tried to explore some part of the cultural politics of how class is reproduced and resisted.

Women have experienced themselves and have been experienced as without class, while in reality they are and always have been class subjects whose access to the cultural and economic resources of class (cultural capital and paid labor) has been shaped and mediated by gender and racial projects. But the androcentrism of the class concept as it exists in social theory and popular discourse precludes their visibility.

CONSTRUCTING CLASS

The consequence of these discursive displacements is, once again, that class remains obscure and often absent from the repertoire of possible cultural and political subjectivities, though it is, of course, a salient social force. To the extent that a class identity existed at all among Waretown girls, it appeared less as class conscience than as a "sense of place." This sense of class-place was constructed through consumption as much as production and in social relations involving family and community as much as paid labor. While distinct expressive cultural practices among working-class people can be identified, they vary by race/ethnicity, gender, and region, making class cultural identities difficult to describe. Moreover, these cultural practices do not necessarily correspond to the formation of a working-class political culture and identity. Consequently, a kind of obscure class struggle is often waged over modes of identity expression more than explicit political ideologies.

Given that our experiences and identities are constructed via the discursive frameworks available to us, and that class discourse is largely absent, it is difficult to have an articulate cultural or political class identity in contemporary historical context. It is the political project of progressive cultural studies and of public intellectuals to make it one. We might begin by looking for class "where it lives" (Ortner 1991), to locate the hidden cultural class identity that exists within discourses of success, money, intelligence, race, style, sexuality, and so forth. It is wrong to conclude that class meaning is totally absent for people if the categories they use are not named and known as class. Class is omnipresent even as it is discursively invisible. It is important to locate instances of class cultural awareness, to make visible the everyday politics of resentment, and to go beyond this to provide a discourse which offers to transform that into a politicized class identity, alongside other political positionings.

Weis explains that "at least part of the reason why females in occupational ghettos have not been as organized historically as males . . . is precisely because women have envisioned and lived out a marginalized wage labor identity" (1990, 204), an identity made possible by a gender order that dictated occupational sex-segregation and female economic dependence on men. But "working-class" girls today, who cannot depend on men, and don't want to, may be more inclined to center their wage-labor identity and be primed for the facilitation of a class subjectivity. An identity as workers is not made available to them, obviously, from capital or from conservatives who offer retrograde gender and family ideology, but neither is it made available from androcentric organized labor and progressives or from a version of feminism that essentializes them only as gendered subjects. A feminist cultural studies that eschews an analytical focus on class participates in making and keeping class invisible and limits progressive politics; it is remiss when it fails to provide a politicized class subjectivity for women. What would it mean for progressive politics if we were to locate, create, and strengthen counterhegemonic narratives and discourses that construct women as class subjects?

Changing educational policy was not a key goal when I set out to do this work, but given that my site for studying women and class identity was a school, and knowing that educators and educational policy makers will want to know how to create more upwardly mobile working-class exceptions, how to turn around "at risk" youth, I can offer a few insights based on what I observed at Waretown High. I saw that the presence of programs that focus on the concerns of particular racial/ethnic groups of color (such as MEChA, MESA, and AVID) have the potential to reach both middle-class youth of color and students of color who are upwardly mobile working-class exceptions, enabling them to construct middle-class racial/ethnic identities that are not experienced as colonized. Moreover, a version of affirmative action that uses race/ethnicity as one among many criteria can help these qualified students of color populate university classrooms to the benefit of themselves, their communities, white students, and the overall project of a multicultural democracy.

But apart from the desirability of securing the place of middle-class students of color and mobility for working-class students of all colors, the fact remains that capital needs workers and workers need living wages. A liberal version of multicultural education that provides attention to racial/ethnic, gender, and sexual inequalities only as a consequence of individual acts of discrimination and prejudice, that offers only tolerance as a remedy, and that fails to explore the political histories of our differences and examine how race/ethnicity, gender, and sexuality are at once institutionalized *in* class inequality and exist *outside* of and apart from class inequality, is inadequate. Also inadequate is a multicultural education that teaches cultural sensitivity but leaves identity categories unified and static in its analysis, failing to think through cultural hybridity. Moreover, multicultural education can no longer be nation-centered but must offer an analysis of racialization and gender and class formation as global processes. Of course, no single institution, like schools, is the cause of or the cure for structural inequalities that exist along multiple axes. Other factors outrank the failure of schools as the cause, for example, of growing economic disparity, including "the globalization of the economy, the rapid advent of new technologies, the changing nature of work, the investment in arms over domestic spending, [and] the failure to organize unions in the newly emergent industries" (Fraser 1997, 19). But schools are one useful site for social change. Acknowledging that it may ring as "naive optimism," James Fraser (1997) argues that the primary purpose of education in a democracy should be to reproduce and expand democracy, not to serve capital and other systems of domination. Yet this is what happens when schools, intentionally or not, ensure that some students "fail" the goal of attending college and are channeled into a curriculum that prepares them for low-wage service economy jobs, because there are "simply not enough good jobs to go around" (MacLeod 1995, 239). A "focus on preparing future workers for world markets deflects schools from the real role they should play in the economic crisis, preparing citizens who can envision a different economic and social order and who have the courage and will to bring their vision into existence" (Fraser 1997, xv).

Schools could prepare such citizens via a progressive curriculum for *all* students, vocational-track and college-preparatory alike, which would include the study of labor's history and present conditions and provide a discourse on class that might produce subjects who see themselves as "workers" in a global economy.[7] Necessary to any kind of social change is an education that "fosters a critical understanding of social problems and their structural causes" (MacLeod 1995, 264).[8] It is tragic that many, if not most, "educated people" (and, particularly relevant here, school professionals) do not have the ability, the literacy, to articulate a description of the world in social structural terms. Repeatedly, I could see the utility for students of an understanding of their lives that brought into focus structural rather than individual causes. Understanding structural class inequality would be beneficial to the "self-esteem" of working-class students across race. Motivation based on indignation at the workings of power and the failures of democracy rather than on self-blame or other-blame is a prerequisite to the formation of class alliances.

It is the schools' obligation to prepare students as global citizens, and an education on the uneven distribution of social goods must be a part of that. Since nationally the new service-sector working class is largely composed of women and men of color and white women, gender and race must be organizing principles within the study of labor history, as they must be a part of labor organizing, in order to manifest an understanding of how race, gender, and sexual identity movements have and can continue to "enrich our conception of class, not move us away from it" (Kelley 1997, 123).

More important than including class as a part of a multicultural education, or more important than anything schools might do, is the need for inclusive unions that make class visible by constructing Americans and global citizens as politicized class subjects in the struggle for living wages. U.S. organized labor has historically been crippled not only by corporate power but by its own racism and androcentrism: the biases of a labor movement that has too long failed to conceptualize low-wage service economy jobs filled with women and men of color and white women as "working-class."[9]

Reflexive ethnography demands the recognition that the knowledges we produce are not neutral, but can have unanticipated political effects, ramifications for institutions, policies, and individuals. It is important, then, to try to avoid being naively drawn into the direct service of the very forces of social domination one is arguing against. There are risks in suggesting a renewed focus on class. If the absence of a discourse on class precludes the potential for the kind of class alliance across axes of difference necessary for a widespread labor movement, so too does a leftist discourse on class that is noninclusive. What is needed is a less exclusionary reformulation of class than has before been offered by the left. As Robin Kelley explains, historically the left has refused to be inclusive of race, gender, and sexuality, because "they either do not understand or refuse to acknowledge that class is *lived through* race and gender" (1997, 109; emphasis mine). Because experiences of class are always racialized and gendered, there is no monolithic, authentic, culturally distinct and bound class identity. Just as there is no universal racial, gender, or sexual identity, there is no universal class identity (Kelley 1997). The same essentialized understanding of race, gender, and sexuality that makes class invisible in popular thinking is too often present in leftist thinking, where envisioning class as a universal identity is the product of the failure to treat race, gender, and sexuality as constructs. This tendency toward essentialism and universalism promotes the belief that "movements focused on race, gender, or sexuality necessarily undermine class unity and, by definition, cannot be emancipatory for the whole" (109), when in fact, race, gender, and sexuality can be "the ground upon which class conflicts are enacted" (202).

The risk in suggesting a renewed focus on class comes not only from the left's historic tendency to formulate noninclusive class politics, but now, perhaps more significantly, comes from the political right. The attendant dangers were never more clear to me than when I observed the most conservative, white (often male) students in my university classroom, whom I usually have to work hard to convince that class inequality exists at all, begin nodding their heads in ready agreement with me as if they were born marxists. Their easy agreement was bewildering at first, until I understood that they were nodding their heads for the wrong reason. In previous years such students had identified themselves as class-privileged and had positioned themselves on the defensive when faced with classroom learning about economic injustice. But now, I realized, the newfound conservative political discourse on class enabled them to position themselves as disadvantaged class (read white) subjects. They were nodding their heads, not because they understood institutionalized class inequality, but because on the surface, a gloss of class theory sounded reminiscent of the discourse of Proposition 209 they had readily latched onto. This points to how *imperative* it is that the progressive left conceptualize class directly in relationship to race and gender so that it cannot be mistaken as a code for "white" or a code for "white male." We see here that, like gender, race, and sexuality, class too is a site of discursive struggle; it too is never finished.

In embarking on a project that foregrounded class, and aware that an author's words continue to signify in spite of and sometimes against her own intentions, I feared and still fear unwittingly providing ammunition to those who would chose to employ it in ways with which I disagree. It is wise to remember always to "evaluate the motivations behind the deployment" of any given category (Fuss 1989, 32), to query who is utilizing it and under what circumstances, how it is deployed, and what the political goals and consequent effects are.

I set out not to privilege class but to demonstrate that it is an element of contemporary feminist and cultural theory that is often discursively present but analytically absent or that at best makes cameo appearances. It is ironic that class remains invisible in public discourse, and too often in critical social theory, under postindustrial conditions: a period when gender and race have become more salient and marked, and when regressive race- and gender-specific projects are actively shaping class formation itself, making women and men of color and white women primary occupants of low-wage, nonunion working-class categories. But given the androcentrism of the class concept, which includes both the historic meaning of working-class as white masculine industrial labor and the failure to think of women's work as productive, postindustrial conditions do make a U.S. working class hard to locate when so many women fill the ranks. At the same time, these changes can help to expose the historically gendered and raced character of class categories. How to define women in class terms has always been problematic by the conventions of class analysis. Exploring class by beginning with women's lives makes the contemporary salience of class as a cultural identity, and potentially a political one, more visible. Moreover, it enables conceptualizing class in nonreductionist ways that point to the multiple axes of social formation; it permits recognizing the diverse experience of class across other identities; and it points to demographic shifts in the working class.

These historic changes give good cause to renew an interest in class and to imagine nonreductionist ways of retheorizing class in relationship to gender, sexuality, and racial/ethnic identity within this historical context. In spite of the fact that class is not a more fundamental axis of organization and identity than race or gender, those categories are more easily essentialized. In our attempts to explore the ways these processes are and are not parallel, contemporary cultural studies often suggests the need to think of these multiple formations *evenly*. But we might consider that social actors do not see them this way, and explore how the meanings people actually give to these categories render class invisible. It is crucial to look at the nature of these entanglements and to theorize class in race and gendered terms. Class analysis should not displace contemporary work on race, gender, and sexuality; rather, we need to rethink the meaning of class by starting with women. Because women, like men, are never without class.

Notes

CHAPTER 1: PORTRAYING WARETOWN HIGH

1. A note on terminology. Race is a term that has historically been used to categorize human physical types based on perceived biological differences or a supposed genetic heritage but that in reality is socially, historically, and politically constructed. Thus, it does not have a fixed meaning, but is always under transformation and is currently used in multiple ways in popular and political discourse. Social scientists widely recognize that race as a biological category is a falsehood and contemporarily use the term to represent socially constructed categories, as I do here. Ethnicity refers to a common cultural heritage. But one source of the common cultural heritage of a diaspora of people is simply that they have been historically defined as a racial group; that is, what is held in common is having been falsely named and treated as a distinct "race" of people. On the one hand, group labels (like Chicanos, Latinos, Asian Americans, African Americans) among both voluntary and involuntary immigrant populations in the United States collapse important distinctions within each population. On the other hand, people within each of these populations do have in common the experience of having been defined and treated as a racial group, so the labels are, in the end, meaningful. At times, I use "race" in conjunction with "ethnicity" (i.e., "race/ethnicity," or "racial/ethnic") to indicate the relationship between a people having been socially constructed as a race and the creation of a common culture based on that group experience. At other times, for stylistic reasons, I use the term "race" apart from "ethnicity," leaving the relationship implicit. I use "color" when I mean to point specifically to the salience of phenotype.

2. Others have also addressed this transition, most notably Gilligan 1982; Brown and Gilligan 1992; Orenstein 1994; Eder, Evans, and Parker 1995; and

Taylor, Gilligan, and Sullivan 1995. I discuss a wider array of recent books on girls in chapter 2.

3. In California, community colleges (formerly known as junior colleges and often still so called by students) fulfill the state's guarantee that every Californian should have an opportunity to attend college, by providing a two-year program in which any high school graduate can prepare to transfer to a four-year institution. (The colleges also offer two-year associate degree programs and many other classes for job skills and lifelong learning.) California has two university systems, the California State Universities and the more selective University of California system, both of which require that applicants have completed certain coursework. In keeping with the students' usage, I often refer to community college as junior college or JC; I use "state universities and UC schools" to refer to the four-year institutions.

4. Moreover, the left grounds its "claims in secular social science instead of religious authority" (Stacey 1996, 52). See Stacey for a full account of how questionable social science has been employed to make the centrist case.

5. See Acland 1995 and Males 1996 for analyses of the social construction of "youth crisis."

6. For Gramsci (1971), "common-sense" is not merely "false consciousness" but contradictory, containing elements of both truth and ideology (negatively conceptualized).

7. "Cultural capital" refers to class-based knowledge, skills, linguistic and cultural competencies, and a worldview that is passed on via family and is related more to educational attainment than to occupation. See Bourdieu and Passeron 1977 and Bourdieu 1984.

8. By "habitus" Bourdieu means unconsciously enacted, socially learned dispositions and habits.

9. The Bracero Program was a joint project between the United States and Mexico that allowed the legal migration of Mexican men into the States as contract farmworkers. During the program's twenty-two years, 4.8 million Mexican men worked on U.S. farms to help make up for the decline in the labor force during World War II. Though these jobs were seasonal and the program did not provide for resident status, many braceros never returned to Mexico.

10. See Vigil 1988. Also see Acland 1995 on the social construction of "gangs" as a social problem. Acland suggests that media accounts too readily apply the description "gang-related activity" to crime within minority communities. Likewise Miller 1995 suggests that "gang member" is a label applied too readily to youth of color and operates as a form of social control. It is important to note that the description of youth gangs and the function they serve is remarkably similar to the characteristics Eckert 1989 gives for groups of working-class white youth; that is, an age-stratified cohort, friendships based on neighborhoods more than school activities, and the use of older peers as links to the job market. In spite of these similarities across race, it is primarily youth of color who are labeled "gangs."

11. "Matured out" refers to a change in orientation toward more conventional lives (Vigil 1988). Vigil's account of "hard-core" versus "fringe" gang members parallels Howell's (1973) distinction between hard and settled living.

Whereas temporary, peripheral, or situational gang members who tend to mature out early come from relatively stable backgrounds, long-term members tend to come from less stable backgrounds and are more willing to engage in illegal income-generating strategies (Vigil 1988).

12. See Clifford and Marcus 1986; Clifford 1988; Stacey 1988; Mascia-Lees, Sharpe, and Cohen 1989; Gluck and Patai 1991; Kirby 1991; Visweswaran 1994; and Behar and Gordon 1995, among many others.

13. hooks 1984; Mohanty 1988, 1991, 1997; Spelman 1988; Zavella 1989; Alarcón 1990; and Trinh 1991, among many others.

14. See Moraga 1983; Anzaldúa 1987, 1990; Zavella 1987, 1993, 1994; S. Hall 1992; Alarcón 1993; and A. Garcia 1997, among many others.

15. Epstein 1987; Escoffier 1991; Harding 1991; and Gamson 1995, among others.

16. Personal communication, 1997; see also Newton and Stacey 1992.

CHAPTER 2: WOMEN WITHOUT CLASS

1. See McNall, Levine, and Fantasia 1991; Ortner 1991; Rorty 1991; Dimock and Gilmore 1994; Bullock 1995; Gitlin 1995; Gibson-Graham 1996, 2001; James and Berg 1996; Kadi 1996; Tomasky 1996; J. R. Hall 1997; Ellis 1998; Felski 2000; Gibson-Graham, Resnick, and Wolff 2000; and hooks 2000, among others.

2. Likewise, ignoring women in the study of race and ethnic relations means failing to see women as racial/ethnic national subjects. Feminists of color have long been critical about this. Most notably Hull, Scott, and Smith made the point with their anthology *All the Women Are White, All the Men Are Black, But Some of Us Are Brave* (1981). Fregoso (1987) and A. M. Garcia (1989) speak directly to the fact that Chicanas have been missing as nationalist subjects in Chicano nationalism.

3. See Cohen 1972; Hall and Jefferson 1976; Willis 1977; Hebdige 1979; and, in the United States, MacLeod 1987; and Foley 1990.

4. Class categories themselves have long been interrogated by feminist criticism because a gendered division of labor and occupational segregation create an obstacle to any single classification (Crompton 1993). Also see Garnsey 1982 for discussions of individual vs. family as a unit of analysis and of the problematic distinction between blue- and white-collar and manual and nonmanual labor in thinking through women's class location.

5. See early works such as Gans 1962; E. P. Thompson 1963; Sennett and Cobb 1972; Aronowitz 1973; Howell 1973; and, later, Halle 1984, and Ryan and Sackrey 1984. See L. B. Rubin 1976 for an early corrective to the almost exclusionary focus on men and for an analysis of the links between work and family. But even here definitions of class remain masculine, in that the "working-class" sample of women studied were selected because they were the wives of blue-collar men. L. B. Rubin 1994 later provides a corrective to this in that blue-collar and pink-collar workers, as well as low-level white-collar service workers, are included and defined as "working-class."

6. See for example, Brown and Gilligan 1992; Orenstein 1994; Pipher 1994; Eder, Evans, and Parker 1995; and Taylor, Gilligan, and Sullivan 1995.

7. Mohanty (1991) offers a definition of "third-world women" that parallels the way "women of color" is often used to designate a constituency of women who share a "common context of struggle." Both terms are often meant to point to a community of potential alliances among women of color in the third world and women of color in the United States. See also Hull, Scott, and Smith 1981; Moraga and Anzaldúa 1981; B. Smith 1983; Anzaldúa 1987, 1990; Asian Women United of California 1989; Alarcón 1990; de la Torre and Pesquera 1993; Hurtado 1996; Sandoval 1998; Trujillo 1998; and Ruiz and DuBois 2000.

8. Critical race feminism takes up "critical race theory," a body of scholarship (stemming from critical legal theory) that works to expose color-blind and race-neutral public policy and practice, revealing the ways in which white privilege is maintained through liberal concepts of legal equality and neutrality. See Delgado 1995; Crenshaw et al. 1995; Ladson-Billings and Tate 1995; and Nebeker 1998, among others.

9. It should be noted that lesbian feminists also made a significant intervention into and transformation of the gender assumptions often made in early second-wave feminism.

10. This trend both continues in and is challenged by the proliferating literature on whiteness, which is uneven in its degree of attentiveness to unpacking class differences among whites. Historical works on whiteness appear to grapple with class fairly consistently, because the very invention of whiteness is seen as a response to class inequities (e.g., Roediger 1991, 1994; Allen 1994, 1997). Works that focus on the contemporary operations of whiteness, however, are more inconsistent in their treatment of class (e.g., Frankenberg 1993, 1997; Daniels 1997; Fine et al. 1997; Wray and Newitz 1997; Lipsitz 1998). Notable exceptions include Hartigan 1997a, 1997b; P. Cohen 1997; and Twine 1997.

11. See Spelman 1988; Alarcón 1990; and Bettie 2001.

12. Writings by feminists of color often contribute to thinking through the subjective experience of class difference as it intersects with racial/ethnic difference. See Hull, Scott, and Smith 1981; Moraga and Anzaldúa 1981; B. Smith 1983; Anzaldúa 1987, 1990; Asian Women United of California 1989; de la Torre and Pesquera 1993; Hurtado 1996; Trujillo 1998; and Ruiz and DuBois 2000. Similar anthologies that include writings by white working-class women (Zandy 1990; Tokarczyk and Faye 1993; and Mathony and Zmroczek 1997) help demonstrate the similarity and difference of working-class experience across race. Works that promote anti-essentialist understandings of race by working to deconstruct racial/ethnic "authenticity" (see Zavella 1989; hooks 1990, 1992, 1994; S. Hall 1992, among others) and by pointing to diversity *within* group categories also help to foreground class difference along with other differences like gender, generation, and geography.

13. Bowles and Gintis 1976; Bourdieu and Passeron 1977.

14. See Holland and Eisenhart 1990 for a clear overview of reproduction, production, and practice theories.

15. See Gordon 1976, 1988, 1994; Stacey 1983, 1990; Zavella 1987; Acker

1988; Scott 1988; Mohanty 1991, 1997; Ware 1992; Chang 1994; and Lowe 1996, among others.

16. See Zavella 1987; Mohanty 1991, 1997; Roediger 1991; Almaguer 1994; Chang 1994; Lowe 1996; and Frank 1999, among others, for accounts of the ways in which class hierarchy and racial order are mutually constitutive.

17. It is constructive to consider the potential overlap between Sennett and Cobbs's (1972) conceptualization of hidden injuries and Bourdieu's (1977) notion of symbolic violence, whereby social control manifests indirectly via culture rather than directly via coercion. This happens primarily through indoctrination in school settings, where one culture or meaning system (e.g., a middle-class cultural form) is imposed upon the lower classes, is constructed as the only culture that is legitimate, and is internalized and thus misrecognized as legitimate, so that the power relations behind the imposition are obscured. This internalized sense that one's own cultural forms are illegitimate might be said to produce the social psychological status anxiety and injury to dignity that Sennett and Cobb describe.

18. By this Williams meant the "affective elements of consciousness and relationships" in a given historical moment, arguing that meanings and values are "actively lived and felt" (1977, 132).

19. Some of what I label "cultural capital" for the sake of simplicity throughout this text might be more accurately labeled "symbolic capital" or "social capital." Symbolic capital refers to prestige and social honor; social capital, to forms of social support provided by a person's interpersonal network. See Stanton-Salazar and Dornbusch 1995 and Stanton-Salazar 1997, 2001 for a detailed exploration of the barriers faced by Mexican-American students that hinder their access to social capital and institutional support and therefore to educational success. See Lamont and Lareau 1988 for an overview of the multiple and contradictory usages of the concept "cultural capital," especially as applied to the United States. Many have explored the utility of Bourdieu's concepts to the study of racial/ethnic and gender difference. Whereas in Bourdieu's work, cultural capital too readily determines class location, other axes of identity and social processes might account for exceptions to this rule. For instance, McCall (1992) considers the utility of Bourdieu's work to feminist theory and the study of gender; Gándara (1995) suggests that among upwardly mobile working-class Chicana/os family stories of exceptionalism and lost fortunes work as a kind of cultural capital to aid in mobility; MacLeod (1995) notes that "habitus," which refers to systems of learned dispositions based on class, might also be applied to think through gender and racial/ethnic dispositions and demonstrates this difference in his study of black and white boys; Holland and Eisenhart (1990) and Skeggs (1997) consider women's sexual attractiveness as a form of capital.

20. I find "status group" limited in its utility as an analytical category, perhaps causing more confusion than clarity. Too often it is used as a catchall term in which gender and race are placed as membership categories alongside, say, "Shriners," as if they are the same. The definition of status groups as having a collective sense of honor does not resonate with race and gender identity generally, but only when those are politicized identities. See my discussion of the

distinction students make between "hicks" and "farmers" in chapter 4 for further explanation.

21. See S. Cohen 1972; Hall and Jefferson 1976; Willis 1977; Hebdige 1979.

22. In Becker's *The Outsiders* (1963), for example, the analysis centers on deviance from norms and not on class or race consciousness, resistance, or power differentials. There have been some exceptions to this "deviance and delinquency" frame in the study of "gangs" and of the race-class consciousness of "style"; for example Vigil 1988; Cosgrove 1989; Jankowski 1991; and Ferrell and Sanders 1995. It is also present in some analyses of popular culture, for example, Lipsitz 1994a. See Brake 1980 for an overview of both U.S. and British sociologies of youth and youth subcultures; for more contemporary analyses, see Austin and Willard 1998.

23. Using hip hop as a case study, Rose suggests that in reality subcultural ruptures never actually take place outside of commodity culture, and thus the distinction between an early authentic/original moment and a later moment of commercial exploitation is artificial. Subcultural challenges are always "articulated via commodities and engaged in the revision of meanings attached to them" (1994, 82–83).

24. While girls have been largely missing from the ethnographic study of subcultures (McRobbie and Garber 1976 and McRobbie 1978 are early exceptions), there is a growing interest in them now. See Bhavani, Kent, and Twine 1998 (a special issue of *Signs* on Feminisms and Youth Culture). Ethnographic work and textual analyses of girls and subcultures, as well as studies of girls and schooling, often overlap. See McRobbie and McCabe 1981, McRobbie and Nava 1984, McRobbie 1991 and 1994, Roman 1988, and LeBlanc 1999 for ethnographic work on girl punks; Rose 1990, 1994 on black women rappers; and Walkerdine 1997 on girls and talent shows. See also Fregoso 1995 for a textual analysis of homegirls, cholas, and pachucas in the film *Mi Vida Loca* and L. Lewis 1990 on girls' consumption of music videos.

There is a growing interest in female gangs but no real literature yet other than the few pages in each book on male gangs. The absence of girls from the literature on gangs is less likely to reflect the absence of girls in gang activity than the failure to see girls as racial/ethnic-class subjects. But see Horowitz 1983 and Campbell 1984.

25. McRobbie and Garber (1976) wrote about girls and subculture in *Resistance through Rituals*. Others have begun this work or made a call for it. Steedman (1986) has suggested feminists need to theorize women's class subjectivity through sites other than work and production, such as family and social relations and the terrain of style. Ortner (1991, 1993, 1998) too has renewed an interest in class along these lines.

26. While Mohanty (1992) uses the terms "inherited" and "chosen" to refer to cultural and political identities respectively, I use the terms to refer in both instances to *cultural* identities, not political ones. By inherited identity I mean to point to those cultural resources received from one's family of origin, and by chosen identity I mean to point to those cultural resources not inherited but desired and emulated.

27. Foley (1990) also explores class as a performance, employing Goffman and Habermas, but he limits his analysis to the ways in which varying "speech performances" express class membership. See also Bernstein's classic work (1975) on the distinction between a middle-class "elaborated" speech code and a working-class "restricted" speech code.

28. For critiques, see Collins et al. 1995. See also Bordo 1992 and Hood-Williams and Harrison 1998 for a discussion of Butler's work and phenomenological sociologies. Similarly, poststructuralist theories have been at times critiqued for conceptualizing the practioner of theory as a subject who is entirely free-floating and indeterminate, exercising more choice than is actually possible in self-fashioning an identity. As Bordo explains it, the objectivist epistemology of "The View from Nowhere" has been replaced with "The View from Everywhere," in which the deconstructionist assumes "seemingly inexhaustive vantage points none of which are owned" (1990, 142).

29. Although I present many of the social structural forces that work against school success, many more have already been documented at great length by sociologists and anthropologists of education and are taken for granted as a backdrop to the analysis of identity and that I offer. In particular see Stanton-Salazar 1997 and Phelan, Davidson, and Yu 1993. The latter distinguish between sociocultural barriers (where the culture of one's ethnic community is cast as inferior in the schooling environment), socioeconomic barriers, linguistic barriers (when bilingualism is obstructed), and structural barriers (lack of institutional resources). Beyond these are teachers' low expectations of students of color, schools' failure to protect students from exploitation by proprietary (for-profit vocational) schools, and schools' investment in tracking and in alternative routes to a diploma for "at risk" youth. See also Darder, Torres, and Gutíerrez 1997.

30. Many have begun to note that contemporary cultural theory often does not do an adequate job of theorizing just how discourse enters and constructs the subject in social psychological terms, or "the practices of meaning-making and the inner mindful and imaginative dimensions of those practices" (Lembo 2000, 86). That is, "identity" is conceptualized as an effect of discourse and at the same time as the source of agency, thus explaining little. Where Butler attempts to deal with interiority using psychoanalytic theory, Lembo provides a useful attempt to rebuild the agent by synthesizing Butler's poststructuralism with Mead's and Goffman's symbolic interactionist sociology, suggesting that mindfulness ("an internal process of thinking, of reflexive engagement"; 2000, 91) in performance is not based on an unchanging essence, does not suggest a prediscursive "I," and might usefully be combined with a poststructuralist focus on power and discourse. This problem of interiority is the same as the question of structure versus agency, since the interior is the site where the subject as an active agent, "a person who is understood to be capable of initiating thought and action" (89) would manifest. Bourdieu's concept of "habitus" is an attempt to bridge the structure/agency divide but ends up more squarely on the side of structure, given that it is used to refer to unconscious habits and dispositions that inform practices, more than consciously learned rules. Moreover, habitus

remains a "black box" in Bourdieu's work, as he too "neglects the actual process whereby external forces and internal consciousness wrestle with each other" (MacLeod 1987, 255).

31. Here I am paraphrasing Bordo (1992), who poses these same questions about race in her review of Butler 1990.

32. For some examples of such explorations see Allison 1994; Penelope 1994; Kadi 1996; and Raffo 1997. Among British feminists, see Steedman 1986; Mathony and Zmroczek 1997; Skeggs 1997; and Walkerdine 1997.

CHAPTER 3: HOW WORKING-CLASS CHICAS GET WORKING-CLASS LIVES

1. A quinceañera is a celebration of a girl's fifteenth birthday, thought to signal the time when she enters adulthood and becomes a woman, has reached sexual maturity, and/or is ready for marriage.

2. For a parallel kind of analysis see Banks 2000 on black women and the cultural politics of hair.

3. The distinction I make here between dissident and school-sanctioned femininity is an oversimplification. Another variation of dissident femininity not characterized by feminine sexual display is discussed in chapter 4.

4. See also Enstad 1999.

5. Horowitz 1983 and S. Thompson 1994 also found girl fights not reducible to heterosexual tensions.

6. *Coconut* is used to signify "brown on the outside but white on the inside."

7. See Blake 1997; Zavella 1997; and Hurtado 1998, among many others, for discussions of Chicana sexuality. It is certainly the case that my status as a cultural outsider shaped the conversations I had with Mexican-American girls on the topic of sexuality. There were no particular incidents or remarks that made a lack of intersubjectivity or girls' discomfort apparent to me, but nonetheless I want to acknowledge here this likelihood.

8. See S. Thompson 1995 for a sophisticated account of "teenage girls' tales of sex, romance and pregnancy." See also Tolman 1994.

9. See Fine 1988 for a fuller discussion of the "missing discourse of desire" in sex education courses and how anti-sex rhetoric arrests the development of sexual responsibility among adolescents.

10. Fine summarizes the status of proprietary schools in the state of New York, where the State Department of Education's 1985 report "found that proprietary schools [were] involved in violation of entry requirements; questionable recruitment practices; high dropout rates; less than quality standards; inadequate record keeping; and failure to offer instructional programs approved by the State Department of Education" (1991, 91).

11. Fordham and Ogbu (1986) and Fordham (1996, 1999) address the meanings of the phrase "acting white" among black students. The content of "acting white" in their subjects' accounts is often (but not always) coded middle class (e.g., attending the Smithsonian or the symphony, playing golf, going to the country club, and doing volunteer work). Fordham and Ogbu show that academic success is equated with whiteness and that the fear of being accused

of "acting white" can lead to underachievement and various other strategies that are employed to "cope with the burden of acting white." See also Cousins 1999 and Matute-Bianchi 1991, who discusses "acting Anglo" among Mexican-American students. Setting aside the students' meanings, when I refer to a student as "acting white" here I do not, of course, mean that they are really Mexican-American in a modernist, realist, essentialist way. Rather, white and Mexican-American are historically constructed, racialized subjectivities that are only temporarily fixed categories of identity, in that social actors embrace them as real and they are real in their consequences. Likewise, there is no "authentic" racial/ethnic self, but only an ideology of essentialized authenticity that is mobilized by actors to achieve various effects.

12. It is not apparent what the content of whiteness as a cultural identity is in social science discourse either. For many writers on whiteness (Roediger 1991, 1994; Allen 1994, 1997; Lipsitz 1998), whiteness is conceptualized as a system of domination, where whiteness is described as a politicized racial positioning in the struggle over resources. When whiteness is viewed as nothing more than an oppressive ideology, it is seen as culturally bereft. Whiteness as a *cultural* identity is less explored in whiteness studies, but notable exceptions include Hartigan who, pointing to regional and class differences among whites, argues that "while whiteness may be fixed as a unified or unifying phenomenon when regarded ideologically at the national level, on the ground that unity quickly becomes illusory" (1997b, 180). Twine (1997) also points to white cultural identity as the product of everyday negotations in her interviews with multiracial women of known African descent who acquired a white cultural identity in childhood. Activities such as family conversations and silences, dating, consumerism, and friendships were central to the shifting racial identities of these women. See also P. Cohen 1997 and Perry 2001. Whiteness as an identity outside of middle-classness is discussed again in chapter 6.

13. Vigil (1988) explains the link between pachuco style and low income, noting that starched and creased khaki pants, for example, originated in military and penal institutions, sites central to working-class life. Likewise, Dickie is a brand of work clothing, which has been appropriated and has come to signify group membership.

14. For example, Oulette (1999) keenly describes how Helen Gurley Brown's intent in creating *Cosmopolitan* magazine was to instruct pink-collar working-class women how to present themselves as middle-class in order to attract a superior (read, middle-class) man and enable their mobility via marriage.

CHAPTER 4: HARD-LIVING HABITUS, SETTLED-LIVING RESENTMENT

1. See Bettie 1995 and Wray and Newitz 1997 for explorations of the race and class meanings of "poor white trash."

2. By postfeminist I mean that they take certain feminist gains for granted, such as the right to have a career and a family both, but they fail to see these as political achievements of a women's movement (see Stacey 1990).

3. This theme was reflected at the time in the movie *The Craft* (1996) about

three marginalized high school girls who enact revenge on popular students through their use of witchcraft. This film reflects a genre of popular culture about subordinate girls' empowerment, much like the 1976 film *Carrie.*

4. B. Thompson's (1994) interview study challenges the popular belief that eating disorders are experienced primarily by women who are young, white, heterosexual, and middle- or upper-class. She suggests that the rate of eating disorders among working-class women, women of color, and lesbians is hard to measure, given that physicians may too often assume that such disorders are common only to white, middle-class, heterosexual women and so may misdiagnose working-class women, women of color, and lesbians. While not refuting the salience of gender identity and the impact of media images on girls and women, Thompson demonstrates that eating disorders cross the boundaries of race, class, sexuality, and generation and cannot be understood solely in terms of gender. She argues that such disorders are in "response to myriad injustices including racism, sexism, homophobia, classism, the stress of acculturation, and emotional, physical, and sexual abuse" (2).

5. Between 1960 and 1980, the U.S. divorce rate increased sharply, from 2.2 to 5.2 divorces per thousand population. Since then, the divorce rate has stabilized and in 1996 was 4.4 divorces per thousand population (U.S. Bureau of the Census 1966). Evidence that divorce is drastically injurious to children rests, as Stacey explains, on "social scientific sleights-of-hand" (1996, 60): widely cited studies (Wallerstein and Kelly 1980; Wallerstein and Blakeslee 1989) that argue that children of divorce are worse off than those whose parents do not divorce fail to provide control groups of children whose parents experience conflict in their marriages but do not divorce. There is much evidence that family conflict is a more important variable than family structure in assessing children's well-being (Furstenburg and Cherlin 1991; Demo 1992). (See Fassel 1991 for an account of the positive strengths and behaviors children acquire from witnessing parental divorce.) In fact, "when other parental resources—like income, education, self-esteem, and a supportive social environment—are roughly similar, signs of two-parent privilege largely disappear" (Stacey 1996, 60). This suggests that it is not divorce per se that is problematic for kids but the poverty of women, especially working-class women, which is a consequence of the loss of male income from the family.

6. See Stacey 1996 for an account of the "revisionist" campaign on family values.

7. This argument was made notorious by Daniel Patrick Moynihan in the 1965 "Moynihan Report," which suggested that black poverty was the consequence of a "tangle of pathology," a different value system among African Americans. Focusing on family structure, his report suggested that the prevalence of female-headed black families was due to black cultural difference, failing to consider that the structure of black families might be an adaptation to harsh socioeconomic conditions, as later researchers argued (Stack 1974; Gutman 1976; White 1985).

8. Often studies of the reproduction of inequality in schools fail to consider family as a site of the production of class identity, focusing instead on the role of schooling and peer culture and emphasizing structural constraints over cul-

tural difference. At times authors (see Halle 1984; MacLeod 1995) explain that they fear a focus on family will suggest to readers a culture of poverty argument. But this, of course, is not an adequate reason for the failure to give any priority to family as a site for the production of class subjectivity. Some have recognized this and called for more work in this area (see Weis 1990; MacLeod 1995.) See also Lareau 1987.

9. The character Roseanne occasionally referred to her family as "white trash" on the television show of the same name (see Bettie 1995). A 1994 "This World" insert from the *San Francisco Chronicle* was titled "White Trash Nation" and featured photos of Tanya Harding and Joey Buttafuoco on the cover with a subtitle that read "America's fast-growing underclass is setting ever-lower standards of behavior." The same year *Rolling Stone* identified "White Trash" as the new "hot subculture," mentioning Roseanne and Tom Arnold, John Wayne Bobbitt, Clint Black, Hank Williams Jr., and Brett Butler as representatives.

10. See Hebdige's 1979 classic work on British punks.

11. See Brake 1980; Street 1986; and Fox 1987 for discussions of how U.S. punk culture lacks a clearly articulated class politics. See Roman 1988 and LeBlanc 1999 on appropriations of punk by girls in the United States. See also White's (1995) account of the emergence of "rriot girls," whose political articulations of gender defiance through style are, at times, somewhat sophisticated. Rriot girls (or grrls) juxtapose elements of conventional girl culture like baby doll dresses, Barbie lunch boxes, and barrettes with a heavy handed critique of male control over female sexuality. Rriot girls recognize contradiction as a powerful way to articulate such a critique and reappropriate elements of girl culture while naming bands Bikini Kill, Babes in Toyland, and Seven Year Bitch and singing songs like "Dead Men Don't Rape." According to White, the rriot girl movement was largely a white middle-class movement of college women, and their focus on gender and sexuality excluded race and class concerns. Rriot girl culture was not something the girls I studied were familiar with.

CHAPTER 5: BORDER WORK BETWEEN CLASSES

1. See Willis 1977; Eckert 1989; Foley 1990; Weis 1990; Brantlinger 1993; and MacLeod 1995, among others.

2. As feminists have pointed out, domestic violence exists across class categories, but its occurrence is easier for middle-class families to hide, given their economic resources and access to private treatment rather than public services. The same is true with regard to substance abuse. See Reinarman and Levine 1997.

3. There is little research to draw upon in answering the question of whether working-class girls have higher academic achievement than their male counterparts. The American Association of University Women study (1992, 1994) on girls and schooling did not compare boys' and girls' graduation rates or grades, but compared them only on six subjective "self-esteem" measures, arguing that girls suffer from lower self-esteem than boys in almost all cases. Although some attention was paid to racial differences (African-American girls scored higher

on self-esteem than Latinas and white girls, but lower on the academic self-esteem measure), the findings failed to analyze class differences among girls at all. Moreover, given that self-esteem is a context-specific phenomenon, it is not clear what we learn from this methodological approach. The more recent AAUW report on Latinas (2001), in recognition of the problems with trying to measure "self-esteem," uses the concept "possible selves" as an alternative. The report shows that persistence rates are roughly equal for Latina/o girls and boys, but that between ninth and twelfth grade, girls have a lower persistence rate than boys. Also, while Latinas start out school with higher self-esteem than any other group, theirs decreases the most in comparison to white and African-American girls toward young adulthood. Gándara (1995) found that low-income Chicanas who were upwardly mobile academically outperformed their male peers. See Valenzuela 1999a for an account of how working-class Chicanas promoted a pro-school ethic among their male peers.

4. See Steinitz and Solomon 1986 for further discussion of how class interacts in important ways with geography.

5. Studies that explore the variable of generation on high school graduation present conflicting results. Most studies that explore the impact of generational status on high school graduation among Latinos suggest that children of immigrants have higher levels of achievement than second- and third-generation youth (Nielsen and Fernandez 1982; Fernandez and Nielsen 1986; Buriel and Cardoza 1988; Portes and Rumbaut 1990; Chavez 1991; Matute-Bianchi 1991; Ogbu 1991; Suarez-Orozco 1991; Landsman et al. 1992; Portes and Zhou 1993; Buriel 1994; Kao and Tienda 1995; Zsembik and Llanes 1996; and Valenzuela 1999b). Other studies find that third-generation students have higher rates of high school graduation and college attendance than second- and first-generation (immigrant) students (Featherman and Hauser 1978; Baral 1979; McCarthy and Valdez 1985; Chapa 1988; and Hurtado et al. 1992). Yet other studies show no impact of generation on dropping out of high school (Fernandez, Paulsen, and Hirano-Nakanishi 1989; Romo and Falbo 1996). No studies are comprehensive enough to control for all the variables that need to be considered, including generation, socioeconomic status of the family before immigration, socioeconomic status in the United States, ethnicity (i.e., disaggregating the category Latina/o), gender, language fluency (see Rumberger and Larson 1998), and whether academic achievement (represented by completion of high school or grade reports) is disaggregated by vocational and college-prep curriculums. Studies usually explore only one or two of these variables. Moreover, the use of different measurements makes cross-study comparisons difficult. To my knowledge there is no parallel literature that explores in an extensive way the causes of white working-class upward mobility. But for accounts of the subjective experience of upward mobility among whites, see Sennett and Cobb 1972; Ryan and Sackrey 1984; Zandy 1990; Tokarczyk and Faye 1993; Skeggs 1997; Reay 1998; and Lawler 1999.

6. This is also akin to MacLeod's (1995) naming of an "achievement ideology."

7. Although, unfortunately, he argues against bilingual education, Rodri-

guez (1982) still provides a compelling account of the loss of language and culture as one of the potential (but not inevitable) costs of class mobility.

8. Mehan, Hubbard, and Villanueva (1994) also found that some nonimmigrant Latinos combined achievement with a critical consciousness of structural inequality rather than perceiving school success as assimilationist.

9. I don't mean to over-romanticize MEChA, wherein identity production is actually quite complex. Its participants, at times, promote an essentialized notion of racial/ethnic identity based on uncontested origins, raising a number of questions about the efficacy of identity politics as a political strategy—namely, when belonging is hinged on the notion of an "authentic" cultural identity and not on political identification. Nonetheless, in the context of Waretown High, it proved a valuable and empowering tool for some students by offering them pride in Chicana/o identity and skills for mobility.

10. Valenzuela also keenly addresses generation and style among Mexican-American youth and how students' use of it is commonly misinterpreted by teachers and, at times, parents. See also Darder's (1991) critique of traditional pedagogy, her discussion of the variety of student responses to the biculturation process, and her elaboration of an alternative critical bicultural pedagogy.

11. As Valenzuela (1999b) rightly points out, the focus on student attitudes found in the Ogbu tradition at times causes researchers to lose sight of the institution and to fail to point to schools' accountability for student achievement. Gándara (1995) notes that the upwardly mobile Chicana/os in her study benefited from a view that achievement is not symbolically opposed to the affirmation of cultural identity. The research of Portes and Zhou (1993) also suggests that those students who remain closely allied to their parents' culture are the most academically successful. See also Flores-Gonzales 1999.

12. Sennett and Cobb 1972; Rodriguez 1982; Horowitz 1983; Ryan and Sackrey 1984; hooks 1989; Baca Zinn et al. 1990; Childers and hooks 1990; Zandy 1990; Granfield 1991; Tokarczyk and Faye 1993; Cuádraz and Pierce 1994; Kadi 1996; Reay 1998; Cuádraz 1999; Lawler 1999; and Mullen 1999, among others. These authors address the issue directly, but much of the vast body of literature produced by third-world feminists speaks implicitly to class as a subjective experience.

13. See Bettie 1995, 2000. Class origins can be signified by teeth (revealing whether one has access to dental care), weight (in the United States weight is inversely correlated with socioeconomic status), clothing, and grammar.

14. As has been found among black Americans, studies show that Mexican Americans with lighter skin color and European features have more years of education and higher earnings than darker-complected Mexican Americans (Arce, Murguia, and Frisbie 1987; Telles and Murguia 1990; Bloom 1991).

CHAPTER 6: SAMENESS, DIFFERENCE, AND ALLIANCE

1. In May 2001 the University of California Regents voted unanimously to repeal SP1 and SP2, resolutions that had prohibited affirmative action in admissions and hiring. However, it is still too soon to tell what effects this will

have on actual future admissions and hiring in the UC system, as Proposition 209, despite legal challenges, was deemed constitutional by federal courts.

2. People of color are now the majority of the population in California, with whites constituting 49.86 percent of the total state population, Latinos 31.56 percent, and other racial/ethnic groups less than 13 percent each (U.S. Bureau of the Census 2000).

3. Since the implementation of Proposition 209, undergraduate admission of Latino, African-American, and Native-American students has decreased significantly at the top University of California campuses, dropping from 22.2 percent in fall 1997 to 10.2 percent in fall 1998 at UC Berkeley and from 19.7 percent in fall 1997 to 12.5 percent in fall 1998 at UCLA. See University of California 1998.

4. Gilligan 1982; Holland and Eisenhart 1990; Brown and Gilligan 1992; Orenstein 1994; Eder 1995; and Taylor, Gilligan, and Sullivan 1995.

5. The Personal Responsibility and Work Opportunity Reconcilement Act signed into law by President Clinton in 1996 has meant that welfare assistance is now limited to a lifetime total of five years per person, without regard for the availability of paid employment, and recipients are forced to work or perform community service in exchange for assistance. States are required to implement strategies that reduce pregnancies outside of marriage, to increase statutory rape convictions, and to enforce paternity and child support rules that reduce or terminate assistance for mothers deemed "non-cooperative." For a more detailed analysis of welfare reform, see Mink 1998, which argues that welfare reform is an attack not only on the rights of women in poverty but on the rights of all women because of the patriarchal morality encoded in welfare reform's attack on reproductive and vocational freedoms. Since the implementation of the act, it appears that the number of people on welfare has decreased substantially as recipients move from "welfare-to-work," but the evidence does not suggest they have found living-wage jobs. A joint report by the Children's Defense Fund and the National Coalition on Homelessness (Sherman et al. 1998) found that 71 percent of former welfare recipients who had found work were earning less than the poverty level for a three-person household ($250 per week). Further, these low-paying jobs rarely provided benefits, and many former recipients lacked food, medical care, and stable housing. Moreover, in some states up to 50 percent of former welfare recipients had not found employment, and many families were denied cash assistance through no fault of their own.

6. Proposition 187, meant to withhold a number of social services from undocumented immigrants (including public education, emergency health care, and prenatal care), was passed by California voters in 1994. It was challenged by the American Civil Liberties Union and the League of United Latin American Citizens and was put on hold in 1997 by U.S. District Court Judge Marina Pfaelzer, who declared it unconstitutional. Governor Pete Wilson appealed the judge's decision in 1999, but his successor, Governor Gray Davis, signed an agreement with civil rights groups stating that he would not appeal the judge's decision. This effectively killed the measure, and ultimately Proposition 187 was never fully implemented.

CHAPTER 7: CONCLUSION

1. Because the majority of children usually live with their mother after divorce, because women's earning power is generally less than men's, and because court-decreed child support awards are often insufficient or are not met by fathers, women's standard of living drops dramatically upon divorce (Weitzman 1985); family income, on average, declines by 37 percent when the father moves out of the household (Seltzer 1994).

2. The concept *experience* has been a source of angst and debate in feminist theory over the past decade, as theorists who promote an antifoundationalist epistemology (e.g., Scott 1990; Butler 1990, 1993) have critiqued others ("standpoint theorists," in particular) for their suggestion that the source of knowledge is "experience," conceptualized as raw, objective, and unmediated by meaning systems. Postmodern theorists suggest instead that while the source of knowledge is indeed "experience," that experience and identity are discursively constructed. Here, neither the subject, identity, nor experience exists in some form prior to or outside of discourse. That is, there is no unified subject that exists prior to discourse and that can have experiences which are transparent to herself. For a discussion, see Collins 1987; Harding 1987; Hartsock 1987; Hekman 1987; and D. E. Smith 1987, all of which are in the symposium on "standpoint theory revisited" in *Signs* 22, no. 2 (winter 1997). See also Alcoff 1988; Bordo 1990; and Fuss 1989.

3. See Bowles and Gintis 1976; Bourdieu and Passeron 1977.

4. Even according to Eric Olin Wright (1982), chronicler of the U.S. class structure, "the majority of the working class in the United States consists of women" (53.6 percent).

5. Weis's (1990) research suggests that with deindustrialization and the increasing importance placed on a college education for all students, working-class boys are beginning to rework working-class masculinity such that schooling is no longer viewed as emasculating.

6. See, for example, Fregoso 1987; A. M. Garcia 1989; and hooks 1990, among others.

7. See Anyon 1983, 1996 for a critical analysis of the absence of class from curricula.

8. See the work of Freire (1990) and Giroux (1983) on critical literacy.

9. For accounts of the exclusion of women and people of color in the history of American labor, see, e.g., Hartmann 1979; Zavella 1987; Scott 1988; Frank 1994; Lipsitz 1994b; Roediger 1994; Wellman 1995; Kelley 1997.

References

Acker, Joan. 1988. “Class, Gender and the Relations of Distribution.” *Signs: Journal of Women in Culture and Society* 13, no. 3 (spring): 473–97.

Acland, Charles R. 1995. *Youth, Murder, Spectacle: The Cultural Politics of “Youth in Crisis.”* Boulder, Colo.: Westview Press.

Alarcón, Norma. 1990. “The Theoretical Subject(s) of *This Bridge Called My Back* and Anglo-American Feminism.” In *Making Face, Making Soul / Haciendo Caras: Creative and Critical Perspectives by Women of Color,* edited by Gloria Anzaldúa, 356–69. San Francisco: Aunt Lute Foundation.

———, ed. 1993. *Chicana Critical Issues.* Berkeley, Calif.: Third Woman Press.

Alcoff, Linda. 1988. “Cultural Feminism versus Post-Structuralism: The Identity Crisis in Feminist Theory.” *Signs: Journal of Women in Culture and Society* 13, no. 3 (spring): 405–36.

Allen, Theodore W. 1994. *The Invention of the White Race.* Vol. 1, *Racial Oppression and Social Control.* London and New York: Verso.

———. 1997. *The Invention of the White Race.* Vol. 2, *The Origin of Racial Oppression in Anglo America.* London and New York: Verso.

Allison, Dorothy. 1994. *Skin: Talking About Sex, Class, and Literature.* Ithaca, N.Y.: Firebrand Books.

Almaguer, Tomás. 1994. *Racial Fault Lines: The Historical Origins of White Supremacy in California.* Berkeley: University of California Press.

American Association of University Women. 1992. *How Schools Shortchange Girls: The AAUW Report: A Study of Major Findings on Girls and Education.* Washington, D.C.: AAUW Educational Foundation, National Education Association.

———. 1994. *Shortchanging Girls, Shortchanging America: Executive Summary.* Washington, D.C.: American Association of University of Women.

———. 2001. *Si Se Puede! Yes, We Can: Latinas in School.* Washington, D.C.: American Association of University Women.

Anyon, Jean. 1983. "Workers, Labor, and Economic History, and Textbook Content." In *Ideology and Practice in Schooling,* edited by Michele Apple and Lois Weis, 37–60. Philadelphia: Temple University Press.

———. 1984. "Intersections of Gender and Class: Accommodation and Resistance by Working-Class and Affluent Females to Contradictory Sex-Role Ideologies." *Journal of Education* 166, no. 1: 27–48.

———. 1996. "Social Class and the Hidden Curriculum of Work." In *Transforming Curriculum for a Culturally Diverse Society,* edited by Etta Hollins, 179–203. Mahwah, N.J.: Lawrence Erlbaum Associates.

Anzaldúa, Gloria. 1987. *Borderlands / La Frontera: The New Mestiza.* San Francisco: Spinsters/Aunt Lute Foundation.

———, ed. 1990. *Making Face, Making Soul / Haciendo Caras: Creative and Critical Perspectives by Women of Color.* San Francisco: Aunt Lute Foundation.

Arce, Carlos H., Edward Murguia, and William Parker Frisbie. 1987. "Phenotype and Life Chances among Chicanos." *Hispanic Journal of Behavioral Science* 9, no. 1 (March): 19–32.

Aronowitz, Stanley. 1973. *False Promises: The Shaping of American Working-Class Consciousness.* New York: McGraw-Hill.

Asian Women United of California, ed. 1989. *Making Waves: An Anthology of Writings By and About Asian American Women.* Boston: Beacon Press.

Austin, Joe, and Michael Nevin Willard. 1998. *Generations of Youth: Youth Cultures and History in Twentieth Century America.* New York: New York University Press.

Baca Zinn, Maxine, Lynn Weber Cannon, Elizabeth Higginbotham, and Bonnie Thorton Dill. 1990. "The Costs of Exclusionary Practices in Women's Studies." In *Making Face, Making Soul / Haciendo Caras: Creative and Critical Perspectives by Women of Color,* edited by Gloria Anzaldúa, 29–41. San Francisco: Aunt Lute Foundation.

Banks, Ingrid. 2000. *Hair Matters: Beauty, Power, and Black Women's Consciousness.* New York: New York University Press.

Baral, David P. 1979. "Academic Achievement of Recent Immigrants from Mexico." *NABE Journal* 3, no. 3 (spring): 1–13.

Becker, Howard. 1963. *The Outsiders: Studies in the Sociology of Deviance.* New York: The Free Press.

Behar, Ruth, and Deborah Gordon. 1995. *Women Writing Culture / Culture Writing Women.* Berkeley: University of California Press.

Bernstein, Basil B. 1975. *Class, Codes, and Control.* London: Routledge and Kegan Paul.

Bettie, Julie. 1995. "Class Dismissed? Roseanne and the Changing Face of Working-Class Iconography." *Social Text* 13, no. 4 (winter): 125–49.

———. 2000. "Women without Class: Chicas, Cholas, Trash, and the Presence/Absence of Class Identity." *Signs: Journal of Women in Culture and Society* 26, no. 1 (autumn):1–35.

———. 2001. "Changing the Subject: Male Feminism, Class Identity, and the Politics of Location." In *Identity Politics in the Women's Movement,* edited by B. Ryan, 109–19. New York: New York University Press.

Bhavnani, Kum-Kum, Kathryn R. Kent, and France Winddance Twine, eds. 1998. *Signs: Journal of Women in Culture and Society* 23, no. 3 (spring), special issue titled *Feminisms and Youth Culture.*

Blake, Debra J. 1997. *The Right to Passion: Chicana Sexuality Refigured.* PhD. diss., University of Iowa.

Bloom, Gilda Maria. 1991. "The Effects of Speech Style and Skin Color on Bilingual Teaching Candidates' and Bilingual Teachers' Attitudes toward Mexican-American Pupils." Ph.D. diss., Stanford University.

Bordo, Susan. 1990. "Feminism, Postmodernism, and Gender-Scepticism." In *Feminism/Postmodernism,* edited by Linda J. Nicholson, 133–56. New York: Routledge.

———. 1992. "Postmodern Subjects, Postmodern Bodies." Review of *Gender Trouble,* by Judith Butler. *Feminist Studies* 18, no. 1 (spring): 159–75.

Bourdieu, Pierre. 1977. *Outline of A Theory of Practice.* New York: Cambridge University Press.

———. 1984. *Distinction: A Social Critique of the Judgment of Taste.* Cambridge, Mass.: Harvard University Press.

Bourdieu, Pierre, and Jean-Claude Passeron. 1977. *Reproduction in Education, Society, and Culture.* London: Sage Publications.

Bowles, Samuel, and Howard Gintis. 1976. *Schooling in Capitalist America: Educational Reform and the Contradictions of Economic Life.* New York: Basic Books.

Brake, Mike. 1980. *The Sociology of Youth Subcultures: Sex and Drugs and Rock 'n' Roll.* London: Routledge and Kegan Paul.

Brantlinger, Ellen. 1993. *The Politics of Social Class in Secondary School: Views of Affluent and Impoverished Youth.* New York: Teachers College Press.

Brice Heath, Shirley. 1983. *Ways with Words: Language, Life, and Work in Communities and Classrooms.* New York: Cambridge University Press.

Brown, Lyn Mikel. 1998. *Raising Their Voices: The Politics of Girls' Anger.* Cambridge, Mass: Harvard University Press.

Brown, Lyn Mikel, and Carol Gilligan. 1992. *Meeting at the Crossroads.* New York: Ballantine Books.

Brumberg, Joan Jacobs. 1997. *The Body Project: An Intimate History of American Girls.* New York: Random House.

Bullock, Heather. 1995. "Class Acts: Middle-Class Responses to the Poor." In *The Social Psychology of Interpersonal Discrimination,* edited by Bernice Lott and Diane Maluso, 118–59. New York: Guilford Press.

Buriel, Raymond. 1994. "Immigration and Education of Mexican-Americans." In *The Educational Achievement of Latinos: Barriers and Successes,* edited by Aida Hurtado and Eugene E. Garcia, 197–226. Santa Cruz: Regents of the University of California, University of California, Santa Cruz.

Buriel, Raymond, and Desdemona Cardoza. 1988. "Sociocultural Correlates of Academic Achievement among Three Generations of Mexican American High School Seniors." *American Educational Research Journal* 25, no. 2 (summer): 177–92.

Butler, Judith. 1990. *Gender Trouble: Feminism and the Subversion of Identity.* New York: Routledge.

———. 1993. *Bodies That Matter: On the Discursive Limits of "Sex."* New York: Routledge.

Campbell, Anne. 1984. *The Girls in the Gang: A Report from New York City.* New York: Blackwell Publishers.

Chabram, Angie. 1990. "Chicano Studies as Oppositional Ethnography." *Cultural Studies* 4, no. 3 (Oct.): 228–47.

Chang, Grace. 1994. "Undocumented Latinas: The New 'Employable Mothers.'" In *Mothering: Ideology, Experience, and Agency,* edited by Evelyn Nakano Glenn, Grace Chang, and Linda Rennie Forcey, 259–85. New York: Routledge.

Chapa, Jorge. 1988. "The Question of Mexican American Assimilation: Socioeconomic Parity of Underclass Formation?" *Public Affairs Comment* 35, no. 1.

Chavez, Linda. 1991. *Out of the Barrio: Towards a New Politics of Hispanic Assimilation.* New York: Academic Press.

Childers, Mary, and bell hooks. 1990. "A Conversation about Race and Class." In *Conflicts in Feminism,* edited by Marianne Hirsch and Evelyn Fox Keller, 60–81. New York: Routledge.

Clarke, John. 1991. *New Times and Old Enemies: Essays on Cultural Studies and America.* London: HarperCollins Academic.

Clifford, James. 1988. *The Predicament of Culture: Twentieth-Century Ethnography, Literature, and Art.* Cambridge, Mass.: Harvard University Press.

Clifford, James, and George Marcus. 1986. *Writing Culture: The Poetics and Politics of Ethnography.* Berkeley: University of California Press.

Cockburn, Alexander. 1996. "The War on Kids." *The Nation* 262, no. 22 (June 3): 7.

Cohen, Phil. 1997. "Laboring under Whiteness." In *Displacing Whiteness: Essays in Social and Cultural Criticism,* edited by Ruth Frankenberg, 244–82. Durham, N.C.: Duke University Press.

Cohen, Stanley. 1972. *Folk Devils and Moral Panics: The Creation of the Mods and Rockers.* Bungay, Suffolk: MacGibbon and Kee Ltd.

Collins, Patricia Hill. 1997. "Truth and Method: Feminist Standpoint Theory Revisited: Where's the Power? Comment." *Signs: Journal of Women in Culture and Society* 22, no. 2 (winter): 375–81.

Collins, P. H., L. A. Maldonado, D. Y. Takagi, B. Thorne, L. Weber, and Howard Winant. 1995. "Symposium: On West and Fenstermaker's 'Doing Difference.'" *Gender and Society* 9, no. 4 (Aug.): 491–506.

Connell, Robert W. 1987. *Gender and Power: Society, the Person, and Sexual Politics.* Stanford, Calif.: Stanford University Press.

Connell, Robert W., D. J. Ashenden, S. Kessler, and G. W. Dowsett. 1982. *Making the Difference: Schools, Families, and Social Division.* Boston: George Allen and Unwin.

Cosgrove, Stuart. 1989. "The Zoot Suit and Style Warfare." In *Zoot Suits and Second-Hand Dresses: An Anthology of Fashion and Music,* edited by Angela McRobbie, 3–22. London: Macmillan.

Cousins, L. H. 1999. "Playing between Classes: America's Troubles with Class,

Race, and Gender in a Black High School and Community." *Anthropology and Education Quarterly* 30, no. 3 (Sept.): 294–316.
Crenshaw, Kimberle, Neil Gotanda, Gary Peller, and Kendall Thomas. 1995. *Critical Race Theory: The Key Writings That Formed the Movement.* New York: The New Press.
Crompton, Rosemary. 1993. *Class and Stratification.* Cambridge: Polity Press.
Cuádraz, Gloria Holguin. 1999. "Stories of Access and 'Luck': Chicanas/os, Higher Education, and the Politics of Incorporation." *Latino Studies Journal* 10, no. 1 (winter): 100–123.
Cuádraz, Gloria H., and Jennifer L. Pierce. 1994. "From Scholarship Girls to Scholarship Women: Surviving the Contradictions of Class and Race in Academe." *Explorations in Ethnic Studies* 17, no. 1 (Jan.): 21–44.
Daniels, Jessie. 1997. *White Lies: Race, Class, Gender, and Sexuality in White Supremacist Discourse.* London: Routledge.
Darder, Antonia. 1991. *Culture and Power in the Classroom: A Critical Foundation for Bicultural Education.* New York: Bergin and Garvey.
Darder, Antonia, Rodolfo D. Torres, and Henry Gutierrez. 1997. *Latinos and Education: A Critical Reader.* New York: Routledge.
De La Torre, Adela, and Beatriz M. Pesquera, eds. 1993. *Building with Our Hands: New Directions in Chicana Studies.* Berkeley: University of California Press.
Delgado, Richard. 1995. *The Rodrigo Chronicles: Conversations about America and Race.* New York: New York University Press.
Demo, David H. 1992. "Parent-Child Relations—Assessing Recent Changes." *Journal of Marriage and the Family* 54, no. 1 (Feb.): 104–17.
Dimock, Wai Chee, and Michael T. Gilmore. 1994. *Rethinking Class: Literary Studies and Social Formations.* New York: Columbia University Press.
Du Bois, W. E. B. 1935. *Black Reconstruction: An Essay toward a History of the Part Which Black Folk Played in the Attempt to Reconstruct Democracy in America, 1860–1880.* New York: Harcourt, Brace.
Eckert, Penelope. 1989. *Jocks and Burnouts: Social Categories and Identity in the High School.* New York: Teachers College Press.
Eder, Donna, Catherine Colleen Evans, and Stephen Parker. 1995. *School Talk: Gender and Adolescent Culture.* New Brunswick, N.J.: Rutgers University Press.
Ehrenreich, Barbara. 1989. *Fear of Falling: The Inner Life of the Middle Class.* New York: Pantheon Books.
Ellis, Jacqueline. 1998. *Silent Witnesses: Representations of Working-Class Women in the United States.* Bowling Green, Ohio: Bowling Green State University Popular Press.
Enstad, Nan. 1999. *Ladies of Labor, Girls of Adventure: Working Women, Popular Culture, and Labor Politics at the End of the Twentieth Century.* New York: Columbia University Press.
Epstein, Steven. 1987. "Gay Politics, Ethnic Identity: The Limits of Social Constructionism." *Socialist Review* 17, no. 3–4 (May–Aug.): 9–54.
Escoffier, Jeffrey. 1991. "The Limits of Multiculturalism." *Socialist Review* 21, no. 3–4 (July–Dec.): 61–74.

Fassel, Diane. 1991. *Growing Up Divorced: A Road to Healing for Children of Divorce*. New York: Pocket Books.
Featherman, David, and Robert M. Hauser. 1978. *Opportunity and Change*. New York: Academic Press.
Felski, Rita. 2000. "Nothing to Declare: Identity, Shame, and the Lower Middle Class." *PMLA* 115 (Jan.): 33–45.
Fernandez, Roberto M., and Francois Nielsen. 1986. "Bilingualism and Hispanic Scholastic Achievement: Some Baseline Results." *Social Science Research* 15, no. 1 (March): 43–70.
Fernandez, Roberto M., Ronelle Paulsen, and Marsha Hirano-Nakanishi. 1989. "Dropping Out among Hispanic Youth." *Social Science Research* 18, no. 1 (March): 21–52.
Ferrel, Jeff, and Clinton R. Sanders, eds. 1995. *Cultural Criminology*. Boston: Northeastern University Press.
Fine, Michelle. 1988. "Sexuality, Schooling, and Adolescent Females: The Missing Discourse of Desire." *Harvard Educational Review*, 58, no. 1: 29–53.
———. 1991. *Framing Dropouts: Notes on the Politics of an Urban Public High School*. Albany: State University of New York Press.
Fine, Michelle, Lois Weis, Linda C. Powell, and L. Mun Wong. 1997. *Off White: Readings on Race, Power, and Society*. New York: Routledge.
Flores-Gonzales, Nilda. 1999. "Puerto Rican High Achievers: An Example of Ethnic Academic Identity Compatibility." *Anthropology and Education Quarterly* 30: 343–62.
Foley, Douglas. 1990. *Learning Capitalist Culture: Deep in the Heart of Tejas*. Philadelphia: University of Pennsylvania Press.
Fordham, Signithia. 1996. *Blacked Out: Dilemmas of Race, Identity, and Success at Capital High*. Chicago: University of Chicago Press.
———. 1999. "Dissin' the Standard: Ebonics as Guerrilla Warfare at Capital High." *Anthropology and Education Quarterly* 30, no. 3 (Sept.): 272–93.
Fordham, Signithia, and John Ogbu. 1986. "Black Students' School Success: Coping with the Burden of 'Acting White.'" *Urban Review* 18, no. 3: 176–206.
Fox, Kathryn Joan. 1987. "Real Punks and Pretenders: The Social Organization of a Counterculture." *Journal of Contemporary Ethnography* 16, no. 3 (Oct.): 344–70.
Frank, Dana. 1994. *Purchasing Power: Consumer Organizing, Gender, and the Seattle Labor Movement, 1919–1929*. Cambridge: Cambridge University Press.
———. 1999. *Buy American: The Untold Story of Economic Nationalism*. Boston: Beacon Press.
Frankenberg, Ruth. 1993. *White Women, Race Matters: The Social Construction of Whiteness*. Minneapolis: University of Minnesota Press.
———, ed. 1997. *Displacing Whiteness: Essays in Social and Cultural Criticism*. Durham, N.C.: Duke University Press.
Fraser, James W. 1997. *Reading, Writing, and Justice: School Reform as if Democracy Matters*. Albany: State University of New York Press.

Fregoso, Rosa Linda. 1987. *The Bronze Screen: Chicana and Chicano Film Culture.* Minneapolis: University of Minnesota Press.
———. 1995. "Homegirls, Cholas, and Pachucas in Cinema: Taking Over the Public Sphere." *California History* 74, no. 3 (fall): 316–27.
Fregoso, Rosa Linda, and Angie Chabram. 1990. "Introduction. Chicana/o Cultural Representations: Reframing Alternative Critical Discourses." *Cultural Studies* 4, no. 3 (Oct.): 203–12.
Freire, Paulo. 1990. *Pedagogy of the Oppressed.* New York: The Continuum Publishing Company.
Furstenburg, Frank F., Jr., and Andrew J. Cherlin. 1991. *Divided Families: What Happens to Children When Parents Part.* Cambridge, Mass.: Harvard University Press.
Fuss, Diana. 1989. *Essentially Speaking: Feminism, Nature, and Difference.* New York: Routledge.
Gaines, Donna. 1990. *Teenage Wasteland: Suburbia's Dead End Kids.* New York: Pantheon Books.
Gamson, Joshua. 1995. "Must Identity Movements Self-Destruct? A Queer Dilemma." *Social Problems* 42, no. 3: 390–407.
Gándara, Patricia. 1995. *Over the Ivy Walls: The Educational Mobility of Low-Income Chicanos.* Albany: State University of New York Press.
Gans, Herbert. 1962. *The Urban Villagers: Group and Class in the Life of Italian-Americans.* New York: Free Press of Glencoe.
Garcia, Alma M. 1989. "The Development of Chicana Feminist Discourse, 1970–1980." *Gender and Society* 3, no. 2 (June): 217–38.
———, ed. 1997. *Chicana Feminist Thought: The Basic Historical Writings.* New York: Routledge.
Garcia, Robert J. 1998. "The Racial Politics of Proposition 187." In *The Latino/a Condition: A Critical Reader,* edited by Richard Delgado and Jean Stefancic. New York: New York University Press.
Garnsey, Elizabeth. 1982. "Women's Work and Theories of Class and Stratification." In *Classes, Power, and Conflict: Classical and Contemporary Debates,* edited by Anthony Giddens and David Held, 425–45. Berkeley: University of California Press.
Geertz, Clifford. 1973. *The Interpretation of Cultures: Selected Essays.* New York, Basic Books.
Gibson, Margaret A. 1988. *Accommodation without Assimilation: Sikh Immigrants in an American High School.* Ithaca, N.Y.: Cornell University Press.
Gibson-Graham, J. K. 1996. *The End of Capitalism (As We Knew It): A Feminist Critique of Political Economy.* Malden, Mass.: Blackwell Publishers.
Gibson-Graham, J. K., Stephen A. Resnick, and Richard D. Wolff, eds. 2000. *Class and Its Others.* Minneapolis: University of Minnesota Press.
———, eds. 2001. *Re/Presenting Class: Essays in Postmodern Marxism.* Durham, N.C.: Duke University Press.
Gilligan, Carol. 1982. *In a Different Voice: Psychological Theory and Women's Development.* Cambridge, Mass.: Harvard University Press.
Giroux, Henry A. 1983. *Theory and Resistance in Education: A Pedagogy for the Opposition.* South Hadley, Mass.: Bergin & Garvey.

Gitlin, Todd. 1995. *Twilight of Our Common Dreams: Why America Is Wracked by Culture Wars.* New York: Metropolitan Books.

Gluck, Sherna Berger, and Daphne Patai, eds. 1991. *Women's Words: The Feminist Practice of Oral History.* New York: Routledge.

Goffman, Erving. 1959. *The Presentation of Self in Everyday Life.* Garden City, N.Y.: Doubleday.

———. 1967. *Interaction Rituals: Essays in Face-to-Face Behavior.* Chicago: Aldine Publishing Company.

———. 1974. *Frame Analysis: An Essay on the Organization of Experience.* New York: Harper and Row.

Gordon, Linda. 1976. *Woman's Body, Woman's Right: A Social History of Birth Control in America.* New York: Grossman.

———. 1988. *Heroes of Their Own Lives: The Politics and History of Family Violence.* New York: Viking.

———. 1994. *Pitied but Not Entitled: Single Mothers and the History of Welfare, 1890–1935.* New York: Free Press.

Gramsci, Antonio. 1971 [1891–1937]. *Selections from the Prison Notebooks of Antonio Gramsci.* Edited and translated by Quintin Hoare and Geoffrey Nowell Smith. London: Lawrence & Wishart.

Granfield, Robert. 1991. "Making It by Faking It: Working-Class Students in an Elite Academic Environment." *Journal of Contemporary Ethnography* 20, no. 3 (Oct.): 331–52.

Gray, Herman. 1995. *Watching Race: Television and the Struggle for "Blackness."* Minneapolis: University of Minnesota Press.

Grubb, W. Norton. 1991. "The Decline of Community College Transfer Rates: Evidence from National Longitudinal Surveys." *Journal of Higher Education* 62, no. 2 (March/April): 194–222.

Gutman, Herbert G. 1976. *The Black Family in Slavery and Freedom.* New York: Pantheon Books.

Hall, John R., ed. 1997. *Reworking Class.* Ithaca, N.Y.: Cornell University Press.

Hall, Stuart. 1992. "What Is This 'Black' in Black Popular Culture?" In *Black Popular Culture,* edited by Gina Dent, 21–33. Seattle: Bay Press.

———. 1996. "Introduction: Who Needs Identity?" In *Questions of Cultural Identity,* edited by Stuart Hall and Paul du Gay, 1–17. London and Thousand Oaks, Calif.: Sage.

Hall, Stuart, and Tony Jefferson, eds. 1976. *Resistance through Rituals: Youth Subcultures in Post-War Britain.* London: Hutchinson.

Halle, David. 1984. *America's Working Man: Work, Home, and Politics among Blue-Collar Property Owners.* Chicago: University of Chicago Press.

Haraway, Donna. 1988. "Situated Knowledges: The Science Question in Feminism and the Privilege of Partial Perspective." *Feminist Studies* 14, no. 3 (fall): 575–600.

Harding, Sandra. 1991. *Whose Science? Whose Knowledge? Thinking from Women's Lives.* Ithaca, N.Y.: Cornell University Press.

———. 1997. "Truth and Method: Feminist Standpoint Theory Revisited:

Whose Standpoint Needs the Regimes of Truth and Reality? Comment." *Signs: Journal of Women in Culture and Society* 22, no. 2 (winter): 382–91.

Hartigan, John, Jr. 1997a. "Green Ghettos and the White Underclass." *Social Research* 64, no. 2 (summer): 339–65.

———. 1997b. "Locating White Detroit." In *Displacing Whiteness: Essays in Social and Cultural Criticism,* edited by Ruth Frankenberg, 180–213. Durham, N.C.: Duke University Press.

Hartmann, Heidi. 1979. "The Unhappy Marriage of Marxism and Feminism: Towards a More Progressive Union." *Capital and Class* no. 8 (summer): 1–33.

Hartsock, Nancy C. M. 1997. "Truth and Method: Feminist Standpoint Theory Revisited: Truth or Justice? Comment." *Signs: Journal of Women in Culture and Society* 22, no. 2 (winter): 367–74.

Hebdige, Dick. 1979. *Subculture: The Meaning of Style.* London: Methuen.

Hekman, Susan. 1997. "Truth and Method: Feminist Standpoint Theory Revisited." *Signs: Journal of Women in Culture and Society* 22, no. 2 (winter): 341–65.

Hemmings, Annette. 1996. "Conflicting Images? Being Black and a Model High School Student." *Anthropology and Education Quarterly* 27, no. 1: 20–50.

Higginbotham, Elizabeth, and Lynn Weber. 1992. "Moving Up with Kin and Community: Upward Social Mobility for Black and White Women." *Gender and Society* 6, no. 3 (Sept.): 416–40.

Holland, Dorothy C., and Margaret Eisenhart. 1990. *Educated in Romance: Women, Achievement, and College Culture.* Chicago: University of Chicago Press.

Hood-Williams, John, and Wendy Cealey Harrison. 1998. "Trouble with Gender." *The Sociological Review* 46, no. 1 (Feb.): 73–94.

hooks, bell. 1984. *Feminist Theory: From Margin to Center.* Boston: South End Press.

———. 1989. *Talking Back: Thinking Feminist, Thinking Black.* Boston: South End Press.

———. 1990. *Yearning: Race, Gender, and Cultural Politics.* Boston: South End Press.

———. 1992. *Black Looks: Race and Representation.* Boston: South End Press.

———. 1994. *Outlaw Culture: Resisting Representation.* New York: Routledge.

———. 2000. *Where We Stand: Class Matters.* New York: Routledge.

Horowitz, Ruth. 1983. *Honor and the American Dream: Culture and Identity in a Chicano Community.* New Brunswick, N.J.: Rutgers University Press.

Howell, Joseph. 1973. *Hard Living on Clay Street: Portraits of Blue-Collar Families.* Garden City, N.Y.: Anchor.

Hudson, Barbara. 1984. "Femininity and Adolescence." In *Gender and Generation,* edited by Angela McRobbie and Mica Nava, 31–53. London: Macmillan.

Hull, Gloria T., Patricia Bell Scott, and Barbara Smith, eds. 1981. *All the Women Are White, All the Blacks Are Men, But Some of Us Are Brave: Black Women's Studies.* Old Westbury, N.Y.: Feminist Press.

Hurtado, Aida. 1996. *The Color of Privilege: Three Blasphemies on Race and Feminism.* Ann Arbor: The University of Michigan Press.

———. 1998. "The Politics of Sexuality in the Gender Subordination of Chicanas." In *Living Chicana Theory,* edited by Carla Trujillo, 383–428. Berkeley, Calif.: Third Woman Press.

Hurtado, Aida, David E. Hayes-Bautista, R. Burciaga Valdez, and Anthony C. R. Hernandez. 1992. *Redefining California: Latino Social Engagement in a Multicultural Society.* Los Angeles: UCLA Chicano Studies Research Center.

James, David E., and Rick Berg. 1996. *The Hidden Foundation: Cinema and the Question of Class.* Minneapolis: University of Minnesota Press.

Jankowski, Martin Sanchez. 1991. *Islands in the Street: Gangs and American Urban Society.* Berkeley: University of California Press.

Kadi, Joanna. 1996. *Thinking Class: Sketches From a Cultural Worker.* Boston: South End Press.

Kao, Grace, and Marta Tienda. 1995. "Optimism and Achievement: The Educational Performance of Immigrant Youth." *Social Science Quarterly* 76, no. 1 (March): 1–19.

Kelley, Robin. 1990. *Hammer and Hoe: Alabama Communists during the Great Depression.* Chapel Hill: University of North Carolina Press.

———. 1997. *Yo' Mama's Disfunktional!: Fighting the Culture Wars in Urban America.* Boston: Beacon Press.

Kirby, Vicki. 1991. "Comment on Mascia-Lees, Sharpe, and Cohen's 'The Post-Modernist Turn in Anthropology: Cautions From a Feminist Perspective.'" *Signs: Journal of Women in Culture and Society* 16, no. 2 (winter): 394–400.

Ladson-Billings, Gloria, and William F. Tate. 1995. "Toward a Critical Race Theory of Education." *Teachers College Record* 97, no. 1 (fall): 47–69.

Lamont, Michele. 1992. *Money, Morals, and Matters: The Culture of the French and American Upper Class.* Chicago: University of Chicago Press.

Lamont, Michele, and Annette Lareau. 1988. "Cultural Capital: Allusions, Gaps, and Glissandos in Recent Theoretical Developments." *Sociological Theory* 6, no. 2 (fall): 153–68.

Landsman, M. A., A. M. Padilla, P. H. Leiderman, C. Clark, P. Ritter, and S. Dornbusch. 1992. "Biculturalism and Academic Achievement among Asian and Hispanic Adolescents." Unpublished manuscript, School of Education, Stanford University.

Lareau, Annette. 1987. "Social Class Differences in Family-School Relationships: The Importance of Cultural Capital." *Sociology of Education* 60, no. 2 (April): 73–85.

Lawler, Steph. 1999. " 'Getting Out and Getting Away': Women's Narratives of Class Mobility." *Feminist Review* 63 (autumn): 3–24.

Lazreg, Marnia. 1988. "Feminism and Difference: The Perils of Writing as a Woman on Women in Algeria." *Feminist Studies* 14, no. 1 (spring):81–108.

Leblanc, Lauraine. 1999. *Pretty in Punk: Girls' Gender Resistance in a Boys' Subculture.* New Brunswick, N.J.: Rutgers University Press.

Lembo, Ron. 2000. *Thinking Through Television.* Cambridge: Cambridge University Press.

Lesko, Nancy. 1988. "The Curriculum of the Body: Lessons From a Catholic High School." In *Becoming Feminine: The Politics of Popular Culture,* edited by Leslie G. Roman, Linda K. Christian-Smith, and Elizabeth Ellsworth, 123–42. Philadelphia: The Falmer Press.

Lewis, Lisa. 1990. "Consumer Girl Culture: How Music Video Appeals to Girls." In *Television and Women's Culture,* edited by Mary Ellen Brown, 89–101. London: Sage.

Lewis, Oscar. 1959. *Five Families: Mexican Case Studies in the Culture of Poverty.* New York: Basic Books.

Lipsitz, George. 1994a. *Dangerous Crossroads: Popular Music, Postmodernism, and the Poetics of Place.* New York: Verso.

———. 1994b. *A Rainbow at Midnight: Labor and Culture in the 1940s.* Urbana, Ill: University of Illinois Press.

———. 1998. *The Possessive Investment in Whiteness: How White People Profit from Identity Politics.* Philadelphia: Temple University Press.

Long, Elizabeth. 1989. "Feminism and Cultural Studies." *Critical Studies in Mass Communication* 6, no. 4 (Dec.): 427–35.

Lowe, Lisa. 1996. *Immigrant Acts: On Asian American Cultural Politics.* Durham, N.C.: Duke University Press.

Luker, Kristin. 1996. *Dubious Conceptions: The Politics of Teenage Pregnancy.* Cambridge, Mass: Harvard University Press.

Luttrell, Wendy. 1993. " 'The Teachers, They All Had Their Pets': Concepts of Gender, Knowledge, and Power." *Signs: Journal of Women in Culture and Society* 18, no. 3 (spring): 505–46.

———. 1997. *School-Smart and Mother-Wise: Working-Class Women's Identity and Schooling.* New York: Routledge.

MacLeod, Jay. 1987. *Ain't No Makin' It: Aspirations and Attainment in a Low-Income Neighborhood.* Boulder, Colo.: Westview Press.

———. 1995. *Ain't No Makin' It: Aspirations and Attainment in a Low-Income Neighborhood.* 2nd ed. Boulder, Colo.: Westview Press.

Males, Mike A. 1996. *The Scapegoat Generation: America's War on Adolescents.* Monroe, Me.: Common Courage Press.

———. 1998. *Framing Youth: Ten Myths about the Next Generation.* Monroe, Me.: Common Courage Press.

Mascia-Lees, Frances E., Patricia Sharpe, and Colleen Ballerino Cohen. 1989. "The Postmodernist Turn in Anthropology: Cautions from a Feminist Perspective." *Signs: Journal of Women in Culture and Society* 15, no. 1 (autumn): 7–33.

Mathony, Pat, and Christine Zmroczek. 1997. *Class Matters: Working-Class Women's Perspectives on Social Class.* London: Taylor and Francis.

Matute-Bianchi, Maria Eugenia. 1991. "Situational Ethnicity and Patterns of School Performance among Immigrant and Nonimmigrant Mexican-Descent Students." In *Minority Status and Schooling: A Comparative Study of Immigrant and Involuntary Minorities,* edited by Margaret A. Gibson and John U. Ogbu, 205–48. New York: Garland Publishing.

McCall, Leslie. 1992. "Does Gender Fit? Bourdieu, Feminism, and Conceptions of Social Order." *Theory and Society* 21, no. 6 (Dec.): 837–67.

McCarthy, Kevin, and R. Burciaga Valdez. 1985. *Current and Future Effects of Mexican Immigration in California: Executive Summary*. Santa Monica, Calif.: RAND Company.

McNall, Scott G., Rhonda F. Levine, and Rick Fantasia, eds. 1991. *Bringing Class Back In: Contemporary and Historical Perspectives*. Boulder, Colo.: Westview Press.

McRobbie, Angela. 1978. "Working Class Girls and the Culture of Femininity." In *Women Take Issue: Aspects of Women's Subordination,* edited by the Women's Studies Group, Centre for Contemporary Cultural Studies, University of Birmingham. London: Hutchinson.

———. 1984. "Dance and Social Fantasy." In *Gender and Generation,* edited by Angela McRobbie and Mica Nava. London: Macmillan.

———. 1991. *Feminism and Youth Culture*. London: Macmillan.

———. 1994. *Postmodernism and Popular Culture*. London: Routledge.

McRobbie, Angela, and Jenny Garber. 1976. "Girls and Subcultures: An Exploration." In *Resistance through Rituals: Youth Subcultures in Post-War Britain,* edited by Stuart Hall and Tony Jefferson. London: Hutchinson.

McRobbie, Angela, and Trisha McCabe. 1981. *Feminism for Girls: An Adventure Story*. London: Routledge.

McRobbie, Angela, and Mica Nava. 1984. *Gender and Generation*. London: Macmillan.

Mehan, Hugh, Lea Hubbard, and Irene Villanueva. 1994. "Forming Academic Identities: Accommodation without Assimilation among Involuntary Minorities." *Anthropology and Education Quarterly* 25 (2): 91–117.

Miller, Jody A. 1995. "Struggles over the Symbolic: Gang Style and the Meaning of Social Control." In *Cultural Criminology,* edited by Jeff Ferrell and Clinton R. Sanders, 213–34. Boston: Northeastern University Press.

Mink, Gwendolyn. 1998. *Welfare's End*. Ithaca, N.Y.: Cornell University Press.

Mohanty, Chandra Talpade. 1988. "Under Western Eyes: Feminist Scholarship and Colonial Discourses." *Feminist Review* 30 (autumn): 60–88.

———. 1991. "Cartographies of Struggle: Third World Women and the Politics of Feminism." In *Third World Women and the Politics of Feminism,* ed. Chandra Mohanty, Ann Russo, and Lourdes Torres, 1–47. Bloomington: Indiana University Press.

———. 1992. "Feminist Encounters: Locating the Politics of Experience." In *Destabilizing Theory: Contemporary Feminist Debates,* edited by Michele Barrett and Anne Phillips, 74–92. Cambridge: Polity Press.

———. 1997. "Women Workers and Capitalist Scripts: Ideologies of Domination, Common Interests, and the Politics of Solidarity." In *Feminist Genealogies, Colonial Legacies, Democratic Futures,* edited by M. Jaqui Alexander and Chandra Talpade Mohanty. New York: Routledge.

Moraga, Cherrie. 1983. *Loving in the War Years: Lo Que Nunca Paso Por Sus Labios*. Boston: South End Press.

Moraga, Cherrie, and Gloria Anzaldúa, eds. 1981. *This Bridge Called My Back: Writings by Radical Women of Color*. New York: Kitchen Table: Women of Color Press.

Mouffe, Chantal, ed. 1979. *Gramsci and Marxist Theory*. Boston: Routledge & Kegan Paul.
Moynihan, Daniel Patrick. 1965. *The Negro Family: The Case for National Action*. Washington, D.C.: U.S. Department of Labor.
Mullen, Carol A., ed. 1999. *Latino Studies Journal* 10, no. 1 (winter), special issue titled *Remembering to Tell Success Stories of Latino/a Identity*.
Nebeker, Kristen Crosland. 1998. "Critical Race Theory: A White Graduate Student's Struggle with This Growing Area of Scholarship." *Qualitative Studies in Education* 11, no. 1: 25–41.
Newton, Judith, and Judith Stacey. 1992. "Learning Not to Curse, or, Feminist Predicaments in Cultural Criticism by Men: Our Movie Date with James Clifford and Stephen Greenblatt." *Cultural Critique* 3 (winter): 51–82.
Nielson, Francois, and Roberto M. Fernandez. 1982. "Achievement of Hispanic Students in American High Schools: Background Characteristics and Achievement." *Contractor's Report to the National Center for Educational Statistics*. Washington, D.C.: U.S. Government Printing Office.
Oakes, Jeannie. 1985. *Keeping Track: How Schools Structure Inequality*. New Haven: Yale University Press.
Ogbu, John U. 1991. "Immigrant and Involuntary Minorities in Comparative Perspective." In *Minority Status and Schooling: A Comparative Study of Immigrant and Involuntary Minorities,* edited by Margaret A. Gibson and John U. Ogbu, 3–33. New York: Garland Publishing.
Ogbu, John U., and Maria Eugenia Matute-Bianchi. 1986. "Understanding Sociocultural Factors: Knowledge Identity and School Adjustment." In *Beyond Language: Social and Cultural Factors in Schooling Language Minority Students,* developed by the Bilingual Education Office, California State Department of Education, 73–142. Los Angeles: Evaluation Dissemination and Assessment Center, California State University, Los Angeles.
Omi, Michael, and Howard Winant. 1986. *Racial Formation in the United States: From the 1960's to the 1980's*. New York: Routledge and Kegan Paul.
Orenstein, Peggy. 1994. *School Girls: Young Women, Self-Esteem, and the Confidence Gap*. New York: Doubleday.
Ortner, Sherry. 1991. "Reading America: Preliminary Notes on Class and Culture." In *Recapturing Anthropology: Working in the Present,* edited by Richard G. Fox, 73–42. Santa Fe: School of American Research Press.
———. 1993. "Ethnography among the Newark: The Class of '58 of Weequahic High School." *Michigan Quarterly Review* 32, no. 3 (summer): 410–29.
———. 1996. *Making Gender: The Politics and Erotics of Culture*. Boston: Beacon Press.
———. 1998. "Identities: The Hidden Life of Class." *Journal of Anthropological Research* 54, no. 1 (spring): 1–17.
Oulette, Laurie. 1999. "Inventing the Cosmo Girl: Class Identity and Girl-Style American Dreams." *Media, Culture, and Society* 21, no. 3 (May): 359–83, 428.
Patai, Daphne, ed. 1988. *Brazilian Women Speak: Contemporary Life Stories*. New Brunswick, N.J.: Rutgers University Press.

Penelope, J. 1994. *Out of the Class Closet: Lesbians Speak*. Freedom, Calif.: The Crossing Press.

Perry, Pamela. 2001. "White Means Never Having to Say You're Ethnic: White Youth and the Construction of 'Cultureless' Identities." *Journal of Contemporary Ethnography* 30, no. 1 (Feb.): 56–91.

Persell, Caroline. 1977. *Education and Inequality: A Theoretical and Empirical Synthesis*. New York: Free Press.

Pfiel, Fred. 1994. "No Basta Teorizar." In *Scattered Hegemonies: Postmodernity and Transnational Feminist Practices,* edited by Inderpal Grewel and Caren Kaplan, 197–230. Minneapolis: University of Minnesota Press.

Phelan, P., A. L. Davidson, and H. C. Yu. 1993. "Students' Multiple Worlds: Navigating the Borders of Family, Peer, and School Cultures." In *Renegotiating Cultural Diversity in American Schools,* edited by P. Phelan and A. L. Davidson, 52–88. New York: Teachers College Press.

Pipher, Mary. 1994. *Reviving Ophelia: Saving the Selves of Adolescent Girls*. New York: Putnam.

———. 1996. *The Shelter of Each Other: Rebuilding Our Families*. New York: Ballantine Books.

Portes, Alejandro, and Ruben G. Rumbaut. 1990. *Immigrant America: A Portrait*. Berkeley: University of California Press.

Portes, Alejandro, and Min Zhou. 1993. "The New Second Generation: Segmented Assimilation and Its Variants." *Annals of the American Academy of Political and Social Science* 530 (Nov.): 74–96.

Raffo, Susan, ed. 1997. *Queerly Classed: Gay Men and Lesbians Write about Class*. Boston: South End Press.

Rapp, Rayna. 1978. "Family and Class in Contemporary America: Notes toward an Understanding of Ideology." *Science and Society* 42, no. 3: 278–300.

Reay, Diane. 1998. "Surviving in Dangerous Places: Working-Class Women, Women's Studies, and Higher Education." *Women's Studies International Forum* 21, no. 1 (Jan.–Feb.): 11–19.

Reinarman, Craig, and Harry G. Levine, eds. 1997. *Crack in America: Demon Drugs and Social Justice*. Berkeley: University of California Press.

Rodriguez, Richard. 1982. *Hunger of Memory: The Education of Richard Rodriguez, an Autobiography*. New York: Bantam Books.

Roediger, David R. 1991. *The Wages of Whiteness: Race and the Making of the American Working Class*. New York: Verso.

———. 1994. *Towards the Abolition of Whiteness: Essays on Race, Politics, and Working Class History*. New York: Verso.

Roman, Leslie G. 1988. "Intimacy, Labor, and Class: Ideologies of Feminine Sexuality in the Punk Slam Dance." In *Becoming Feminine: The Politics of Popular Culture,* edited by Leslie G. Roman, Linda K. Christian-Smith, and Elizabeth Ellsworth, 143–84. New York: The Falmer Press.

Romo, Harriet, and Toni Falbo. 1996. *Latino High School Graduation: Defying the Odds*. Austin: University of Texas Press.

Rorty, Richard. 1991. *Objectivity, Relativism, and Truth*. Cambridge: Cambridge University Press.

Rose, Tricia. 1990. "Never Trust a Big Butt and a Smile." *Camera Obscura* 23 (May): 109–31.

———. 1994. "A Style Nobody Can Deal With: Politics, Style, and the Postindustrial City in Hip Hop." In *Microphone Fiends: Youth Music and Youth Culture,* edited by Andrew Ross and Tricia Rose, 71–88. New York: Routledge.

Rubin, Gayle. 1975. "The Traffic in Women: Notes on the 'Political Economy' of Sex." In *Toward an Anthropology of Women,* edited by Rayna R. Reiter, 157–210. New York: Monthly Review Press.

———. 1984. "Thinking Sex: Notes for a Radical Theory of the Politics of Sexuality." In *Pleasure and Danger: Exploring Female Sexuality,* edited by Carol S. Vance, 267–319. New York: Routledge.

Rubin, Lillian B. 1976. *Worlds of Pain: Life in the Working-Class Family.* New York: Basic Books.

———. 1994. *Families on the Faultline: America's Working Class Speaks Out about the Family.* New York: HarperCollins.

Ruiz, Vicki L., and Ellen Carol DuBois, eds. 2000. *Unequal Sisters: A Multicultural Reader in U.S. Women's History.* 3rd ed. New York: Routledge.

Rumberger, Russell W., and Katherine A. Larson. 1998. "Toward Explaining Differences in Educational Achievement among Mexican American Language Minority Students." *Sociology of Education* 71, no. 1 (Jan.): 68–93.

Ryan, Jake, and Charles Sackrey. 1984. *Strangers in Paradise: Academics From the Working Class.* Boston: South End Press.

Sandoval, Chela. 1998. "Mestizaje as Method: Feminists-of-Color Challenge the Canon." In *Living Chicana Theory,* edited by Carla Trujillo, 352–70. Berkeley, Calif.: Third Woman Press.

Scott, Joan. 1988. *Gender and the Politics of History.* New York: Columbia University Press.

———. 1990. "Experience." In *Feminists Theorize the Political,* edited by Judith Butler and Joan W. Scott, 22–40. New York: Routledge.

Seltzer, Judith A. 1994. "Consequences of Marital Dissolution for Children." *Annual Review of Sociology* 20: 235–66.

Sennett, Richard, and Jonathan Cobb. 1972. *The Hidden Injuries of Class.* New York: Vintage Books.

Sherman, Arloc, Cheryl Amey, Barbara Duffield, Nancy Ebb, and Deborah Weinstein. 1998. *Welfare to What? Early Findings on Family Hardship and Well-Being.* Washington, D.C.: Children's Defense Fund and National Coalition on Homelessness.

Skeggs, Beverley. 1997. *Formations of Class and Gender: Becoming Respectable.* London: Sage.

Smith, Barbara. 1983. *Home Girls: A Black Feminist Anthology.* New York: Kitchen Table Women of Color Press.

Smith, Dorothy E. 1997. "Truth and Method: Feminist Standpoint Theory Revisited—Comment." *Signs: Journal of Women in Culture and Society* 22, no. 2 (winter): 392–98.

Spelman, Elizabeth V. 1988. *Inessential Woman: Problems of Exclusion in Feminist Thought.* Boston: Beacon Press.

Stacey, Judith. 1983. *Patriarchy and Socialist Revolution in China.* Berkeley: University of California Press.

———. 1988. "Can There Be a Feminist Ethnography?" *Women's Studies International Forum* 11, no. 1: 21–27.

———. 1990. *Brave New Families: Stories of Domestic Upheaval in Late Twentieth Century America.* New York: Basic Books.

———. 1996. *In the Name of the Family: Rethinking Family Values in the Postmodern Age.* Boston: Beacon Press.

Stack, Carol B. 1974. *All Our Kin: Strategies for Survival in a Black Community.* New York: Harper and Row.

Stanton-Salazar, R. D. 1997. "A Social Capital Framework for Understanding the Socialization of Racial Minority Children and Youths." *Harvard Educational Review* 67, no. 1 (spring): 1–40.

———. 2001. *Manufacturing Hope and Despair: The School and Kin Support Networks of U.S.-Mexican Youth.* New York: Teachers College Press.

Stanton-Salazar, R. D., and S. M. Dornbusch. 1995. "Social Capital and the Reproduction of Inequality: Information Networks among Mexican-Origin High School Students." *Sociology of Education* 68, no. 2 (April): 116–35.

Steedman, Carolyn. 1986. *Landscape for a Good Woman: A Story of Two Lives.* New Brunswick, N.J.: Rutgers University Press.

Steinitz, Victoria Anne, and Ellen Rachel Solomon. 1986. *Starting Out: Class and Community in the Lives of Working-Class Youth.* Philadelphia: Temple University Press.

Street, John. 1986. *Rebel Rock: The Politics of Popular Music.* New York: Blackwell.

Sturm, Susan, and Lani Guinier. 1996. "The Future of Affirmative Action: Reclaiming the Innovative Ideal." *California Law Review* 84, no. 4 (July): 953–1036.

Suarez-Orozco, Marcelo M. 1991. "Immigrant Adaptation to Schooling: A Hispanic Case." In *Minority Status and Schooling: A Comparative Study of Immigrant and Involuntary Minorities,* edited by Margaret A. Gibson and John U. Ogbu, 37–62. New York: Garland Publishing.

Swidler, Ann. 1986. "Cultures in Action: Symbols and Strategies." *American Sociological Review* 51 (April): 273–86.

Takagi, Dana Y. 1992. *The Retreat from Race: Asian-American Admissions and Racial Politics.* New Brunswick, N.J.: Rutgers University Press.

Taylor, Jill McLean, Carol Gilligan, and Amy M. Sullivan, eds. 1995. *Between Voice and Silence: Women and Girls, Race and Relationship.* Cambridge, Mass.: Harvard University Press.

Telles, Edward E., and Edward Murguia. 1990. "Phenotypic Discrimination and Income Differences among Mexican Americans." *Social Science Quarterly* 71, no. 4 (Dec.): 682–93.

Thompson, Becky. 1996. *A Hunger So Wide and Deep: American Women Speak Out on Eating Problems.* Minneapolis: University of Minnesota Press.

Thompson, E. P. 1963. *The Making of the English Working Class.* London: Penguin.

Thompson, Sharon. 1994. "What Friends Are For: On Girls' Misogyny and

Romantic Fusion." In *Sexual Cultures and the Construction of Adolescent Identities,* edited by Janice Irvine, 228–49. Philadelphia: Temple University Press.

———. 1995. *Going All the Way: Teenage Girls' Tales of Sex, Romance, and Pregnancy.* New York: Hill and Wang.

Tokarczyk, Michelle M., and Elizabeth A. Faye, eds. 1993. *Working Class Women in the Academy: Laborers in the Knowledge Factory.* Amherst: University of Massachusetts Press.

Tolman, Deborah L. 1994. "Daring to Desire: Culture and the Bodies of Adolescent Girls." In *Sexual Cultures and the Construction of Adolescent Identities,* edited by Janice Irvine, 250–84. Philadelphia: Temple University Press.

Tomasky, Michael. 1996. *Left for Dead: The Life, Death, and Possible Resurrection of Progressive Politics in America.* New York: The Free Press.

Trinh, T. Minh-Ha. 1991. *When the Moon Waxes Red: Representation, Gender, and Cultural Politics.* New York: Routledge.

Trujillo, Carlos, ed. 1998. *Living Chicana Theory.* Berkeley, Calif.: Third Woman Press.

Turner, Brenda. 1996. "Culture Crash." *USA Weekend,* April 26–28.

Twine, France Winddance. 1997. "Brown-skinned White Girls: Class, Culture, and the Construction of White Identity in Suburban Communities." In *Displacing Whiteness: Essays in Social and Cultural Criticism,* edited by Ruth Frankenberg, 214–43. Durham, N.C.: Duke University Press.

U.S. Bureau of the Census. 1996. *Statistical Abstract of the United States 1996.* Washington, D.C.: U.S. Government Printing Office.

———. 2000. Population Estimates for States by Race and Hispanic Origin: July 1, 1999 (ST-99-32). Washington, D.C.: Population Estimates Program, Population Division, U.S. Census Bureau.

University of California. 1998. "UC Admits More Students for 1998–99 Academic Year. Table of Ethnic Distribution of Freshmen Admitted to the University of California, Fall 1998(1) and Fall 1997(2)." University of California News Release, May 5.

Valenzuela, Angela. 1997. "Mexican American Youth and the Politics of Caring." In *From Sociology to Cultural Studies: New Perspectives,* edited by Elizabeth Long, 322–50. Malden, Mass.: Blackwell Publishers.

———. 1999a. "Checkin' Up on My Guy: Chicanas, Social Capital, and the Culture of Romance." *Frontiers: A Journal of Women Studies* 20, no. 1: 60–79.

———. 1999b. *Subtractive Schooling: U.S.-Mexican Youth and the Politics of Caring.* Albany, N.Y.: State University of New York Press.

Vigil, James Diego. 1988. *Barrio Gangs: Street Life and Identity in Southern California.* Austin: University of Texas Press.

Visweswaran, Kamala. 1994. *Fictions of Feminist Ethnography.* Minneapolis: University of Minnesota Press.

Wagner, Venise. 1996. "Crossover." *San Francisco Examiner Magazine* (Nov. 10): 8–32.

Walkerdine, Valerie. 1997. *Daddy's Girl: Young Girls and Popular Culture.* Cambridge, Mass.: Harvard University Press.

Wallerstein, Judith S., and Sandra Blakeslee. 1989. *Second Chances: Men, Women, and Children a Decade after Divorce.* New York: Ticknor and Fields.
Wallerstein, Judith S., and Joan Berlin Kelly. 1980. *Surviving the Breakup: How Children and Parents Cope With Divorce.* New York: Basic Books.
Ware, Vron. 1992. *Beyond The Pale: White Women, Racism, and History.* New York: Verso.
Weedon, Chris. 1987. *Feminist Practice and Poststructuralist Theory.* New York: Blackwell.
Weis, Lois. 1990. *Working Class without Work: High School Students in a De-industrializing Economy.* New York: Routledge.
Weitzman, Lenore J. 1985. *The Divorce Revolution: The Unexpected Social and Economic Consequences for Women and Children in America.* New York: Free Press.
Wellman, David. 1995. *The Union Makes Us Strong: Radical Unionism on the San Francisco Waterfront.* Cambridge: Cambridge University Press.
West, Candace, and Sarah Fenstermaker. 1995. "Doing Difference." *Gender and Society* 9, no. 1 (Feb.): 8–37.
White, Deborah Gray. 1985. *Ain't I a Woman: Female Slaves in the Plantation South.* New York: Norton.
White, Emily. 1995. "Revolution Girl Style Now." In *Rock She Wrote,* edited by E. McDonell and A. Powers, 396–408. New York: Delta.
Williams, Patricia. 1991. *The Alchemy of Race and Rights.* Cambridge, Mass.: Harvard University Press.
Williams, Raymond. 1970. *The English Novel from Dickens to Lawrence.* Forgmore, St. Albans, Herts., U.K.: Paladin.
———. 1977. *Marxism and Literature.* New York: Oxford University Press.
Willis, Paul. 1977. *Learning to Labour: How Working Class Kids Get Working Class Jobs.* Farnborough, U.K.: Saxon House.
Winant, Howard. 1995. "Symposium: On West and Fenstermaker's 'Doing Difference.'" *Gender and Society* 9, no. 4 (Aug.): 491–506.
Wolf, Naomi. 1997. *Promiscuities: The Secret Struggle for Womanhood.* New York: Random House.
Wray, Matt, and Annalee Newitz, eds. 1997. *White Trash: Race and Class in America.* New York: Routledge.
Wright, Erik Olin. 1985. *Classes.* London: Verso.
Wright, Eric Olin, Cynthia Costello, David Hachen, and Joey Sprague. 1982. "The American Class Structure." *American Sociological Review* 47, no. 6 (Dec.): 709–26.
Zandy, Janet, ed. 1990. *Calling-Home: Working-Class Women's Writings.* New Brunswick, N.J.: Rutgers University Press.
Zavella, Patricia. 1987. *Women's Work and Chicano Families: Cannery Workers of the Santa Clara Valley.* Ithaca, N.Y.: Cornell University Press.
———. 1989. "The Problematic Relationship of Feminism and Chicana Studies." *Women's Studies* 17, no. 1–2 (Nov.): 25–37.
———. 1993. "Feminist Insider Dilemmas: Constructing Ethnic Identity with 'Chicana' Informants." *Frontiers* 13, no. 3 (spring): 53–77.

———. 1994. "Reflections on Diversity among Chicanas." In *Race,* edited by Steven Gregory and Roger Sanjek. New Brunswick, N.J.: Rutgers.
———. 1997. "Playing with Fire: The Gendered Construction of Chicana/Mexicana Sexuality." In *The Gender/Sexuality Reader,* edited by Roger N. Lancaster and Micaela di Leonardo. New York: Routledge.
Zsembik, Barbara A., and David Llanes. 1996. "Generational Differences in Educational Attainment among Mexican Americans." *Social Science Quarterly* 77, no. 2 (June): 363–74.

SUPPLEMENTARY REFERENCES

Ahmed, Sara. 2004. *The Cultural Politics of Emotion.* Edinburgh: Edinburgh University Press.
Almaguer, Tomás. 2012. "Race, Racialization, and Latino Populations in the United States." In *Racial Formation in the Twenty-First Century,* edited by Daniel HoSang, Oneka LaBennett, and Laura Pulido, 89–101. Berkeley: University of California Press.
Banet-Weiser, Sara. 2012. *Authentic™: The Politics of Ambivalence in a Brand Culture.* New York: New York University Press.
Berlant, Lauren. 1997. *The Queen of America Goes to Washington City: Essays on Sex and Citizenship.* Durham, N.C.: Duke University Press.
———. 2008. *The Female Complaint: The Unfinished Business of Sentimentality in American Culture.* Durham, N.C.: Duke University Press.
———. 2011. *Cruel Optimism.* Durham, N.C.: Duke University Press.
Bernstein, Elizabeth. 2010. *Temporarily Yours: Intimacy, Authenticity, and the Commerce of Sex.* Chicago: University of Chicago Press.
Bettie, Julie. 2014. "Shopping for a Textuality: Writing on Sexual Commerce as Public Sociology." Paper in progress.
Bilge, Sirma. 2013. "Intersectionality Undone: Saving Intersectionality from Feminist Intersectionality Studies." *Du Bois Review* 10, no. 2: 405–24.
Butler, Judith. 2004. *Undoing Gender.* New York: Routledge.
———. 2006. *Gender Trouble: Feminism and the Subversion of Identity.* New York: Routledge.
———. 2010. "Performative Agency." *Journal of Cultural Economy* 3, no. 2 (July): 147–61.
Caballero, Chamio, Jo Haynes, and Leon Tikly. 2007. "Researching Mixed Race in Education: Perceptions, Policies and Practices." *Race, Ethnicity and Education* 10, no. 3 (Sept.): 345–62.
Cantú, Lionel, Jr. 2009. *The Sexuality of Migration: Border Crossings and Mexican Immigrant Men.* Edited by Nancy A. Naples and Salvador Vidal-Ortiz. New York: New York University Press.
Carbado, Devon W., Kimberlé Williams Crenshaw, Vickie M. Mays, and Barbara Tomlinson. 2013. "Intersectionality: Mapping the Movements of a Theory." *Du Bois Review* 10, no. 2: 303–12.
Carbado, Devon W., and Mitu Gulati. 2013. *Acting White? Rethinking Race in Post-Racial America.* Oxford: Oxford University Press.

———. 2003. "The Law and Economics of Critical Race Theory." *Yale Law Review* 112, no. 7: 1757–828.

Carter, Prudence L. 2005. *Keepin' It Real: School Success beyond Black and White.* Oxford: Oxford University Press.

Chadderton, Charlotte. 2013. "Towards a Research Framework for Race in Education: Critical Race Theory and Judith Butler." *International Journal of Qualitative Studies in Education* 26, no. 1 (Jan.): 39–55.

Choo, Hae Yeon, and Myra Marx Ferree. 2010. "Practicing Intersectionality in Sociological Research: A Critical Analysis of Inclusions, Interactions, and Institutions in the Study of Inequalities." *Sociological Theory* 28, no. 2 (June): 129–49.

Clough, Patricia, and Jean Halley, eds. 2007. *The Affective Turn: Theorizing the Social.* Durham, N.C.: Duke University Press.

Cobble, Dorothy Sue. 2005. *The Other Women's Movement: Workplace Justice and Social Rights in Modern America.* Princeton, N.J.: Princeton University Press.

Coole, Diana, and Samantha Frost, eds. 2010. *New Materialisms: Ontology, Agency, and Politics.* Durham, N.C.: Duke University Press.

Crenshaw, Kimberlé. 1989. "Demarginalizing the Intersection of Race and Sex: A Black Feminist Critique of Antidiscrimination Doctrine, Feminist Theory and Antiracist Politics." *University of Chicago Legal Forum* 140: 139–67.

———. 1991. "Mapping the Margins: Intersectionality, Identity Politics, and Violence against Women of Color." *Stanford Law Review* 43, no. 6 (July): 1241–99.

Cvetkovich, Ann. 2003. *An Archive of Feelings: Trauma, Sexuality, and Lesbian Public Cultures.* Durham, N.C.: Duke University Press.

———. 2012. *Depression: A Public Feeling.* Durham, N.C.: Duke University Press.

Davis, Angela. 2014. "(Un)Occupy." In *Occupy! Scenes from Occupied America,* edited by Astra Taylor, Keith Gessen, and editors from *n* + *1*, 132–33. London: Verso.

Deleuze, Gilles, and Felix Guattari. 1983. *Anti-Oedipus: Capitalism and Schizophrenia.* Translated by Robert Hurley, Mark Seem, and Helen R. Lane. London: Athlone.

Denner, Jill, and Nora Dunbar. 2004. "Negotiating Femininity: Power and Strategies of Mexican American Girls." *Sex Roles* 50, no. 5 (March): 301–14.

Driscoll, Catherine. 2002. *Girls: Feminine Adolescence in Popular Culture and Cultural Theory.* New York: Columbia University Press.

Duggan, Lisa. 2002. "The New Homonormativity: The Sexual Politics of Neoliberalism." In *Materializing Democracy: Toward a Revitalized Cultural Politics,* edited by Russ Castronovo and Dana D. Nelson, 175–94. Durham, N.C.: Duke University Press.

———. 2012. *The Twilight of Equality? Neoliberalism, Cultural Politics, and the Attack on Democracy.* Boston: Beacon Press.

Dyson, Michael Eric. 2011. "Tour(é)ing Blackness." In *Who's Afraid of Post-Blackness? What It Means to Be Black Now*, by Touré, xiii–xx. New York: Simon and Schuster.

Egan, R. Danielle. 2013. *Becoming Sexual: A Critical Appraisal of the Sexualization of Girls*. Hoboken, N.J.: John Wiley and Sons.

Ehlers, Nadine. 2003. "Passing Phantasms/Sanctioning Performatives: (Re)Reading White Masculinity in *Rhinelander v. Rhinelander*." *Studies in Law, Politics, and Society* 27: 63–91.

———. 2006. "'Black Is' and 'Black Ain't': Performative Revisions of Racial 'Crisis.'" *Culture, Theory and Critique* 47, no. 2 (Nov.): 149–63.

———. 2012. *Racial Imperatives: Discipline, Performativity, and Struggles against Subjection*. Bloomington: Indiana University Press.

Espiritu, Yen Le. 2001. "'We Don't Sleep Around like White Girls Do': Family, Culture, and Gender in Filipina American Lives." *Signs: Journal of Women in Culture and Society* 26, no. 2 (winter): 415–40.

Ferguson, Roderick A. 2004. *Aberrations in Black: Toward a Queer of Color Critique*. Minneapolis: University of Minnesota Press.

Fleetwood, Nicole R. 2011. *Troubling Vision: Performance, Visuality, and Blackness*. Chicago: University of Chicago Press.

Garcia, Lorena. 2012. *Respect Yourself, Protect Yourself: Latina Girls and Sexual Identity*. New York: New York University Press.

Gibson-Graham, J. K. 1996. "Querying Globalization." *Rethinking Marxism* 9, no. 1 (Jan.): 1–27.

Gilbert, David. 2006. "Interrogating Mixed-Race: A Crisis of Ambiguity?" *Social Identities* 11, no. 1 (Aug.): 55–74.

Gonzalez, Roberto G. "Learning to Be Illegal: Undocumented Youth and Shifting Legal Contexts in the Transition to Adulthood." *American Sociological Review* 76, no. 4 (2011): 602–19.

Gould, Deborah B. 2009. *Moving Politics: Emotion and ACT UP's Fight against AIDS*. Chicago: University of Chicago Press.

Grzanka, Patrick R., ed. 2014. *Intersectionality: A Foundations and Frontiers Reader*. Boulder, Colo.: Westview Press.

Halberstam, Judith. 2005. *In a Queer Time and Place: Transgender Bodies, Subcultural Lives*. New York: New York University Press.

———. 2013. *Gaga Feminism: Sex, Gender, and the End of Normal*. Boston: Beacon Press.

Hall, Stuart. 2000. "Old and New Identities, Old and New Ethnicities." In *Theories of Race and Racism*, edited by Les Back and John Solomos, 199–208. London: Routledge.

Heath, Melanie. 2012. *One Marriage under God: The Campaign to Promote Marriage in America*. New York: New York University Press.

Higgenbotham, Evelyn Brooks. 1993. *Righteous Discontent: The Women's Movement in the Black Baptist Church, 1880–1920*. Cambridge, Mass.: Harvard University Press.

Hochschild, Arlie. 1983. *The Managed Heart: The Commercialization of Human Feeling*. Berkeley: University of California Press.

HoSang, Daniel, Oneka LaBennett, and Laura Pulido. 2012. *Racial Formation in the Twenty-First Century.* Berkeley: University of California Press.
Ibrahim, Habiba. 2012. *Troubling the Family: The Promise of Personhood and the Rise of Multiculturalism.* Minneapolis: University of Minnesota Press.
Jackson, John L., Jr. 2001. *Harlemworld: Doing Race and Class in Contemporary Black America.* Chicago: University of Chicago Press.
Johnson, E. Patrick. 2003a. *Appropriating Blackness: Performance and the Politics of Authenticity.* Durham, N.C.: Duke University Press.
———. 2003b. "Race, Ethnicity, and Performance." *Text and Performance Quarterly* 23, no. 2 (April): 105–6.
Jones, Nikki. 2009. *Between Good and Ghetto: African American Girls and Inner-City Violence.* Piscataway, N.J.: Rutgers University Press.
Kandaswamy, Priya. 2012. "Gendering Racial Formation." In *Racial Formation in the Twenty-First Century,* edited by Daniel HoSang, Oneka LaBennett, and Laura Pulido, 23–43. Berkeley: University of California Press.
Kim, Richard. 2011. "The Audacity of Occupy Wall Street." *Nation* 293, no. 21 (Nov.): 15–21.
Lancaster, Roger N. 2011. *Sex Panic and the Punitive State.* Berkeley: University of California Press.
Lopez, Nancy. 2002. *Hopeful Girls, Troubled Boys: Race and Gender Disparity in Urban Education.* New York: Routledge.
Mahtani, Minelle. 2002. "Tricking the Border Guards: Performing Race." *Environment and Planning D: Society and Space* 20, no. 4 (Aug.): 425–40.
Marshall, Elizabeth. 2007. "Schooling Ophelia: Hysteria, Memory and Adolescent Femininity." *Gender and Education* 19, no. 6 (Oct.): 707–28.
Massumi, Brian. 2002. *Parables for the Virtual: Movement, Affect, Sensation.* Durham, N.C.: Duke University Press.
McCall, Leslie. 2005. "The Complexity of Intersectionality." *Signs: Journal of Women in Culture and Society* 30, no. 3 (spring): 1771–800.
McRobbie, Angela. 1991. *Feminism and Youth Culture: From "Jackie" to "Just Seventeen."* London: Macmillan.
———. 2008. *The Aftermath of Feminism: Gender, Culture and Social Change.* London: Sage Publications.
Milkman, Ruth, Stephanie Luce, and Penny Lewis. 2013. "Changing the Subject: A Bottom-Up Account of Occupy Wall Street in New York City." New York: The Murphy Institute, City University of New York.
Miller, Jody. 2008. *Getting Played: African American Girls, Urban Inequality, and Gendered Violence.* New York: New York University Press.
Mirón, Louis F., and Jonathan Xavier Inda. 2000. "Race as a Kind of Speech Act." *Cultural Studies* 5: 85–107.
Moore, Mignon. 2011. *Invisible Families: Gay Identities, Relationships, and Motherhood among Black Women.* Berkeley: University of California Press.
Nayak, Anoop. 2006. "After Race: Ethnography, Race and Post-Race Theory." *Ethnic and Racial Studies* 29, no. 3 (Aug.): 411–30.
Nichols, John. 2011. "The Spirit of Wisconsin: How Scott Walker's Union-busting Spurred a Popular Uprising." *Nation* 292, no. 12 (March): 13–16.

Omi, Michael, and Howard Winant. 2012. "Conclusion—Racial Formation Rules: Continuity, Instability, and Change." In *Racial Formation in the Twenty-First Century*, edited by Daniel HoSang, Oneka LaBennett, and Laura Pulido, 302–31. Berkeley: University of California Press.

Pascoe, Cheri J. 2011. *Dude, You're a Fag: Masculinity and Sexuality in High School*. Berkeley: University of California Press.

Pruitt, Lisa R. 2011. "The Geography of the Class Culture Wars." *Seattle University Law Review* 34, no. 3 (Feb.): 767–812.

Puar, Jasbir K. 2007. *Terrorist Assemblages: Homonationalism in Queer Times*. Durham, N.C.: Duke University Press.

———. 2012. "I Would Rather Be a Cyborg than a Goddess: Becoming-Intersectional in Assemblage Theory." *philoSOPHIA* 2, no. 1: 49–66.

Puri, Jyoti. 1999. *Woman, Body, Desire in Post-Colonial India: Narratives of Gender and Sexuality*. New York: Routledge.

———. 2004. *Encountering Nationalism*. Malden, Mass.: Blackwell Publishers.

Ravitch, Diane. 2011. *The Death and Life of the Great American School System: How Testing and Choice Are Undermining Education*. New York: Basic Books.

———. 2013. *Reign of Error: The Hoax of the Privatization Movement and the Danger to American's Public Schools*. New York: Knopf.

Renold, Emma, and Jessica Ringrose. 2011. "Schizoid Subjectivities? Re-Theorizing Teen Girls' Sexual Cultures in an Era of 'Sexualization.'" *Journal of Sociology* 47, no. 4 (Dec.): 389–409.

Rich, Camille Gear. 2004. "Performing Racial and Ethnic Identity: Discrimination by Proxy and the Future of Title VII." *New York University Law Review* 79 (Oct.): 1134–2417.

Ringrose, Jessica. 2013. *Postfeminist Education? Girls and the Sexual Politics of Schooling*. London: Routledge.

Rockquemore, Kerry Ann, and David L. Brunsma. 2007. *Beyond Black: Biracial Identity in America*. Lanham, Md.: Rowman and Littlefield.

Rosenfeld, Michael J., and Byung-Soo Kim. 2005. "The Independence of Young Adults and the Rise of Interracial and Same-Sex Unions." *American Sociological Review* 70, no. 4 (Aug.): 541–62.

Roth, Wendy. 2012. *Race Migrations: Latinos and the Cultural Transformation of Race*. Stanford, Calif.: Stanford University Press.

Rottenburg, Catherine. 2004. "Salome of the Tenements, the American Dream and Class Performativity." *American Studies* 45, no. 1 (spring): 65–83.

Santos, Jose Luis, Nolan L. Cabrera, and Kevin J. Fosnacht. 2010. "Is 'Race-Neutral' Really Race-Neutral? Adverse Impact towards Underrepresented Minorities in the UC System." *Journal of Higher Education* 81, no. 6 (Nov./Dec.): 675–701.

Stacey, Judith. 2012. *Unhitched: Love, Marriage, and Family Values from West Hollywood to Western China*. New York: New York University Press.

Stout, Noelle. 2013. "Close to Home: Personal Failure and Public Affect in the Mortgage Crisis." Paper presented at the American Anthropological Association Meeting, San Francisco.

Tienken, Christopher, and Donald Orich. 2013. *The School Reform Landscape: Fraud, Myth, and Lies*. Lanham, Md.: Rowman and Littlefield Education.

Touré. 2011. *Who's Afraid of Post-Blackness? What It Means to Be Black Now*. New York: Simon and Schuster.

Valocchi, Stephen. 2005. "Not Yet Queer Enough: The Lessons of Queer Theory for the Sociology of Gender and Sexuality." *Gender and Society* 19, no. 6 (Dec.): 750–70.

Veninga, Catherine. 2009. "Fitting In: The Embodied Politics of Race in Seattle's Desegregated Schools." *Social and Cultural Geography* 10, no. 2 (March): 107–29.

Vogel, Richard D. 2006. "Harder Times: Undocumented Workers and the U.S. Informal Economy." *Monthly Review* 58, no. 3: 29–39.

Walley, Christine J. 2013. *Exit Zero: Family and Class in Postindustrial Chicago*. Chicago: University of Chicago Press.

Ward, Rebecca. 2008. *Respectably Queer: Diversity Culture in LGBT Activist Organizations*. Nashville: Vanderbilt University Press.

Williams, Joan. 2010. *Reshaping the Work-Family Debate: Why Men and Class Matter*. Cambridge, Mass.: Harvard University Press.

Willis, Jessica L. 2008. "Sexual Subjectivity: A Semiotic Analysis of Girlhood, Sex, and Sexuality in the Film *Juno*." *Sexuality and Culture* 12, no. 4 (Sept.): 240–56.

Youdell, Deborah. 2006. *Impossible Bodies, Impossible Selves: Exclusions and Student Subjectivities*. Dordrecht, Netherlands: Springer.

Zhao, Yong. 2012. *World Class Learners: Educating Creative and Entrepreneurial Students*. Thousand Oaks, Calif.: Corwin.

Index